W9-ADK-420

The Inclusion of the Other

Studies in Contemporary German Social Thought (partial listing)
Thomas McCarthy, general editor

James Bohman, *Public Deliberation: Pluralism, Complexity, and Democracy*
James Bohman and Matthias Lutz-Bachmann, editors, *Perpetual Peace: Essays on Kant's Cosmopolitan Ideal*
Craig Calhoun, editor, *Habermas and the Public Sphere*
Maeve Cooke, *Language and Reason: A Study of Habermas's Pragmatics*
Jürgen Habermas, *Between Facts and Norms: Contributions to a Discourse Theory of Law and Democracy*
Jürgen Habermas, *Justification and Application: Remarks on Discourse Ethics*
Jürgen Habermas, *On the Logic of the Social Sciences*
Jürgen Habermas, *The Inclusion of the Other: Studies in Political Theory*
Jürgen Habermas, *Moral Consciousness and Communicative Action*
Jürgen Habermas, *The New Conservatism: Cultural Criticism and the Historians' Debate*
Jürgen Habermas, *The Philosophical Discourse of Modernity: Twelve Lectures*
Jürgen Habermas, *Philosophical-Political Profiles*
Jürgen Habermas, *Postmetaphysical Thinking: Philosophical Essays*
Jürgen Habermas, *On the Pragmatics of Communication*
Jürgen Habermas, *The Structural Transformation of the Public Sphere: An Inquiry into a Category of Bourgeois Society*
Jürgen Habermas, editor, *Observations on "The Spiritual Situation of the Age"*
Axel Honneth, *The Critique of Power: Reflective Stages in a Critical Social Theory*
Axel Honneth, *The Struggle for Recognition: The Moral Grammar of Social Conflicts*
Axel Honneth and Hans Joas, editors, *Communicative Action: Essays on Jürgen Habermas's* The Theory of Communicative Action
Axel Honneth, Thomas McCarthy, Claus Offe, and Albrecht Wellmer, editors, *Cultural-Political Interventions in the Unfinished Project of Enlightenment*
Axel Honneth, Thomas McCarthy, Claus Offe, and Albrecht Wellmer, editors, *Philosophical Interventions in the Unfinished Project of Enlightenment*
Maurizio Passerin d'Entrèves and Seyla Benhabib, editors, *Habermas and the Unfinished Project of Modernity: Critical Essays on* The Philosophical Discourse of Modernity
Ernst Tugendhat, *Self-Consciousness and Self-Determination*
Albrecht Wellmer, *Endgames: Essays and Lectures on the Irreconcilable Nature of Modernity*
Albrecht Wellmer, *The Persistence of Modernity: Essays on Aesthetics, Ethics and Postmodernism*

The Inclusion of the Other

Studies in Political Theory

Jürgen Habermas

edited by Ciaran Cronin and Pablo De Greiff

The MIT Press, Cambridge, Massachusetts

Second printing, 1999

This translation ©1998 Massachusetts Institute of Technology

This work originally appeared in German under the title *Die Einbeziehung des anderen. Studien zur politischen Theorie,* ©1996 by Suhrkamp Verlag, Frankfurt am Main, Germany.

All rights reserved. No part of this book may be reproduced in any form or by any electronic or mechanical means (including photocopying, recording, or information storage and retrieval) without permission in writing from the publisher.

This book was set in New Baskerville by Wellington Graphics and printed and bound in the United States of America.

Library of Congress Cataloging-in-Publication Data

Habermas, Jürgen.
  [Einbeziehung des Anderen. English.]
  The inclusion of the other : studies in political theory / Jürgen Habermas : edited by Ciaran Cronin and Pablo De Greiff.
      p. cm.
  Translation of: Die Einbeziehung des Anderen.
  Includes bibliographical references (p.   ) and index.
  ISBN 0-262-08267-5 (hc : alk. paper)
  1. Political science. 2. Liberalism. 3. State, The. 4. Human rights. 5. Democracy. I. Cronin, Ciaran. II. De Greiff, Pablo. III. Title.
JA68.H23 1998
320.51'3—dc21   98-21601
                                                                           CIP

Contents

Contents

Editors' Introduction

The wide-ranging essays collected in this volume provide an overview of Jürgen Habermas's work in political philosophy over the past decade together with a number of important elaborations of its basic themes in connection with current political debates. One of the distinctive features of this work has been its approach to the problem of political legitimacy through a sustained reflection on the dual legitimating and regulating function of modern legal systems. Eschewing the revolutionary utopianism of traditional socialism while remaining true to its emancipatory aspirations, Habermas has focused on the claim to legitimacy implicitly raised by the legal and political institutions of the modern constitutional state and has asked how this claim can be grounded in an appropriate theory of democracy. Extending his discourse theory of normative validity to the legal-political domain, he defends a proceduralist conception of deliberative democracy in which the burden of legitimating state power is borne by informal and legally institutionalized processes of political deliberation. Its guiding intuition is the radical democratic idea that the legitimacy of political authority can only be secured through broad popular participation in political deliberation and decision-making or, more succinctly, that there is an internal relation between the rule of law and popular sovereignty.[1] In the present volume Habermas brings this discursive and proceduralist analysis of political legitimacy to bear on such urgent contemporary issues as the enduring legacy of the welfare state, the future of the nation state, and the prospects for a global politics of human rights.

Habermas's political philosophy is marked by a dual focus that mirrors a duality inherent in modern law itself. Modern legal orders are distinguished, on the one hand, by the "facticity" of their enactment and their enforcement by the state (i.e., by their positive and coercive character) and, on the other, by their claim to "validity."[2] Thus a political philosophy that attaches central importance to the legal system must approach the legal and political institutions of the constitutional state simultaneously from two distinct though interrelated perspectives. In the first place, it must address the question of legitimacy: What is the ground of the validity of the principles of justice that form the core of modern democratic constitutions?[3] This is, of course, the central question of modern political philosophy in both the liberal and civic republican traditions. Habermas's theory of political legitimation is deeply indebted to both, but he takes his immediate orientation from a discursive analysis of questions of normative validity. He first developed this approach in his discourse theory of morality and now extends it to the legal domain in a way that is sensitive to the formal features of legality that set it apart from morality. This general approach to normative questions is based on the cognitivist premise that certain kinds of action norms admit of reasoned justification in practical discourse and that their validity can as a consequence be elucidated by an analysis of the forms of argumentation through which they are justified.

However, this normative approach to law and politics is in need of supplementation by an analysis of the functional contribution that positive legal orders make to the stabilization and reproduction of modern societies. Modern legal systems developed in response to the problems of social order created by accelerating processes of modernization; the formal features of legality are dictated by this regulative function of modern law. Moreover, Habermas claims that these two approaches to law, the normative and the functional, are inseparable. The problem of the basic principles of a constitutional democracy cannot be addressed in abstraction from the positive and coercive character of the legal medium in which they are to be realized; and these formal features of modern law are conditioned by the problems of social integration and reproduction to which modern legal orders respond. It is crucial for the analyses of human rights and popular sovereignty that form the core of Habermas's theory of democracy that the parameters of the problem they are intended to solve are laid down by history. If, following Habermas, we approach the problem of legitimacy by asking what rights free and equal citizens have to confer on one another when they deliberate on how they can legitimately regulate their common life by means of law, then the medium or language in which they must answer this question is not something they are free to choose but is imposed by the constraints of the task they are trying to solve. There are no functional alternatives to positive law as a basis for integrating societies of the modern type.

It is not our aim to offer an exhaustive analysis of this wide-ranging theoretical project here. Instead, by way of introduction we will outline the relevant features of Habermas's discourse theory of normative legitimacy as they bear on his theory of legal rights (section 1), before turning to his proceduralist conception of deliberative democracy (section 2). We will then consider the implications of this project for the problems of the future of the nation state, of a global politics of human rights, and of corresponding supranational political institutions (section 3). This will provide the background for some concluding remarks on Habermas's contributions to the debates currently raging on multiculturalism and the rights of cultural minorities (section 4).

1 The Discourse Theory of Morality and Law

Habermas starts from the assumption that in modern, pluralistic societies, social norms can derive their validity only from the reason and will of those whose decisions and interactions are supposed to be bound by them. He shares this starting point with John Rawls, who has emphasized that disagreement over conceptions of the good and questions of ultimate value is likely to be an enduring feature of pluralistic societies and could only be overcome through the repressive imposition of one belief system. Yet their responses to the challenge posed by pluralism differ in important ways. Rawls argues that citizens committed to different and incompatible "comprehensive doctrines" can nevertheless reach an "overlapping consensus" on basic principles of justice which they justify separately within their own evaluative worldviews, assuming that they can draw on certain shared ideals of the person, of society, and of public reason rooted in the tradition of Western liberal democracy.[4] Habermas, by contrast, thinks that there exists a more universal basis for agreement on general normative principles even among members of pluralistic societies who differ on questions of value and the good life. This confidence is grounded in the central role his social theory accords communicative action—that is, that form of social interaction in which the participants act on, or try to reach, a shared understanding of the situation—in regulating and reproducing forms of social life and the identities of social actors.[5] Among the things on which communicative actors are committed to reaching a shared understanding according to this theory are the normative assumptions that inform their actions; hence they are implicitly oriented to practical argumentation concerning the validity of norms as a means of resolving practical disagreements. This leads Habermas to suggest that the grounds of the validity of norms can be elucidated through an analysis of the presuppositions that speakers unavoidably make when they engage in good faith in practical argumentation. Indeed he argues that these unavoidable pragmatic presuppositions of argumentation entail a general principle of discourse, (D), which specifies the conditions that any valid social norm must satisfy: "Just those norms are valid to which all possibly affected persons could agree as participants in rational discourses."[6]

The discourse principle forms the cornerstone of a theory of both moral and legal validity which is intended to rebut noncognitivist skepticism concerning the rational basis of moral and legal norms.[7] The discourse theory holds that at least a certain range of normative questions have genuine cognitive content. In particular, it claims that participants in an ideally inclusive practical discourse could in principle reach an uncoerced agreement on the validity of these kinds of norms on the basis of reasons that are acceptable to all. The idealizations to which this discursive approach appeals lend Habermas's theory a demanding, counterfactual character: the principle of discourse points to an ideal procedure of discursive validation which functions as a normative standard against which existing conditions of discourse can be criticized. Although these idealizations are undoubtedly controversial, the suspicion that they are simply arbitrary, or reflect an idealistic conception of reason that has little practical relevance, can be allayed by noting that they are internally related to the conditions under which actors form and maintain their identities and regulate their interactions.[8]

This discursive analysis of normative questions allows for a sharp differentiation between moral and legal validity. The principle of discourse expresses a general idea of impartiality that finds different, though complementary, expressions in moral and legal norms. Habermas's differentiation between law and morality challenges the traditional assumption that morality represents a higher domain of value in which basic legal and political principles must be grounded. With the emergence of modern societies organized around a state and a positive legal order, the understanding of the basis of political legitimacy underwent a profound transformation: modern natural law or social contract theory broke with traditional natural law in arguing that political authority flows from the will of those who are subject to it rather than from a divinely ordained moral order. Nevertheless, the assumed priority of morality over law continued to play a central, if not always critically examined, role in both the liberal and communitarian traditions of modern political thought. Whereas classical liberalism in the Lockean tradition accords primary importance to prepolitically grounded rights of individual liberty, communitarian thinkers appeal to values rooted in inherited national, religious, or ethnic identities as the inescapable background against which all questions of political justice must be answered. Against both traditions, Habermas argues that law and morality stand in a complementary relation. The basic human rights enshrined in modern legal orders are essentially *legal* rights, not moral rights that are imposed as an external constraint on the constitution-founding practice of the citizens, though moral considerations enter into the justification of basic rights.

Habermas construes morality in broadly Kantian terms as a system of duties grounded in the unconditional claim to respect and consideration of all persons. Moral duties are binding on all beings capable of speech and action and hence have unrestricted or universal scope.[9] However, the very nature of morality means that it is limited as a mechanism for regulating social interaction. The unrestricted universality of moral principles, their highly abstract, cognitive claim to validity, and the unconditional character of the duties they impose create a rift between moral judgment and reasoning, on the one hand, and motivation, on the other. Moral norms provide agents with weak cognitive motives grounded in the knowledge that they have no good reason to act otherwise, but provide them with no rational motives to act accordingly. Moreover, the justification and application of moral norms calls for practical discourses whose highly exacting conditions can at best be approximated by real discourses. Thus moral norms are unsuitable for regulating social interactions between strangers where the practical costs in time and effort of establishing and maintaining the relations of mutual trust required for practical discourses are too high.

As a mechanism for regulating interactions between strangers, modern law has a number of important structural advantages over morality. Modern legal systems secure a space of individual liberty in which citizens are free to pursue their private purposes by conferring actionable individual rights on all citizens: whereas in the moral domain duties are prior to rights and entitlements, in the legal domain individual rights are prior to duties in accordance with the Hobbesian principle that whatever is not prohibited is permitted. In addition, whereas morality must rely on the weak sanctions of a guilty conscience, the enforcement of legal norms is ensured by the police and penal power of the state. Though the content of basic legal norms may sometimes be indistinguishable from that of universal moral principles, the fact that legal norms must be enacted and that all legal norms are in principle subject to revision means that their domain of application is limited in the first instance to a particular jurisdiction and its citizenry.

If we are to do justice to the distinctive mode of legitimacy of positive legal orders, Habermas argues, we should begin by asking what basic rights free and equal citizens must confer on one another if they are to regulate their common life by means of positive law. Once the goal of the constitution-founding practice is appropriately characterized, the formal features of the medium in which it must be accomplished—that is, positive, coercive law—set strict limits on the possible outcomes of the procedure. In particular, since legal rights presuppose that citizens have the status of legal subjects, the citizens must first confer on one another certain basic *liberty rights* which guarantee them this artificial status, including rights to the greatest possible measure of equal individual liberties, rights of membership in the political community, and rights guaranteeing individual legal protection.[10] Without these rights of *private autonomy,* which create a space for citizens to pursue their private ends free from interference, morally responsible agents could not reasonably be expected to submit themselves voluntarily to a coercive legal order. But in addition they must grant one another basic *rights of political participation* or rights of *public autonomy* through which the laws that give effect to all of the basic rights, including the political rights themselves, are formulated and enacted. Contrary to classical liberalism, which treats liberty rights as prepolitical endowments and interprets them as negative rights of noninterference, Habermas argues that liberty rights cannot be implemented without broad popular participation in the processes of political opinion-formation of an inclusive public sphere, through which the citizens can influence the definitions of their needs and interests that are embodied in the law.[11] Viewed from this perspective, political rights can be represented as necessary conditions for the realization of the artificial status of legal subject as bearer of rights, because they regulate the implementation of the liberty rights. However, the relation between private and public autonomy can also be interpreted in light of the conception of legitimacy expressed in the principle of discourse. This principle stipulates that laws derive their legitimacy from the presumed rationality of the decisions reached through appropriately regulated procedures of deliberation; thus the legitimacy of a legal order ultimately depends on the institutionalization of the forms of political communication necessary for rational political will-formation, and the liberty rights can be justified as necessary conditions for the institutionalization of the corresponding forms of political communication. Thus neither the liberty rights nor the political rights can be accorded priority but must be regarded as co-original. The principle of the essential interdependence of private and public autonomy or, alternatively, of the co-originality of the rule of law and popular sovereignty, forms the cornerstone of Habermas's proceduralist model of deliberative democracy.

But before turning to this, we should note a number of important features of Habermas's theory of rights. In the first place, it avoids the problems generated by the fiction of the state of nature in social contract theory, problems that arguably still bedevil Rawls's device of the original position. Habermas need not appeal to controversial prepolitical conceptions of human nature and of practical reason, nor need he appeal to conceptions grounded in specific constitutional traditions; on his account, the decision to found a political community is not itself in need of normative justification. The nature of the constitution-founding task and the medium in which it is to be accomplished need only be justified in functional terms— that is, in terms of the regulative functions of modern legal systems—and then the general shape of the theory of rights follows automatically, in conjunction with the discursive account of normative validity. The normative principle on the basis of which participants must decide which rights to grant one another is not grounded in transcendent ideals of reason and the person but is implicit in the presuppositions of communicative action and practical discourse. Thus rights are not treated as moral givens which are imposed as an external constraint on the citizens' political deliberations but are represented as the result of a process of construction, and hence as an expression of the reason and will of the citizens themselves.

However, although he argues that the theory of rights for the constitutional state need not draw on controversial questions of value and the human good, Habermas does not exclude ethical questions from the purview of politics altogether.[12] Political questions of what values and ideals of the good should be politically realized do not admit of rational resolution in the unrestricted sense of questions of justice because they are inseparable from the cultural traditions and historical experiences that shape the identities of groups, and hence can only be answered within the context of an *already constituted* political community. This does not mean that questions of the collective good cannot be rationally debated and resolved; but in pluralistic societies deliberations and decisions concerning what values and ideals of the good should be politically implemented must take place within a constitutional framework that guarantees individual liberty and the right of minorities to dissent from the values of the majority culture and to cultivate their distinctive identities. On the other hand, each political community must realize the system of basic rights within a political culture that reflects shared traditions and historical experiences, though this political culture must not be assimilated to the majority culture.

A further noteworthy feature of Habermas's approach, one with far-reaching implications for issues of international justice, is that the hypothetical procedure of a mutual conferring of rights can be conceived as being performed by groups of different scopes, ranging from the local and the national to the regional and the global.[13] While the basic human rights that must be conferred in order to establish a legitimate constitutional regime are essentially the same in each case, the political institutions required for their implementation would have to reflect the different scope of the practical matters to be regulated and the different composition of the populations subject to the laws enacted. Thus, as we shall see, Habermas's general theory of human rights points to the possibility of a global political order in which sovereignty would be divided and dispersed among local, national, and regional regimes, with a global regime assuming responsibility for the implementation of human rights at the international level.

2   Public Reason and Deliberative Democracy

Habermas's theory of human rights and popular sovereignty calls for the creation of political institutions in which discursive processes of opinion- and will-formation play a central role. This follows from the radically proceduralist orientation of the discourse theory which places the whole weight of political legitimation on informal and legally institutionalized procedures of opinion- and will-formation. On this account, the legitimacy of legal norms is a function of the formal features of procedures of political deliberation and decision making which support the presumption that their outcomes are rational. The resulting requirement that the enactment of legal norms be tied to discursive processes of rational political will-formation applies in different ways to basic constitutional principles and to enacted legal norms and statutes. At the constitutional level, the principle of popular sovereignty requires that the citizens must be able to affirm the basic rights as ones they would confer on one another in a constitution-founding practice. Because in most cases the citizens are born into an already existing state and never actually participate in such a practice, the requirement of their voluntary consent must be given effect through procedures by which existing constitutional principles can be challenged and changed if sufficient political will to do so can be mobilized. In the case of enacted laws, the principle of popular sovereignty requires that the citizens should play an active role in the elaboration and defense of the criteria in accordance with which the basic rights are implemented, most importantly in shaping the definitions of their needs and interests which become incorporated into law. In neither case can the content of legal norms be determined independently of the popular will as expressed in a critical public opinion. Thus the internal relation between the rule of law and popular sovereignty calls for a proceduralist model of deliberative democracy in which all political decision making, from constitutional amendments to the drafting and enactment of legislation, is bound to discursive processes of a political public sphere.

Habermas has specified the basic shape that political institutions would have to take in order to realize this model of deliberative democracy. It calls in the first place for a public sphere of informal political communication whose institutional basis is provided by the voluntary associations of civil society and which depends on inputs of expert information and on open access to the print and electronic media. The informal character of public political discussion, and the fact that it must be responsive to problems as they arise in the lifeworld of everyday interaction, mean that the associations in which it is conducted cannot be directly regulated by law; however, the basic political rights guaranteed by the constitution, such as freedom of association, freedom of speech, and freedom of conscience, are specifically designed to secure the background conditions that make possible a flourishing civil society.[14] The public sphere has as its complement the legally regulated government sphere composed of the legislative, judicial, and administrative branches. The specific tasks of each of these branches call for a complex division of labor in which each branch plays both an enabling and a limiting role vis-à-vis each of the others. For example, the professional judiciary must not preempt the political function of the legislature by creating law; conversely, the institution of judicial review enables the judiciary to restrain the legislature from programming specific legal judgments by enacting laws to that effect.[15]

While this model conforms to the basic institutional arrangements of modern constitutional democracies, Habermas provides an original rationale for these arrangements in terms of the legitimating function of public reason. This he construes in terms of a model of the circulation of power: on the input side, influence generated in the public sphere is transformed through the democratic procedures of elections and parliamentary opinion- and will-formation into communicative power, which in turn is transformed through the legal programs and policies of parliamentary bodies into administrative power; at the output end, administrative programs create the necessary conditions for the existence of civil society and its voluntary associations, and hence of a vibrant political public sphere.[16]

Habermas claims that this proceduralist model of deliberative democracy captures the principle of the interdependence of the rule of law and popular sovereignty better than rival theoretical proposals. The rival position that is perhaps closest to Habermas's is the political liberalism of Rawls, which is discussed at length in the two essays that comprise Part II of this volume. In the first, Habermas outlines three basic criticisms of political liberalism: first, that the devices of the original position and the veil of ignorance do not adequately model the idea of impartiality that informs deontological conceptions of justice; second, that the idea of a public justification of a political conception of justice in terms of an "overlapping consensus" is not commensurate with the epistemic or cognitive validity claim such a theory must raise if it is to claim legitimacy; and, third that Rawls's conception of the political implies a rigid division between the public and nonpublic identities of citizens which leads him to accord the negative liberty rights priority over the rights of political participation.[17] In a reply to this essay Rawls argued forcefully that Habermas's criticisms did not do justice to the complexity of his position, revealing in the process that his position is in some respects closer to Habermas's than the latter may have appreciated.[18] However, in the next essay Habermas reiterates and further clarifies his basic criticisms.

Perhaps the key disagreement between them concerns the appropriate nature and scope of a philosophical conception of practical reason that would be sufficient to ground a theory of justice for a constitutional democracy. Although both take a broadly constructivist approach to practical reason—they represent principles of justice for a constitutional democracy as those that citizens would agree to as the result of an appropriate process of reflection or deliberation—Habermas believes that the conception of legitimacy implicit in modern democratic constitutions calls for a more comprehensive theory of practical reason than Rawls allows. Thus he reiterates his argument that Rawls's idea of reasonable overlapping consensus is not sufficient to ground the legitimacy of the basic constitutional principles because it does not allow for a shared perspective from which the citizens could convince themselves of the validity of the principles *for the same reasons*.[19] Such a perspective, he argues, is implicit in the presuppositions that speakers unavoidably make when they engage in practical argumentation, so that the appropriate normative principles can be grounded in a purely procedural manner. Rawls, by contrast, rejects this approach on the grounds that a political theory of justice must be freestanding, and hence can have no part of theories of reason grounded in comprehensive philosophical doctrines such as Habermas's theory of communicative action.[20]

The significance of their contrasting approaches to practical reason can be brought out by considering their respective analyses of the legitimating function of the public use of reason, an idea that is central to both of their positions. It has emerged from their exchange that public reason undergoes a problematic split in Rawls's political liberalism. In the first place, there is the unrestricted exchange of ideas in the "background culture of civil society" in which all practical and theoretical proposals are open to debate; here participants are free to appeal to whatever considerations they find compelling, including their own comprehensive views, in an attempt to convince their fellows. This is the forum in which justice as fairness and rival political conceptions of justice must prove themselves. However, a much more restricted conception of public reason informs Rawls's idea of the "public justification" of a political conception of justice by "political society" and the related notion of public reason as an *ideal* to which participants in public political life should conform when debating matters of political concern. In public justification of a shared political conception, reasonable citizens, who have already justified the political conception "privately" by embedding it in their various comprehensive doctrines, take account of *the fact* that others have reasonable comprehensive doctrines that likewise endorse the political conception, though for different reasons. What is gained by this "mutual accounting" are not further supporting reasons for the political conception—since the express *content* of comprehensive doctrines plays no normative role in public justification—but a shared recognition that different citizens endorse the same conception for different reasons that must be respected.[21] This mutual recognition finds expression in the ideal of public reason and the corresponding political virtue of civility: when addressing political issues, especially ones that bear on constitutional essentials, citizens, candidates for office, officeholders, judges, and legislators must limit themselves to adducing reasons that their fellow citizens could reasonably accept and hence must refrain from appealing to their own comprehensive doctrines.

Habermas is highly critical of this restricted conception of public reason. The consensus that results from public justification as depicted by Rawls is not "rationally motivated" in a sense that is consonant with the deontological meaning of the basic principles of justice on which modern constitutional regimes are founded. The problem is that the overlapping consensus is not based on shared reasons: citizens simply *observe* that their fellows accept the political conception for their own reasons but cannot judge whether this acceptance has a genuine rational basis. This attenuated conception of public justification means that Rawls must restrict the validity claim publicly associated with the basic constitutional principles to the weak claim to "reasonableness." But this leaves him in the—for Habermas, highly paradoxical—position of holding that publicly defensible reasons can only support a weak claim to "reasonableness," whereas the private reasons mobilized in defense of comprehensive doctrines can ground the stronger claim to "moral truth." Habermas, by contrast, holds that the values and ideals of the good associated with religious and metaphysical worldviews cannot claim the universal validity of basic principles of justice, though they do shape the cultural context within which basic principles must be interpreted and applied. Moreover, he argues that a consistently proceduralist conception of the public use of reason entails that informal political discussion in civil society (i.e., in the "public sphere") and public deliberation bearing on constitutional essentials in legislative and judicial contexts are subject to essentially the *same* rational constraints. In both cases the rationality of outcomes ideally should be solely a function of the reasons adduced, the only difference being that in the public sphere the rationality of debate is assured by a vibrant political culture that facilitates open participation, whereas in the constitutionally regulated governmental sphere it is assured through legally prescribed procedures of judicial and parliamentary deliberation and decision making designed to ensure sufficient approximation to ideal conditions of discursive openness under limitations of time and information. On this account, the legitimacy-conferring function of political deliberation does not have to rely on the civility of citizens, legislators, and jurists who voluntarily refrain from adducing reasons that they think would not be acceptable to their fellow citizens; it can and must be left to the procedural constraints of discourses themselves to determine which reasons ultimately win out.

Although it must be left to the reader to unravel the threads of this intricate debate further,[22] we would like to draw attention to a divergence between Rawls's and Habermas's approaches to issues of international justice, which has a bearing on Habermas's broader concerns in this volume. Rawls's theory of justice is tailored from the beginning to a view of the state as a more or less self-sufficient system of social cooperation that is assumed to exist in perpetuity; hence, it presupposes the conception of the nation-state as exercising exclusive sovereignty over a territory and people enshrined in modern international law. This orientation is reinforced by Rawls's more recent idea of a political conception of justice as one that draws on ideas latent in the political culture of Western liberal democracies. When he turns to the question of how liberal democracies should behave toward nonliberal regimes whose political cultures are not structured by such liberal ideas, the principle of toleration itself dictates that a liberal regime must not insist unilaterally on liberal standards as the basis for judging which regimes it should recognize as legitimate. In other words, Rawls is compelled to apply much weaker standards of political legitimacy to the international domain, and his theory of international justice, at least as currently formulated, seems to allow for only limited protection of the human rights of citizens of authoritarian states.[23]

On Habermas's approach there is no such theoretical break between the application of liberal principles of justice to the national and to the international domains. Rather than accepting the framework of traditional international law which views states as the sole legitimate representatives of their citizens, Habermas advocates a model of *cosmopolitan* law which would supersede international law, confer actionable legal rights *directly* on individuals, and mandate the creation of supranational political agencies and institutions to ensure the implementation of human rights on a global scale. While nation-states would retain limited sovereignty, their citizens would be able to appeal to the coercive legal authority of regional or global agencies, against their own governments if necessary. This extension of the theory of rights and procedural democracy in a cosmopolitan direction raises far-reaching questions concerning the future of the nation-state, to which we now turn.

3   The Future of the Nation-State in an Era of Globalization

The essays collected in Parts III and IV of this volume represent some of Habermas's most significant interventions in the ongoing debates about the nature and future of the nation-state. In contrast to most arguments for cosmopolitanism, however, Habermas's point of departure is neither an attack on the nation-state nor a repudiation of nationalism, but a normative and empirical analysis of their successes as well as their limitations. Briefly, Habermas argues that the nation-state emerged in response to a dual crisis of legitimation and integration that arose with the demise of the old European feudal order and deepened with the acceleration of processes of modernization. After the wars of religion and the emergence of credal pluralism, authority had to be legitimated in a secular fashion. Modernization left in its wake isolated individuals and dislocated communities.[24] The achievement of the nation-state consists precisely in addressing the problems of legitimation and integration at once. By forming states and incorporating democratic constitutional procedures, communities gain a measure of legitimacy for their authoritative political institutions. At the same time, it is precisely the (in most cases deliberate) adoption of the idea of nationhood that creates bonds of mutual solidarity between former strangers and motivates the extension of democratic citizenship, thereby addressing the problem of disintegration.[25]

But if the idea of the nation was historically important in the formation of democratically ordered societies, for Habermas it seems to have outlived its usefulness, at least as traditionally conceived and enshrined in international law. It is not just that the increasing pluralism and relentless processes of economic globalization are rendering obsolete the notion of internally homogeneous and externally sovereign states; in addition an inherent tension between nationalism and republicanism is coming to a head. Whereas nationality depends primarily on ascriptive criteria such as ethnicity, a common language, or a shared history, republicanism is founded on the ideals of voluntary association and universal human rights. Despite the importance of the historical convergence of nationality and republicanism in the formation of the nation-state since the French Revolution, Habermas argues, this was only a contingent link: republicanism is neither conceptually nor practically dependent on nationality, and the twentieth century in particular has provided grotesque examples of the dangers of emphasizing the relationship between ethnos and demos.

Editors' Introduction

Habermas's main target in this discussion is the position that regards a culturally or ethnically homogeneous population as a necessary condition of the effective operation of a constitutional democracy.[26] For Habermas, insisting on this condition implies a failure to acknowledge the importance of legal institutions in the formation of national identities. He reminds us that modern consciousness is not merely a result of membership in prepolitical ancestral communities based on kinship, but is at least in part a function of politics, of the active enjoyment of the status of citizen within a political community.

Attention to the role of legal structures—as opposed to inherited loyalties—in the constitution of national identity helps Habermas to meet one of the objections raised against supranational regimes such as the European Union. According to some critics, in the absence of a genuine supranational identity such regimes suffer from an irresolvable legitimacy deficit: they will inevitably be antidemocratic both in origin and in operation. Habermas, of course, acknowledges that a European identity will not come about merely through legal fiat; but he argues that the genesis of such an identity depends on the institutionalization of supranational democratic procedures. Just as the identity of the French, for example, is based not merely on a shared cultural identity but also on the shared legal-political institutions and practices that are part of the legacy of the Revolution, the identity of Europeans will be at least in part a function of a legal framework that allows for the development of a genuinely European identity. Habermas's model here is that of the slow historical process through which, in the course of the nineteenth century, inherited local and dynastic loyalties became subordinated to the more abstract and legally mediated political identity of citizens of particular nation-states.

In mounting this argument, Habermas makes use of a pair of related distinctions that are becoming important in discussions not just about nationalism but more generally about political justification in multicultural contexts. He distinguishes, on the one hand, between a *civic* and an *ethnic* sense of the nation, and on the other, between a *political* and a *majority* culture. The idea, of course, is to restrict the object of politics so as to make agreement more feasible.

Citizens do not have to agree on a mutually acceptable set of cultural practices but must come to a to more modest though still demanding agreement concerning abstract constitutional principles. As with national identity within pluralistic states, Habermas thinks that a supranational identity might evolve around an agreement about political principles and procedures rather than about culture more generally. The agreement in question amounts to an identification with basic constitutional principles and practices which Habermas (among others) calls "constitutional patriotism." As within the nation-state, inherited regional loyalties could be subordinated to, but not completely replaced by, constitutional patriotism, so a similar process might take shape at the supranational level, provided that the different constitutional traditions of the member states embodied the same set of basic rights.[27]

But Habermas's interest in cosmopolitan structures goes beyond the approving observation that the different republican traditions converge on the same constitutional principles. After all, the classical system of states, up to and including the League of Nations, also included a set of principles that all member countries were supposed to follow.[28] But that system did not give anyone the authority to intervene in defense of the shared principles. In this respect, Habermas's cosmopolitanism is more demanding than Kant's idea of a federation of sovereign states, which is in some ways reflected in the classical conception of international law.[29] On Habermas's view, there is an inconsistency in Kant's dual aspiration to preserve the sovereignty of the associated states, on the one hand, and to maintain peace in the long run, on the other. The tension lies in the fact that the proposed federative scheme exists only insofar, and as long as, the member states *will* to remain in it. However, if peace is to be promoted, Habermas argues, states must be under the *obligation* to act in harmony with the principles of the federation.[30] Although Kant envisaged the possibility of a "universal federal state" (*Völkerstaat*) "based upon enforceable public laws to which each state must submit,"[31] in fact he advocated a "federation of peoples" (*Völkerbund*), a more modest structure whose aim is not to constitute a legal order to increase welfare and justice, but rather only to further the abolition of war.[32] This voluntary association does not give rise to any actionable rights, and hence its permanence remains unexplained.

Moreover, the concern to leave intact the sovereignty of its member states will, predictably, conflict with the need to obligate unruly members to subordinate their own *raison d'état* so that peace may be perpetuated.[33] Thus there is an inherent tension in the dual aim of establishing a regime of enforceable human rights, on the one hand, and of making consent the sole source of obligation of international law, on the other.

An appropriate reformulation of classical international law is in order, then. The thrust of Habermas's proposal is that republicanism needs to be preserved at the supranational level if it is to survive at all. The nation-state suffers three sorts of weaknesses, which are unlikely to be overcome by the nation-state alone. First, individual nation-states do not have the necessary resources to deal with risks on a global scale, including ecological problems, economic inequalities, the arms trade, and international crime. Second, states are becoming helpless in the face of the globalization or denationalization of the economy. It is not only the increased magnitude of the economic activity across national borders but also the rapid mobility of capital that leads to the loss of a large measure of individual states' control over their own economies. This weakness is not merely a pragmatic matter but threatens to undermine the integrative achievements of the nation-state. One of the dangers of the denationalization of economies is a race between several countries to dismantle their welfare systems in the search for competitive advantages. This in turn would accelerate the formation of underclasses even in developed countries, with three fateful consequences: an increasing recourse to repressive politics in a vain attempt to contain the anomic effects of a large underclass; the decay of the infrastructure of expanded areas; and, as a consequence of the foregoing, the collapse of the bonds of social solidarity and political legitimacy, two achievements of the democratic nation-state.[34] Finally, the inherent tension between nationalism and republicanism makes the sovereign state a less than reliable guarantor of the rights that individuals are supposed to have qua human beings, and not only as citizens of particular states.

Supranational regimes, according to Habermas, are more likely to succeed where sovereign states fail. For this reason, he supports supranational institutions with greater executive and judicial powers, so long as these institutions are also more democratic than present international organizations. The aim of these regimes is to constitute an international legal order that at the very least would bind individual governments to respect the basic rights of their citizens, if necessary through the threat or the implementation of sanctions. While increased judicial and executive functions would be necessary to make international institutions effective in the protection of individual rights, for this very reason they would also have to embody greater democratic openness in order to prevent selective and unfair uses of international force.

The same democratic, cosmopolitan orientation can be seen in Habermas's position on the future of Europe. Critics allege that the Union suffers from a serious "democratic deficit" on at least three grounds.[35] First, the Union rests on international treaties, a seemingly shaky basis for institutions and legal precedents that increasingly play a federative role.[36] Second, critics aver that structural impediments to democracy such as the increasing power of the Commission,[37] the poorly developed democratic procedures of the Council,[38] and the relative structural unimportance of the Parliament,[39] make Union decisions appear as impositions on the part of a bureaucratic body that has become dangerously autonomous. Even if member states could "lend" their legitimacy to the institutions of the Union, over time a democratic gap has allegedly opened up, for the overloaded Council has delegated decisions to the European Commission, whose members are not accountable to the particular member states but to the Union itself. Finally, some critics dispute the democratic character of the Union, asserting that a stronger Union would have an even more severe legitimacy deficit because of the nonexistence of a European public.

Habermas's response to the democratic deficit of the Union parallels his suggestions concerning the United Nations. He defends "[n]ew political institutions such as a European Parliament with the usual powers, a government formed out of the Commission, a Second Chamber replacing the Council, and a European Court of Justice with expanded competences."[40] In short, Habermas advocates "a transition of the European Community to a democratically constituted, federal state."[41] For him, the way to make good the democratic deficit of the Union is precisely to strengthen its political institutions while giving it the character of a federal government. To those (like Grimm) who think that a stronger Union would have an even more severe legitimacy deficit because of the nonexistence of an European public, Habermas offers the reminder that the identity of persons as citizens is shaped, at least in part, by the legal and political institutions within which they conduct their lives. It is not unreasonable, then, to expect that "the political institutions that would be created by a European constitution would have a catalytic effect"[42]—that is, that they would contribute to the formation of an authentic European identity, which would in turn promote the democratization of European institutions.

The suggestions for international institutional reform that Habermas offers are provocative, but the focus of his work lies on the normative dimension of cosmopolitanism. At this level, what makes his defense of cosmopolitanism particularly compelling is that it follows from an argument that seeks to reconcile particularism and universalism, *Sittlichkeit* and *Moralität,* by giving each its due. The guiding idea is that cosmopolitan political institutions can be seen as the result of the application of the very same hypothetical construct in terms of which he elucidates the legitimacy of legal rights within the nation state. Just as within states rights are necessary in order to mediate social interactions by means of laws, certain rights become necessary in order to achieve the same goal when the interactions take place across national borders. Since for Habermas the legitimation of law requires sensitivity both to the concrete context of application and to the universalistic thrust of impartial reason, the universality of basic rights, far from thwarting the expression and development of concrete forms of life, actually promotes them, as will become clear in the next section.

4   Multiculturalism and the Rights of Cultural Minorities

Habermas's discussion of multiculturalism serves to illustrate the advantages of his differentiated approach to moral, legal, and political issues and to the complex relationships between them. Both liberals and communitarians charge one another with insensitivity toward difference and hence with difficulties in dealing with some of the pressing issues of contemporary identity politics. Communitarians charge that the liberal emphasis on equal treatment amounts to "an abstract leveling of distinctions, a leveling of both cultural and social differences."[43] Liberals, in turn, claim that many of the characteristic features of communitarianism lead to an exclusion of difference. These include the communitarians' willingness to grant primacy to collective over individual rights and their construal of rights as an expression of values contained in the traditions of particular communities. The strong link between the notion of collective identity and rights is particularly problematic in pluralistic societies, where conflicts inevitably arise concerning the rights of minority groups whose identities and traditions differ from those of the majority group.

The peculiar power and originality of Habermas's theory of political legitimation consists in part in its ability to deal with a broad range of issues within the framework of a single unified theory of human rights and of popular sovereignty. However, it is not immediately evident that his approach is better able to account for politically significant differences between ethnic, religious, and national groups than either communitarianism or classical liberalism. For one thing, the highly abstract theories of human rights and of popular sovereignty on which he proposes to ground democracy at both the national and supranational levels seem to ignore the cultural values that shape the identities of groups. We shall conclude with a few brief remarks on these matters.

(1) The assumption that ethnic and cultural homogeneity are necessary conditions for the proper functioning of a democratic community creates obvious difficulties for justifying equal treatment of minority groups. Habermas's defense of the distinction between ethnos and demos, as we saw above, is directed precisely against this assumption, and this enables him to argue that there is no a priori reason why a constitutional democracy should find itself challenged by ever-increasing ethnic and cultural pluralism. Critics will predictably complain that this very argument underestimates the importance of cultural identities. They will point out that modern constitutional democracies emerged for the most part from struggles for self-determination by groups who saw their political destiny

as a matter of cultivating particular forms of life, customs, and values that distinguished them from other national groups. Habermas, by contrast, seems to treat the question of membership merely as a matter of historical contingency.

Even critics who accept the contingency of political membership could argue, however, that the distinction between ethnos and demos can establish at best the impermissibility of overt discrimination, but that the multiculturalism debate reveals precisely the tension between the principle of equal treatment and the aim of protecting cultural identity. Habermas's related distinction between a shared political culture and diverse subcultures, which emphasizes that political integration is a matter of agreement concerning basic constitutional principles and procedures rather than about concrete forms of life, might add fuel to the objection that he is insufficiently attuned to the importance of culture in politics, that mere agreement about a constitutional tradition, in isolation from the substance of a thick ethical life, is unlikely to lead to the legal protection of minority or formerly unrecognized communities.

While these objections have a certain plausibility, Habermas's social theory provides him with theoretical resources to deal with them. In the first place, he can draw on an account of identity-formation according to which individuation is achieved only through processes of socialization.[44] Briefly, the idea is that personal identity has an irreducibly intersubjective basis because the acquisition and maintenance of a sense of self depends upon the structures of reciprocity and recognition that are built into the presuppositions of communicative action. If identities are always articulated in and through processes of socialization, then protecting the identities of individuals necessarily implies protecting the contexts of interaction in which they define who they are. Because respect for the integrity of individuals thus requires respect for the contexts in which they form and sustain their identities, Habermas is led to defend policies that supporters of multiculturalism also endorse, such as multicultural education, governmental support for the cultural activities of minority groups, and the like.

Although Habermas and his communitarian opponents may support some of the same policies, they differ sharply in the justifications they offer for them. Thus Charles Taylor ultimately appeals to a controversial notion of group rights,[45] whereas Habermas relies on the notion of personal autonomy. For him, multicultural policies not only sustain the conditions for maintaining individual and group identities, but also secure the conditions for exercising autonomous choice. The goal of such policies is to allow citizens to engage in their cultural practices without being penalized, that is, without being discriminated against for their choices.[46] Hence, whatever programs are instituted for the protection of cultural contexts, they ought to be such as to secure the possibility of meaningful cultural choices. To this extent Habermas's proposal is mistrustful of essentialist multiculturalisms that attribute to the members of national or cultural groups what Anthony Appiah has called "tightly scripted identities," or that engage in attempts to dictate to individuals the nature or importance of such group memberships.[47] In a pluralistic context, both collective and personal identities are to some degree open to choice. Habermas's position on multiculturalism, then, endorses difference, but it is also sensitive to the potential threats to personal autonomy entailed by demands for recognizing group identities. The oppressive potential of the politics of recognition derives both from the desire to define what counts as an authentic manifestation of cultural participation and from the expectation that participants should make their membership in national or cultural groups the central, defining feature of their identities.

(2) A second aspect of Habermas's work that undergirds its sensitivity to difference is its highly differentiated approach to the nature of legal-political discussions. Liberals have traditionally tended to treat political discourse as though it were all of a piece and hence have been divided over whether democratic discussion ought to be construed either as purely strategic, a competition among elites for the votes of the citizens (Schumpeter, Bobbio, Zolo), or as conversations that stand under the general rules of morality and hence require special sorts of conversational constraints (Ackerman, Rawls). Habermas's approach is more complex. Starting from his distinction between pragmatic, ethical, and moral uses of practical reason,[48] he offers an analysis of political discourse which underlines the importance of ethical concerns in the political domain. While the legitimacy of the law depends on procedures designed to ensure

harmony between basic legal norms and morality, for Habermas legal norms differ from moral norms in that in addition to moral considerations, pragmatic and ethical considerations, as well as processes of compromise formation and bargaining, play a crucial role in the justification of the former. Though the historical developments of modern constitutional traditions exhibit an unmistakable convergence on universal human rights whose basic content is moral, nonetheless the citizens of each political unit, in legislating for themselves, interpret these basic constitutional principles in light of their own history and their own culturally specific values. In other words, in addition to enshrining universal moral principles, a legal system is one of the prime means by which a people defines who they are and who they want to be and thereby articulate their distinctive cultural identity.

(3) Habermas's clarification of the essential interconnection between legal validity and democratic procedure puts him in a strong position in debates about multiculturalism, for the internal relation between private and public autonomy means that the legitimacy of law is a function not merely of the protection of individual liberties but also of the exercise of participatory rights. Feminists, in particular, have insisted that the rights of women cannot be protected when women are prevented from articulating their needs, and that this is so even where institutions have been designed and budgets allotted for the purpose of such protection. In criticizing welfare schemes that lead to the treatment of clients as passive recipients of public charity, they have emphasized the fragility of individual liberties when they are severed from the participation of those whose needs stand in need of protection. If participation in the definition of needs is wanting, welfare turns into a peculiar kind of charity that is given conditionally on the recipients' acceptance of the administrative supervision of their lives. More broadly, in the domain of struggles for recognition of differences, the aim cannot be the institutionalization from above of protections and benefits for previously disadvantaged groups, but must rather be the realization of full democratic dialogue in which everyone affected has some input into the definition of needs and identities and how these will be promoted or hampered by state action.[49]

In the end, conversations about multiculturalism advance only if participants are not forced to choose between a normatively weak contextualism, on the one hand, and a context-insensitive universalism, on the other. Here as elsewhere, relevant distinctions do make a difference.

Translator's Note

Ciaran Cronin

Of the essays collected in this volume, I am responsible for the translations of chapters 1–5 and 7, though James Bohman kindly showed me an early draft of his translation of chapter 7. The remaining translations are by other hands, though I have made some revisions to all of them, as I have to previously published versions of chapters 1 and 2, to take account of final revisions of the German texts and to ensure an appropriate level of consistency between the essays.

A shorter version of chapter 1 appeared in *Proceedings of the Aristotelian Society* 96 (1996): 335–358. Chapter 6 was published under the title "Remarks on Dieter Grimm's 'Does Europe Need a Constitution,'" translated by Iain L. Fraser and John P. McCormick, in *European Law Journal* 1(3), 1995: 303–307. Chapter 8 was translated by Shierry Weber Nicholsen and appeared in Charles Taylor, *Multiculturalism: Examining the Politics of Recognition,* edited by Amy Gutmann (Princeton University Press: Princeton, NJ, 1994), pp. 107–148; it is reprinted here by permission of the publisher. An earlier version of chapter 9 appeared in *Constellations* 1(1): 1–10. Chapter 10 was translated by William Rehg and appeared in *European Journal of Philosophy* 3 (1): 12–20.

In preparing my own translations I learned something from each of these translations, and especially from Bill Rehg's translation of Habermas's *Between Facts and Norms: Contributions to a Discourse Theory of Law and Democracy,* to which this book is a companion volume. I am indebted to Pablo De Greiff, Vic Peterson, and Bill Rehg for suggestions on various chapters, and especially to Jürgen Habermas who went through a complete draft and made many helpful suggestions. In a number of places he has also revised the text so that the meaning is clearer than it would have been in a more literal translation.

Preface

The studies collected in this volume were written since the appearance of *Faktizität und Geltung* in 1992.[1] They are united by an interest in the question of what conclusions can still be drawn from the universalistic content of republican principles, in particular for pluralistic societies in which multicultural conflicts are becoming more acute, for nation-states that are coalescing into supranational units, and for the citizens of a world society who have been drawn unbeknownst to themselves into an involuntary risk society.

In Part I, I defend the rational content of a morality based on equal respect for everybody and on the universal solidarity and responsibility of each for all. Postmodern suspicion of an indiscriminately assimilating and homogenizing universalism fails to grasp the meaning of this morality and in the heat of controversy obliterates the relational structure of otherness and difference that universalism, properly understood, precisely takes into account. In *The Theory of Communicative Action* I set forth the basic concepts in such a way that they reveal the possibility of conditions of life that escape the false opposition between "*Gemeinschaft*" and "*Gesellschaft*," between "community" and "society." The counterpart to this social-theoretical program in moral and legal theory is a universalism that is highly sensitive to differences. Equal respect for *everyone* is not limited to those who are like us; it extends to the person of the other in his or her otherness. And solidarity with the other *as one of us* refers to the flexible "we" of a community that resists all substantive determinations and extends its permeable boundaries ever further. This moral community constitutes itself solely by way of the negative idea of abolishing discrimination and harm and of extending relations of mutual recognition to include marginalized men and women. The community thus constructively outlined is not a collective that would force its homogenized members to affirm its distinctiveness. Here inclusion does not imply locking members into a community that closes itself off from others. The "inclusion of the other" means rather that the boundaries of the community are open for all, also and most especially for those who are strangers to one another and want to remain strangers.

Part II contains a debate with John Rawls which took place at the invitation of the editors and publishers of *The Journal of Philosophy.* In my contribution I argue that discourse theory is better able to conceptualize the moral intuitions that inform both Rawls's and my work. My reply also attempts to clarify the differences between political liberalism and my understanding of Kantian republicanism.

Part III attempts to shed light on a controversy that has flared up once again in Germany since reunification. Here I take a step further a line of argument I originally developed in the essay "Citizenship and National Identity."[2] The romantically inspired idea of the nation as an ethnically based community of culture and historical destiny that may claim to exist as an independent state continues to provide support to such questionable attitudes as the appeal to an alleged right of national self-determination, the corresponding hostility toward multiculturalism and a politics of human rights, and a distrust of the transfer of sovereignty rights to supranational organizations. The defenders of the ethnic nation (*Volksnation*) overlook the fact that we can take as our guide precisely the impressive historical achievements of the democratic nation state and its republican constitutional principles in dealing with the problems currently posed by the inexorable shift to postnational forms of society.

Part IV deals with the implementation of human rights at both the global and the domestic level. The bicentennial of Kant's essay on *perpetual peace* is a suitable occasion for revising his conception of cosmopolitan law (*Weltbürgerrecht*) in light of our subsequent historical experiences. The once sovereign states have long since forfeited the presumption of innocence conferred on them by international law (*Völkerrecht*) and can no longer appeal to the principle of non-interference in their internal affairs. The challenge of multicultural-ism is precisely analogous to the question of humanitarian intervention. Here too minorities seek protection from their own governments. But in the case of multiculturalism, discrimination takes place within the framework of a broadly legitimate constitu-tional state and takes the more subtle form of domination by a majority culture that has merged with the general political culture. However, against Charles Taylor's communitarian proposal, I argue that a "politics of recognition," which is supposed to ensure the equal right of different subcultures and forms of life to coexist within a single republican polity, must reject collective rights and survival guarantees.

In Part V, I review some basic assumptions of the discourse-theoretical conception of democracy and the constitutional state. In particular, this understanding of deliberative politics allows an ac-count of the co-originality of popular sovereignty and human rights.

I

How Rational Is the Authority of the Ought?

1

A Genealogical Analysis of the Cognitive Content of Morality

I

If moral statements or utterances can be justified, then they have a cognitive content. Thus if we want to determine whether morality has a cognitive content we must examine what it means to justify something morally. In so doing we must distinguish between the *theoretical* question of whether moral utterances indeed express knowledge and, if so, how they can be justified, and the phenomenological question of what cognitive meaning those who participate in moral conflicts themselves associate with their utterances. I will use the term "moral justification" in the first instance in a descriptive manner to refer to the rudimentary practice of justification which has its proper place in the everyday interactions of the lifeworld.

In everyday contexts we make statements through which we demand certain conduct of others (i.e., hold them to an obligation), commit ourselves to a course of action (incur an obligation), reproach ourselves or others, admit mistakes, make excuses, offer to make amends, and so forth. On this first level, moral utterances serve to coordinate the actions of different actors in a binding or obligatory fashion. "Obligation" presupposes the intersubjective recognition of moral norms or customary practices that lay down for a community *in a convincing manner* what actors are obliged to do and what they can expect from one another. "In a convincing manner" means that the members of a moral community appeal to these norms whenever the coordination of action breaks down and present them as prima facie convincing reasons for claims and critical positions. Moral utterances are made against a background of potential *reasons* on which we can draw in moral disputes.

Moral rules operate in a reflexive manner; their power to coordinate action is confirmed on two interconnected levels of interaction. On the first level, they regulate social action immediately by binding the will of actors and orienting it in a particular way; on the second level, they govern the critical positions actors adopt when conflicts arise. The morality of a community not only lays down how its members should act; it also provides grounds for the consensual resolution of relevant conflicts. To the moral language game belong disagreements that can be resolved convincingly from the perspective of participants on the basis of potential justifications that are equally accessible to all. Sociologically speaking, moral obligations recommend themselves by their internal relation to the gentle, persuasive force of reasons as an alternative to strategic, that is, coercive or manipulative, forms of conflict resolution. To put it another way, if morality did not possess a credible cognitive content for members of the community, it would have no advantage over other, more costly forms of action coordination (such as the use of direct force, or the exercise of influence through the threat of sanctions or the promise of rewards).

When we examine moral disagreements, we must include affective reactions in the class of moral utterances. The key concept of obligation refers not only to the content of moral injunctions but in addition to the peculiar character of moral validity (*Sollgeltung*) which is also reflected in the feeling of being obligated. The critical and self-critical stances we adopt toward transgressions find expression in affective attitudes: from the third person perspective, in abhorrence, indignation, and contempt, from the perspective of those affected, in feelings of violation or resentment toward second persons, and from the first person perspective, in shame and guilt.[1] To these correspond the positive emotional reactions of admiration, loyalty, gratitude, etc. Because they express implicit judgments, these feelings in which actors express their pro and con attitudes are correlated with evaluations. We judge actions and intentions to be "good" or "bad," whereas our terms for virtues refer to personal qualities of agents. The claim that moral judgments admit of justification also reveals itself in these moral feelings and evaluations, for they differ from other feelings and evaluations in being tied to obligations that function as reasons. We do not regard them as the expression of mere sentiments and preferences.

From the fact that moral norms are "valid" for the members of a community it does not follow, of course, that they have intrinsic cognitive content. A sociological observer may be able to describe a moral language game as a social fact, and even to explain why members are "convinced" of their moral rules, without himself being in a position to give a plausible reconstruction of their reasons and interpretations.[2] But a philosopher cannot remain content with this. He will pursue the phenomenology of the relevant moral disagreements further in order to comprehend what members of the community do when they justify something morally.[3] Of course, "comprehend" here means something other than simply "understanding" utterances. Reflective reconstruction of the everyday practice of justification in which we ourselves participate as laypersons permits reconstructive translations that foster critical understanding. In this methodological attitude the philosopher extends *from within* the participant perspective beyond the circle of *immediate* participants.

The results of such efforts can be gauged by examining modern programs in moral philosophy. These theories differ in their degrees of hermeneutic openness. Their reconstructions of the cognitive content of our everyday moral intuitions are more or less comprehensive to the extent that they are sensitive to the intuitive moral knowledge of the participants.

Strong noncognitivism tries to unmask the presumed cognitive content of moral language in general as an illusion. It attempts to show that behind the utterances that appear to participants as moral judgments and stances that admit of justification, there lurk mere feelings, attitudes, and decisions. Utilitarianism, which traces the "binding" force of evaluative orientations and obligations back to preferences, arrives at revisionist descriptions similar to those of noncognitivist views such as emotivism (e.g., that of Stevenson) and decisionism (e.g., that of Popper or the early Hare). But in contrast with strong noncognitivism, utilitarianism replaces the unreflective moral self-understanding of participants with a utility calculation undertaken from an observer's point of view and thereby provides a moral-theoretical justification of the moral language game.

In this respect there is an affinity between utilitarianism and forms of *weak noncognitivism* that take into account the self-understanding of morally *acting* subjects, whether by reference to moral feelings (as in the tradition of Scottish moral philosophy) or by reference to an orientation to accepted norms (as in Hobbesian contractualism). However, the self-understanding of morally *judging* subjects succumbs to revision. On such accounts, the supposedly objectively grounded positions and judgments of morally judging subjects in fact merely express rational motives, be they feelings or interests, justified in a purposive-rational manner.

Weak cognitivism leaves intact the self-understanding of the everyday practice of moral justification to the extent that it ascribes an epistemic status to "strong" evaluations. Reflection on what is "good" for me (or for us) all things considered or on what is "authoritative" for my (or for our) consciously pursued life-plan opens up a form of rational assessment of evaluative orientations (in the spirit of Aristotle or Kierkegaard). What in each instance is valuable or authentic forces itself upon us, so to speak, and differs from mere preferences in its binding character, that is, in the fact that it points beyond needs and preferences. However, the intuitive understanding of justice undergoes revision on this view. From the perspective of each individual's conception of the good, justice, which is tailored to interpersonal relations, appears as just one value among others (however pronounced), not as a context-independent standard of impartial judgment.

Strong cognitivism seeks in addition to take account of the categorical validity claim of moral obligations. It attempts to reconstruct the cognitive content of the moral language game across its full scope. The Kantian tradition, unlike neo-Aristotelianism, is not just concerned with clarifying a practice of moral justification that unfolds *within* the horizon of received norms, but seeks to justify a moral

A Genealogical Analysis of the Cognitive Content of Morality

point of view from which such norms can themselves be judged in an impartial fashion. In this tradition, moral theory grounds the possibility of moral justification by reconstructing the point of view that members of posttraditional societies themselves intuitively adopt when they find that they must appeal to reasons to justify problematic moral norms. But in contrast with empiricist varieties of contractualism, this view holds that these reasons are not conceived as agent-relative motives, thereby leaving the epistemic core of moral validity intact.

In what follows I first describe the historical situation in which morality loses its religious foundation (II). This description provides the background for a genealogical exploration of the two variants of classical empiricism (III), two interesting attempts to rehabilitate the empiricist program (IV–V), and the two traditions that originate with Aristotle (VI) and Kant (VII), respectively. We are then in a position to examine two systematic questions: Which moral intuitions admit of rational reconstruction? (VIII) and can the discourse-theoretical standpoint itself be justified? (IX)

II

The various attempts that have been made to explicate the "moral point of view" remind us that, after the breakdown of a universally valid "catholic" worldview and with the subsequent transition to pluralistic societies, moral commands can no longer be publicly justified from a transcendent God's eye point of view. From this latter vantage point beyond the world, the world could be objectified as a whole. The moral point of view is supposed to reconstruct this perspective within the world itself, that is, within the boundaries of our intersubjectively shared world, while preserving the possibility of distancing ourselves from the world as a whole, and hence the universality of the world-encompassing viewpoint. This shift in perspective to a "transcendence from within"[4] raises the question of whether the specific binding force of norms and values can be grounded in the subjective freedom and the practical reason of human beings forsaken by God—and, if so, how the peculiar authority of the moral ought is thereby transformed. In the secular societies of the West, everyday moral intuitions are still shaped by the normative substance of so to speak decapitated, legally privatized, religious traditions, in particular by the contents of the Hebrew morality of justice in the Old Testament and the Christian ethics of love in the New Testament. These contents are transmitted by processes of socialization, though often only implicitly and under different titles. Thus a moral philosophy that views its task as one of reconstructing everyday moral consciousness is faced with the challenge of examining how much of this substance can be rationally justified.

The biblically transmitted prophetic doctrines furnished interpretations and reasons that imbued moral norms with the power to generate public agreement; they explained why God's commands are not arbitrary injunctions but can claim validity in a cognitive sense. Let us assume there is no functional equivalent for morality under modern conditions either, and hence that the moral language game cannot be replaced by a system of purely behavioral controls which are also seen as such. Then the phenomenologically attested cognitive validity of moral judgments and positions poses the problem of whether the power of accepted values and norms to generate rational agreement may not be a form of transcendental illusion, or whether it can still be justified even under postmetaphysical conditions. Moral philosophy does not itself have to provide the reasons and interpretations that, in secularized societies, take the place of the (at least *publicly*) devalued religious reasons and interpretations; but it would have to identify the kinds of reasons and interpretations that can lend the moral language game sufficient rational force even without the backing of religion. With regard to this genealogical problematic, I would like, first, to recall the monotheistic foundation of the validity of our moral norms (1) and, second, to specify in greater detail the challenge posed by the modern historical situation (2).

(1) The bible grounds moral commands in the revealed word of God. These commands are to be obeyed unconditionally because they are backed by the authority of an omnipotent God. But if that were the only source of their authority, their validity would merely have the character of a "must" (*Müssen*), as a reflection of the unlimited power of a sovereign: God can compel obedience. But this

voluntaristic interpretation does not yet endow normative validity with any cognitive significance. It first acquires a cognitive meaning when moral commands are interpreted as expressions of the will of an *all-knowing* and completely *just and loving* God. Moral commands do not spring from the free choice of an Almighty but are the expressions of the will of an all-wise Creator and an all-just and loving Redeemer. We can distinguish two different orders of reasons for the respectworthiness of the divine commands: metaphysical (*ontotheologisch*) reasons grounded in the order of creation and soteriological reasons rooted in the (divinely ordained) history of salvation.

Metaphysical justification appeals to a world order that owes its existence to the wise legislation of the Creator. It accords human beings and the human community a privileged status within creation and thereby endows them with a "calling." Creationist metaphysics gives currency to the conception of natural law underlying cosmologically grounded ethical systems which is also familiar from the impersonal worldviews of the Asiatic religions and of Greek philosophy. On such ethical conceptions, things are *essentially* endowed with teleological significance. Human beings are also part of the order of Being and can deduce from it what they are and what they ought to be. In this way the rational content of moral laws receives ontological confirmation from the rational order of Being as a whole.

The soteriological justification of moral commands, by contrast, appeals to the justice and goodness of a Redeemer; at the end of time he will fulfill his promise of salvation which is contingent on one's leading a moral or lawful life. He is Judge and Redeemer in one person. In light of his commands, God judges each person's life in accordance with his just deserts. His justice ensures that his judgment will be consonant with the unique life history of each individual, while at the same time his goodness allows for human fallibility and for the sinfulness of human nature. Moral commands acquire a rational meaning both from the fact that they point the way to personal salvation and from the fact that they are applied in an impartial manner.

To be sure, speaking of "moral commands" is misleading in that the path to salvation is not predetermined by a system of rules but by a divinely authorized way of life that we are enjoined to emulate. This is what is meant, for example, by an *imitatio Christi*, that is, by following in the footsteps of Christ. Other world religions too, and even philosophy with its ideals of the wise man and the *vita contemplativa*, distill the moral substance of their doctrines into exemplary forms of life. This means that in religious-metaphysical worldviews, the *just* is still interwoven with specific conceptions of the *good life*. How we should treat others in interpersonal relations is laid down by a model of the exemplary life.

Furthermore, the reference to a personal God who sits in judgment on the destiny of each individual at the end of time makes possible an important distinction between two aspects of morality. Every person has a twofold communicative relation to God, first as a member of the community of believers with whom God has entered into a covenant, and second as a unique person individuated by his life history who cannot allow himself to be represented (*vertreten*) by anyone else before God. This communication structure shapes one's moral relation—mediated by God—to one's neighbor under the aspects of *solidarity* and of *justice* (here understood in the narrow sense). As a member of the universal community of believers, I am bound by solidarity to the other as my fellow, as "one of us;" as an unsubstitutable (*unvertretbar*) individual; by contrast, I owe the other equal respect as "one among all" persons who, as unique individuals, expect to be treated justly. The "solidarity" grounded in membership recalls the social bond that unites all persons: one person stands in for the other. The uncompromising egalitarianism of "justice," by contrast, calls for sensitivity to the differences that set each individual apart from others: each person demands that others respect him in his otherness.[5] The Judaeo-Christian tradition regards solidarity and justice as two sides of the same coin: they provide two different perspectives on the same communication structure.

(2) With the transition to a pluralism of worldviews in modern society, religion and the ethos rooted in it disintegrate as a *public* basis of a morality shared by all. At any rate, the validity of *universally binding* moral rules can no longer be accounted for in terms of reasons and interpretations that presuppose the existence and the agency of a transcendent Creator and Redeemer. As a consequence, the metaphysical validation of objectively rational moral laws loses

its force, and with it the soteriological connection between their just application and the objectively desirable good of salvation. Moreover, the devaluation of metaphysical concepts (and the corresponding category of explanations) is also connected with a displacement of epistemic authority from religious doctrines to the empirical sciences. With the dissolution of metaphysical concepts of essences, the internal connection between assertoric statements and corresponding expressive, evaluative, and normative statements also dissolves. What is "objectively rational" can be justified only as long as the just and the good are grounded in a normatively imbued Being itself; and what is "objectively desirable" can be justified only as long as the teleology of the history of salvation guarantees the realization of the state of perfect justice that also involves a concrete good.

In this new situation, moral philosophy depends on a "postmetaphysical level of justification." This means in the first place that, as regards its method, it must renounce the God's eye viewpoint; as regards its content, it can no longer appeal to the order of creation and sacred history; and, as regards its theoretical approach, it cannot appeal to metaphysical concepts of essences that undercut the logical distinctions between different types of illocutionary utterances.[6] Moral philosophy must justify the cognitive validity of moral judgments and positions without drawing on these resources.

Four responses to this situation strike me as too implausible to merit further discussion:

• Moral realism attempts to rehabilitate the ontological justification of norms and values with postmetaphysical means. It defends the idea that we can have cognitive access to something in the world that has the peculiar power to orient our desires and to bind our wills. Since this normative source can no longer be explained in terms of the constitution of the world as a whole, the problem shifts to the epistemological level: a mode of experience analogous to perception—an intuitive grasp or ideal intuition of values—must be postulated as the basis of value judgments which are assimilated to factual statements.[7]

• While utilitarianism does offer a principle in terms of which moral judgments can be justified, its orientation to the anticipated aggregate utility of a course of action does not permit an adequate reconstruction of the meaning of normativity in general. In particular, utilitarianism fails to grasp the individualistic meaning of a morality based on equal respect for everyone.

• As we have seen, metaethical skepticism leads to revisionist descriptions of the moral language game that lose touch with the participants' self-understanding. They cannot explain what they are trying to explain, namely, everyday moral practices, which would break down if the participants thought that their moral disputes did not have any cognitive content.[8]

• Moral functionalism is not traditionalistic in the sense that it reverts to premodern modes of justification. It invokes the authority of uprooted religious traditions for their positive effects in stabilizing moral consciousness. But a functional justification of morality undertaken from the observer perspective not only cannot replace the authority of the reasons that convinced believers; it unintentionally destroys the cognitive content of a religiously grounded morality by treating the epistemic authority of belief as a *mere* social fact.[9]

III

The religious doctrines of creation and the history of salvation provided epistemic reasons for believing that divine commands do not spring from blind authority but are rational or "true." If reason now withdraws from the objective realm of nature or sacred history into the minds of acting and judging subjects, the "objectively rational" reasons for moral judgment and action must be replaced by "subjectively rational" reasons.[10] Once the religious foundation has been undermined, the cognitive content of the moral language game can henceforth be reconstructed only on the basis of the reason and the will of its participants. Hence "will" and "reason" also form the basic concepts of moral theories that set themselves this task. Whereas empiricism conceives of practical reason as the faculty of determining one's choice (*Willkür*) by maxims of prudence, Aristotelianism and Kantianism take account not only of rational motives but also of a will (*Wille*) that is free to bind itself by *insight*.

Empiricism identifies practical reason with instrumental reason. On this view it is rational for an actor to act in one way and not in another if the (anticipated) result of the action is in his interest, satisfies him or gives him pleasure. In a particular situation such reasons carry weight for a particular actor who has specific preferences and goals. We call these reasons "pragmatic" or preferential because they motivate actions and, unlike epistemic reasons, do not immediately support judgments or opinions. They provide rational motives for actions but not for convictions. However, they "affect" the will only to the extent that the actor adopts a corresponding rule of action. This is what differentiates intentional action from spontaneously motivated action in general. An "intention" is also a disposition; but, in contrast with "inclination," it only arises through freedom of will, that is, in virtue of the fact that the actor adopts a rule of action. An actor acts rationally when he acts on *reasons* and knows why he follows a maxim. Empiricism only takes account of pragmatic reasons, in other words, of the case in which an actor lets his will be bound (in Kant's terms) to "rules of skill" or "counsels of prudence" by instrumental reason. In this way he obeys the principle of instrumental rationality: "Whoever wills the end, so far as reason has decisive influence on his action, wills also the indispensably necessary means to it that lie in his power."[11]

Taking this as their basis, the two classical empiricist programs attempt to reconstruct a rational core of morality. Scottish moral philosophy takes moral feelings as basic and conceives of morality as what founds the bonds of solidarity that unite a community (a). Social contract theory begins immediately with interests and conceives of morality as what ensures that social interactions regulated by norms are just (b). Both theories ultimately run up against the same problem: they cannot explain the obligatory character of moral duties, which points beyond the binding force of prudence, in terms of rational motives alone.

(a) Moral attitudes express feelings of approval and disapproval. Hume understands these as the typical sentiments of a third person who judges actors from a benevolent distance. Consequently an agreement in moral judgments concerning a person's character signifies a convergence of feelings. Even if approval and disapproval express sympathy and antipathy and hence are emotional in nature, it is rational for an observer to react in this way. For we esteem someone as virtuous if he shows himself to be useful and agreeable to us and our friends. Moreover, this display of sympathy fills the virtuous person with pride and satisfaction, whereas blame pains the one who is reproached and occasions him displeasure. Thus there are pragmatic reasons even for altruistic action: benevolence that meets with the approval of others gives satisfaction to the useful and agreeable person himself. These affective dispositions provide the basis upon which the socially integrative power of mutual trust can unfold.

However, these pragmatic reasons for moral attitudes and actions are convincing only as long as we think of interpersonal relations in small communities based on solidarity, such as families and neighborhoods. Complex societies cannot be held together solely by feelings like sympathy and trust, which are geared to the local sphere. Moral conduct toward strangers calls for "artificial" virtues, above all a disposition to justice. In the case of abstract networks of action, members of primary reference groups can no longer rely on the familiar reciprocities between performances and rewards and thereby lose their pragmatic reasons for benevolence. Feelings of obligation that bridge the distance between strangers are not "rational for me" in the same sense as are feelings of loyalty toward members of my group on whose cooperation I can rely. Insofar as solidarity is the reverse side of justice, there is nothing wrong in principle with the attempt to explain the *origin* of moral duties as the result of the extension of primary group loyalties to ever larger groups (or in terms of the transformation of personal trust into "system trust").[12] But the validity of a normative theory is not measured by how it deals with questions of moral psychology but rather by how it accounts for the normative priority of duties. It should explain why, in cases of conflict between benevolent feelings and an abstract requirement of justice, it is rational for members of a group to *subordinate* their loyalty toward those they know personally to a solidarity with strangers. But feelings offer too narrow a basis for the solidarity between members of an impersonal community of moral beings.[13]

(b) Social contract theory overlooks the dimension of solidarity from the outset by relating the question of the normative justification of a system of justice directly to the interests of the individual, thereby shifting the focus of morality from duties to rights. The juridical conception of an individual right (*subjektive Recht*) to the legally protected freedom to pursue one's interests within certain domains accords with a strategy of justification that operates with pragmatic reasons and is geared to the question of whether it is rational for the individual to subject his will to a system of rules. Furthermore, the *generalized* notion of the contract derived from private law, which grounds such rights in a symmetrical way, is well suited for the construction of a social order based on agreement. Such an order is just or good in the moral sense when it satisfies the interests of its members equally. The social contract follows from the idea that each candidate must have a rational motive for consenting of his own free will to become a member and subjecting himself to the corresponding norms and procedures. Thus the cognitive content of what makes the order a moral or a just order rests on the aggregated consent of all of the individual members and can be explained more precisely in terms of the rational weighing of goods that each of them performs in light of his own preferences.

This program is open to two objections. First, the assimilation of moral questions to questions of the political justice of an association of individuals under law[14] has the drawback that equal respect for everybody, and hence a universalistic morality, cannot be justified on this basis. Only those who already have an interest in rule-governed interaction with one another have a reason to accept reciprocal obligations. Thus the sphere of those possessing rights will extend only to those from whom reciprocation can be expected because they want to, or have to, cooperate. Second, Hobbesianism wrestles in vain with the familiar problem of the free rider, who engages in a shared practice only with the proviso that he can deviate from the agreed norms when it is to his advantage. The free rider problem shows that an agreement between interested parties cannot itself ground any *obligations*.

This problem has led to an interesting combination of the two empiricist strategies. A mental reservation concerning formally recognized norms is no longer possible once transgressions of norms are punished not by externally imposed sanctions but instead by the *internalized* sanctions manifested in feelings of guilt or shame.[15] But the proposed explanation founders on the prima facie difficulty of explaining self-punishing feelings in a rational manner. One cannot have a rational motive for "wishing to have" inner sanctions of this kind.[16] Apart from anything else, there are conceptual reasons why it cannot be "rational for me" to accept the promptings of a bad conscience unquestioningly and at the same time make them the object of practical reflection, hence nonetheless to question them. When we act morally we do so because we take it to be right or good and not because we want to avoid inner sanctions. We call sanctions "internalized" when we have made them our own. But the process of making them our own cannot itself be explained in a purposive-rational manner, at any rate not from the perspective of the person affected: for him the rationality of an action is not simply its ability to make a functional contribution to the regulation of the commu-nity as a whole.[17]

There is no more a way back from the contractualist justification of a normative order to internalized feelings of disapprobation than there is a direct route from moral feelings of sympathy and rejection to the instrumental justification of duties. Moral feelings give expres-sion to attitudes that imply moral judgments; and in disputes over the validity of moral judgments we do not limit our arguments to pragmatic reasons or preferences. Classical empiricism fails to ac-count for this phenomenon because it excludes epistemic reasons. It cannot ultimately explain the obligatory force of moral norms in terms of preferences.

IV

Two more recent theoretical approaches, which remain committed to empiricist assumptions while attempting to do justice to the phe-nomenology of obligatory norms, respond to this predicament of classical empiricism. Whereas Allan Gibbard remains closer to the expressivist approach of explaining a social life based on solidarity, Ernst Tugendhat remains closer to the contractualist approach of reconstructing a social life based on justice. But both start from the same intuition: viewed in terms of function, every moral system provides a solution to the problem of coordinating actions among beings who are dependent on social interaction. Moral consciousness is the expression of the legitimate demands that members of a cooperative social group make on one another. Moral feelings regulate the observance of the underlying norms. Shame and guilt alert a person that he, in Tugendhat's words, has failed as a "cooperative member" or as a "good social partner."[18] Gibbard remarks of these feelings: "[they are] tied genetically to poor cooperative will—to a special way a social being can fail to be a good candidate for inclusion in cooperative schemes."[19] Both authors seek to demonstrate the rational basis of the emergence or the choice of morality in general, but also of a universalistic morality based on reason (*Vernunftmoral*). Whereas Tugendhat sticks to the subjective perspective of participants, Gibbard takes the objectifying approach of functional explanation.

In contrast with Kant, who understands norms exclusively as maxims of action, Gibbard extends the concept of a norm to all kinds of standards that specify why it is rational to hold an opinion, to express a feeling, or to act in a certain way. Having certain opinions can be rational for me in the same way as can expressing certain feelings or acting on certain intentions. That something is "rational for me" means that I have made certain norms my own in light of which it "makes sense," or is "appropriate," "plausible" or simply "best," to believe, feel, or do something. Gibbard then calls those norms moral that lay down for a community which classes of actions merit spontaneous disapproval. They specify in which cases it is rational for the members to feel ashamed or guilty or to resent the conduct of others. Gibbard's inclusive use of the concept of a norm means that, unlike Kant, he cannot derive the rationality of action (in accordance with the aforementioned principle of purposive rationality) from the actor's reasons for binding his will to this or that maxim. But if *all* rational motives refer to prior standards, it makes no sense to ask in turn why it was rational to internalize such standards in the first place. The fact that someone takes something to be rational *simply expresses* the fact that the standards authorizing this judgment are *his* standards. Hence Gibbard understands rationality judgments, whether moral or nonmoral, as expressive speech acts. They cannot be true or false, but only truthful or untruthful. And the only warrant for the agent-relative bindingness of moral rules is a truthfully expressed mental state.[20]

Given this "expressivist" account of normativity, Gibbard makes two moves. First he offers an evolutionary explanation of moral norms from the observer's perspective and then he tries to make sense of the biological "value" of morality from the participant's perspective, that is, he tries to translate it from the theoretical language of a "biology of interpersonal coordination" into the language of practical deliberation.

According to the proposed neo-Darwinian explanation, moral feelings such as shame, guilt, and resentment developed in the course of the evolution of the human species as regulatory mechanisms to facilitate the coordination of action. The normativity of rules in virtue of which it appears rational to members of cooperating groups to have such feelings, and hence to disapprove of conduct that deviates from norms and to offer or to expect corresponding excuses as reparation for a failure in coordination, is not rationally intelligible to the participants themselves. But the authority which simply *manifests* itself in the rationality judgments of the participants can be *explained* from the observer's perspective in terms of the "reproductive value" of the internalized norms and the corresponding affective dispositions. That these norms and dispositions are advantageous from an evolutionary point of view is supposed to find expression in their subjectively convincing character. On this analysis, the proper task for philosophy is to establish a plausible connection between what is *functional* for the observer and what is taken to be *rational* by the participant. This problem takes on particular urgency when the actors no longer rely on internalized norms but engage in open disputes over which norms they should accept as valid.

Language functions in any case as the most important medium for interpersonal coordination. Moral judgments and positions that rest on internalized norms find expression in an emotionally charged language. But when the normative background consensus breaks down and new norms have to be worked out, a *different* form of communication is required. The participants must then put their trust in the orienting power of "normative discourses": "I shall call this influence *normative governance*. It is in this governance of action, belief, and emotion that we might find a place for phenomena that constitute acceptance of norms, as opposed to merely internalizing them. When we work out at a distance, in community, what to do or think or feel in a situation we are discussing, we come to accept norms for the situation."[21]

But it is not altogether clear what could support the "normative governance" such discourses are supposed to provide. It cannot be good reasons, because they derive their rationally motivating power from internalized standards which must be assumed to have forfeited their authority—otherwise there would be no need to reach an understanding in discourse. What the participants must make an object of discussion cannot simultaneously function as a standard in the discussion. Gibbard cannot represent discursively achieved agreement concerning moral norms on the model of the cooperative search for the truth; rather he must represent it as a process in which participants rhetorically *influence* one another.

A proponent who wants to win agreement for a norm that he believes is worthy of recognition can only truthfully express the subjective state in which he *experiences* the norm as binding. If he manages to do this in an authentic way he can win over his interlocutors by inducing similar affective states in them. Thus in normative discourses reaching a rational agreement is replaced by something like achieving a mutual harmonization of feelings. Interestingly, the public, egalitarian, and noncoercive communicative conditions of a Socratic dialogue are supposed to be most conducive to the exercise of this kind of rhetorical influence. The "conversational demands" governing Socratic dialogue are of a pragmatic kind (with the exception of the requirement that contributions must be coherent).[22] They are supposed to prevent the unjustified exclusion of affected parties and the arbitrary privileging of speakers and topics—in other words, unequal treatment; they are also supposed to preclude repression and manipulation and nonrhetorical forms of influence. These communication conditions are indistinguishable from the pragmatic presuppositions of a cooperative search for truth.[23] So it is hardly surprising that the norms that win agreement under these conditions are ultimately identical to a morality of equal solidaristic responsibility for everybody. But we cannot speak of "justification" here because the discursive process is not geared to the mobilization of the better reasons but to the effectiveness of the more impressive expressions of feelings.

As a result, Gibbard owes us an explanation of why precisely the norms that prove to be the best from the functional perspective of their "survival value" for a particular species should win agreement under the pragmatically privileged conditions of communication: "In normative discussion we are influenced by each other, but not only by each other. Mutual influence nudges us toward consensus, if all goes well, *but not toward any consensus whatsoever.* Evolutionary considerations suggest this: consensus may promote biological fitness, *but only the consensus of the right kind.* The consensus must be mutually fitness-enhancing, and so to move toward it we must be responsive to things that promote our biological fitness."[24] Gibbard recognizes the problem that the results reached from the objective perspective of investigation must be made consistent with the results that the participants in discourse accept as rational from an insider's perspective. But one looks in vain for such an explanation. Gibbard fails to explain why the improbable communicative conditions of normative discourses are "selective" in the same sense, and why they should produce the same result—that is, an increase in the probability of collective survival—as do the mechanisms of natural evolution.[25]

V

Ernst Tugendhat avoids the problematic detour through a functionalist explanation of morality. He first describes how moral rule systems function *in general* and what motives we could have to be moral *at all* (a), and then considers *what form* of morality it would be rational for us to choose under postmetaphysical conditions (b).

(a) In contrast with classical contractualism, Tugendhat begins with a full-fledged concept of the moral community. This concept includes the self-understanding of those who feel themselves bound by moral rules and hence those who "have a conscience," express moral feelings, argue about moral judgments with reasons, and so forth. Members of the community think that they "know" what is "good" and "evil" in the categorical sense. Having outlined this conception, Tugendhat considers whether it is rational for any given candidate to enter into such a moral practice described *as a whole,* that is, to become a cooperating member of a moral community *as such:* "That we want to belong to a moral community at all . . . is ultimately an act of our autonomy for which there can only be good motives, not reasons."[26] By "autonomy" Tugendhat understands only the capacity to act in a rule-governed manner from rational motives. But the practical reasons he goes on to enumerate go beyond the empiricist framework of value-free considerations of prudence. For Tugendhat adduces not premoral interests but value-orientations which could only have developed within the context of a morally constituted community. For example, it is rational for me to enter a moral community because I prefer the status of subject and addressee of rights and duties to the status of an object to which reciprocal instrumentalization would reduce me; or because balanced friendships are better for me than the structural isolation of a strategically acting subject; or because I can experience the satisfaction of being respected by persons who are worthy of moral respect only as a member of a moral community, and so forth.

The preferences that Tugendhat specifies for entry into a moral community are already infused with the values of such a community; they are contingent on *prior,* intersubjectively shared value-orientations. At any rate these motives do not explain how it could be rational for actors *who find themselves in a premoral condition* and know nothing else to make the transition to a moral condition. Someone who arrives at reasons for his decision to pursue a moral life, reasons which can only result from reflection on the prior experience of the advantages of morally regulated interaction, has left behind the egocentric perspective of rational choice and takes his orientation instead from conceptions of the good life. He orients his practical deliberation to the ethical question of what kind of life he should lead, who he is and wants to be, what in the long run is "good" for him all things considered, etc. Reasons that count in light of these considerations have motivating force only insofar as they affect the identity and self-understanding of an actor who has already been formed by a moral community.

Martin Seel also understands (and accepts) the argument in this sense. Although the happiness of a successful life does not necessarily consist in a moral life, a subject who wants to live a good life has good reasons for accepting moral conditions (of whatever kind). It is already clear from the ethical perspective that it is not possible to lead a *good* life outside a *moral* community. Of course, that only means that "there are necessary areas of overlap between a good life and a morally good life, but not that a good life is only possible *within the limits* of a morally good life."[27] But Tugendhat is not so much interested in the *relation* between the good life and morality as in the *ethical justification* for being moral. And this leads to an unavoidable paradox if, like Tugendhat, one rightly insists on the difference between what is good for oneself and moral concern for the interests of others: insofar as an actor only has rational motives for preferring moral to premoral conditions, he undermines the obligatory nature of the moral expectations whose categorical validity he should recognize under these conditions.

Seel recognizes that "moral consideration . . . transcends those preference-based reasons we have for accepting the moral point of view *at all*,"[28] but he does not draw the correct conclusion from this.[29] The thrust of an ethical justification for being moral is not that someone is motivated by preference-based reasons to "confront reasons of a completely different sort" but rather that the moral language loses the illocutionary force of unconditional demands as soon as participation in the moral language game is made dependent on the decision of a rational chooser. If the actor who assures himself of the superiority of a moral way of life is the same as the one who accepts such conditions on the basis of this preference, his ethical justification conditions the moral language game as a whole and changes the character of the moves that are possible within it. For acting morally "out of respect for the law" is incompatible with the ethical proviso of always examining whether the practice as a whole also pays off from the perspective of one's own life plan. For conceptual reasons, the categorical meaning of moral obligations can be upheld only as long as addressees are prevented from stepping outside the moral community, if only in a virtual manner, in order to weigh the advantages and disadvantages of membership from the distance of the first person perspective. Nor, conversely, is there a route from ethical reflection to the justification of morality.

(b) Even if the empiricist dream were to become a reality, and reflection on one's own interests would generate a rationally reconstructable dynamic that would propel one beyond the pursuit of those interests in the direction of unconditional moral concern— even then the essential problem would not be solved. Ethical reasons explain at most why we should engage in some moral language game or other, but not which one. Tugendhat gives this problem a genealogical cast. Having lost the traditional foundation of their shared morality, the participants must reach a shared understanding of which specific moral norms they should adopt. In this process nobody can claim more authority than anyone else; all standpoints from which one could claim privileged access to moral truth have lost their validity. The social contract could not provide a satisfactory response to this challenge because an agreement among contracting partners motivated by interests can lead at best to an externally imposed social regulation of conduct, but not to a binding, let alone a universalistic, conception of the common good. Tugendhat's description of the starting point is similar to the one I have proposed. The members of a moral community are not trying to *replace* morality with a social regulation of behavior that is to everybody's advantage. Their goal is not to replace the moral language game as such, but only its religious foundation.

This line of thought leads to reflection on the conditions of communicative agreement which, *after* religion and metaphysics, represent the only remaining resource on which the justification of a morality of equal respect for everybody can draw: "If the good is no longer laid down in a transcendent manner, the only principle of the good seems to be consideration for members of the community, whose membership in turn can no longer be limited, and hence consideration for all others—which means consideration for their wishes and interests. To put it in the form of a slogan: intersubjectivity thus understood takes the place of the transcendent pregiven. . . . Since the reciprocal demands . . . constitute the form of morality in general, one can also say: inasmuch as the content to which the demands refer is nothing other than consideration for what all want, *the content now fits the form.*"[30]

In this way Tugendhat derives the Kantian principle of universalization from the symmetrical conditions of the initial situation in which the parties, who have been stripped of all privileges and as a result are on an equal footing, come together to agree on basic norms that can be rationally accepted by all participants.[31] However, he fails to recognize that "rational acceptability" thereby takes on a meaning different from something's being "rational for me." If there is no authority for relations of moral recognition higher than the good will and insight of those who come to a shared agreement concerning the rules that are to govern their living together, then the standard for judging these rules must be derived exclusively from the situation in which participants seek to *convince* one another of their beliefs and proposals. By entering into a cooperative communicative practice, they already tacitly accept the condition of symmetrical or equal consideration for everyone's interests. Because this practice only achieves its goal if everyone is willing to convince others and to be convinced by them, every serious participant must examine what is rational for him *under the conditions* of symmetrical and equal consideration of interests. But with the reference to the possibility of an agreement reached by rational discourse (which in Rawls's case is imposed by the structure of the original position), pragmatic reasons take on an epistemic meaning. In this way we transcend the boundaries of instrumental reason. A principle of universalization that cannot be justified by appeal to each individual's interests (or to each individual's conception of the good) serves as the ground of validity of rational morality. We can gain insight into this principle only through reflection on the unavoidable conditions of impartial judgment.

While Gibbard analyzes these conditions as pragmatic presuppositions of normative discourses, he views them solely from the functionalist perspective of their contribution to the coordination of social action. Tugendhat, by contrast, upholds the view that the acceptance of moral rules must be justified from the perspective of the participants themselves; but he too denies the epistemic meaning that this acceptance assumes under conditions of rational discourse.

VI

Weak noncognitivism assumes that an actor's choice can be affected by practical reason in just one way, namely, through deliberations that accord with the principle of instrumental rationality. If, by contrast, practical reason is no longer assimilated to instrumental reason, the constellation of reason and will changes, and hence so does the concept of subjective freedom. Freedom is no longer exhausted by the ability to choose in accordance with maxims of prudence but finds expression in the will's capacity to bind itself through insight. The significance of the term "insight" here is that a decision can be justified in terms of "epistemic" reasons. Since epistemic reasons generally support the truth of assertoric statements, the use of the expression "epistemic" in practical contexts is in need of explanation. Pragmatic reasons depend on the preferences and purposes of each particular person. Only the agent himself, who knows his own preferences and purposes, has the final epistemic authority to judge these "data." Practical reflection can lead to insights only when it goes beyond the subjective world to which the actor has privileged access and pertains to the contents of an intersubjectively shared social world. In this way reflection on shared experiences, practices, and forms of life brings to awareness an ethical knowledge to which we do not have access simply through the epistemic authority of the first person singular.

Bringing to consciousness something implicitly known is not the same as acquiring empirical knowledge.[32] Scientific knowledge is counterintuitive, whereas reflexively achieved insight critically appropriates a pretheoretical know-how by making it explicit, contextualizing it, and testing its coherence.[33] Ethical insights result from the explication of the know-how that communicatively socialized individuals have acquired by growing up in a particular culture. The most general elements of the practical knowledge of a culture have become sedimented in its evaluative vocabulary and in its rules for the use of normative sentences. Actors do not just develop conceptions of themselves and of the life they would like to lead in general in light of their evaluatively charged language games; they also discover attractive and repulsive features of particular situations that they cannot understand without "seeing" how they *ought to* respond to them.[34] Because we have intuitive knowledge of what is attractive and repulsive, right or wrong, and in general of relevance, the moment of insight here can be distinguished from a corresponding disposition or preference. It consists of an intersubjectively shared know-how that has gained acceptance in the lifeworld and has "proved" itself in practice. As the shared possession of a cultural form of life, it enjoys "objectivity" in virtue of its social diffusion and acceptance. Hence the practical reflection which *critically* appropriates this intuitive knowledge requires a *social* perspective that goes beyond the first person singular perspective of somebody acting on his preferences.

Here I want to distinguish from the outset between value-orientations (*Wertorientierungen*) and obligations (*Verpflichtungen*). We judge value-orientations and the evaluative self-understanding of persons or groups from the *ethical* point of view, whereas we judge duties, norms, and categorical imperatives from the *moral* point of view. Ethical questions arise from the first person perspective. Seen from the first person plural point of view, they refer to a shared ethos: what is at issue is how we understand ourselves as members of our community, how we should orient our lives, or what is best for us in the long run and all things considered. Similar questions arise from the first person singular perspective: who I am and who I would like to be, or how I should lead my life. Such existential concerns differ from considerations of prudence not just in view of the extended horizons implied by the formula of what "*in the long run and all things considered* is best for me.*" In these questions the first person perspective does not imply an egocentric restriction to sheer preferences; rather, it points to an individual life history that is always already embedded in intersubjectively shared traditions and forms of life.[35] The attractiveness of the values in light of which I understand myself and my life cannot be explained within the limits of the world of subjective experiences to which I have privileged access. From the ethical point of view, my preferences and goals are no longer simply given but are themselves open to discussion;[36] since they depend on my self-understanding, they can undergo reasoned change through reflection on what has intrinsic value *for us* within the horizon of our shared social world.

From the ethical point of view we clarify clinical questions of the successful, or better, not misspent life, which arise in the context of a particular, collective form of life or of an individual life history. Practical reflection takes the form of a process of hermeneutic self-clarification. It gives expression to strong evaluations in light of which I orient my self-understanding. In this context the critique of self-deceptions and of symptoms of a compulsive or alienated mode of life takes its yardstick from the idea of a conscious and coherent mode of life, where the authenticity of a life-project can be understood as a higher-level validity claim analogous with the claim to truthfulness of expressive speech acts.[37]

How we conduct our lives is determined more or less by how we understand ourselves. Thus ethical insights influence how we orient our lives through the interpretation of our self-understanding. As insights that bind the will, they inform a *conscious* plan of life in which the free will in the ethical sense manifests itself. At the level of ethical reasoning, the freedom to choose, in the sense of rational choice, is transformed into the freedom to decide upon an authentic life.[38]

However, the limits of the ethical point of view become manifest once questions of justice arise: for from this perspective justice is reduced to just one value among others. Moral obligations appear to be more important for one person than they are for another and to have more weight in one context than in another. Within the horizon of ethical consciousness, it is certainly possible to account for the semantic difference between the attractive character of values and the bindingness of moral obligations by giving questions of justice a certain priority over questions of the good life: "Ethical life itself is important, but it can see that things other than itself are important. . . . There is one kind of ethical consideration that directly connects importance and deliberative priority, and this is obligation."[39] But as long as duties are viewed *solely* from the ethical point of view, an *absolute* priority of the right over the good, which alone would be commensurate with the categorical validity of moral duties, cannot be maintained: "These kinds of obligations very often command the highest deliberative priority. . . . However, we can also see how they need not always command the highest priority, even in ethically well-disposed agents."[40] As long as justice is treated as an integral part of a particular conception of the good, there is no ground for the requirement that, in cases of conflict, duties can only be "trumped" by duties and rights by rights (as Dworkin puts it).

Without the priority of the right over the good one cannot have an ethically neutral conception of justice. This deficit would have unfortunate consequences for equal treatment in pluralistic societies. For the equal treatment of different individuals and groups, each of which has its own individual or collective identity, could only be assured by standards that are part of a shared conception of the good equally recognized by all of them. The same condition would hold mutatis mutandis for the just regulation of international relations between states, for cosmopolitan relations between world citizens, and for global relations between cultures. The improbability of this requirement of a globally shared conception of the good shows why neo-Aristotelian approaches fall short of the universalistic content of a morality of equal respect and solidaristic responsibility for everyone. For any attempt to project a universally binding collective good on which the solidarity of all human beings—including future generations—could be founded runs up against a dilemma: a substantive conception that is still sufficiently informative entails an intolerable form of paternalism (at least with regard to the happiness of future generations); but an empty conception that abstracts from all local contexts undermines the concept of the good.[41]

To do justice to the *presumptive* impartiality of moral judgments and to the categorical validity *claim* of binding norms, we must uncouple the horizontal perspective, in which interpersonal relations are regulated, from the vertical perspective, of my or our own life-project, and treat moral questions separately. The abstract question of what is equally in the interest of all *goes beyond* the context-bound ethical question of what is best for me or us. Nevertheless, the intuition that issues of justice result from an idealizing extension of the ethical problematic retains a valid meaning.

If we interpret justice as what is equally good for all, then the "good" that has been extended step by step to the "right" forms a bridge between justice and solidarity. For universal justice also requires that one person should take responsibility for another, and even that each person should stand in and answer for a stranger who has formed his identity in completely different circumstances and who understands himself in terms of other traditions. The remnant of the good at the core of the right reminds us that moral consciousness depends on a particular self-understanding of moral persons who recognize that they *belong* to the moral community. All individuals who have been socialized into any communicative form of life at all belong to this community. Because socialized persons can only stabilize their identities through relations of reciprocal recognition, their integrity is particularly vulnerable and they are consequently in need of special protection. They must be able to appeal to a source of authority beyond their own community—G. H. Mead speaks in this connection of the "ever wider community." Every concrete community depends on the moral community as its "better self," so to speak. As members of this community, individuals expect to be treated equally, while it is assumed at the same time that each person regards every other person as "one of us." From this perspective, solidarity is simply the reverse side of justice.

Here we must avoid the misconception that the right is related to the good as form is to content: "The formal concept of the good constitutes the material kernel of a universalistic morality—it is the object of moral concern."[42] This conception betrays the selective vision of a liberalism that reduces the role of morality—as though it were the sum of negative liberty rights—to the protection of the individual good and thereby erects morality on an ethical foundation.[43] In that case the wherefore of morality—that is, knowledge of the "goods and ills" that are equally "at stake" for everybody in moral conflicts—would have to be prescribed to morality as something given. The participants would have to know already, prior to any moral deliberation, what is equally good for all; at the very least they would have to borrow a concept of the formal good from the philosopher. But nobody can determine directly from the observer's perspective what any person should regard as good. The reference to "any" person masks an abstraction that overburdens even the philosopher.[44] To be sure, morality can be understood as a protective mechanism that compensates for the intrinsic vulnerability of persons. But knowledge of the constitutional vulnerability of a being who can develop an identity only through externalizing himself in interpersonal relations, and who can stabilize it only in relations of intersubjective recognition, derives from an intuitive familiarity with the general structures of our communicative form of life as such. It is a deeply rooted general knowledge of which we become aware only in cases of clinical deviance, through the awareness of those circumstances in which the identity of socialized individuals is threatened. Appealing to a knowledge that is shaped by such negative experiences does not commit us to stating in a positive way what constitutes a good life in general. Only those affected can themselves clarify, from the perspective of participants in practical deliberation, what is equally good for all. The good that is relevant from the moral point of view shows itself in each particular case from the enlarged first person plural perspective of a community that does not exclude anybody. The good that is subsumed by the just is the very form of an intersubjectively shared ethos in general, and hence it is the structure of membership of a community, though one that has thrown off the shackles of any exclusionary community.

This connection between solidarity and justice inspired Kant to elucidate the point of view from which questions of justice can be judged impartially in terms of the Rousseauian model of self-legislation: "Consequently every rational being must act as if by his maxims he were at all times a legislative member of the universal realm of ends."[45] Kant uses the term "realm of ends" to indicate that each of its members regards himself and all other members never merely as means but always also as "ends in themselves." As a legislator, nobody is subordinated to an alien will; but at the same time every person is subject along with everyone else to the laws that he gives himself. By replacing the figure of the contract derived from private law with that of republican legislation derived from public law, Kant can, in morality, *combine* in one and the same person the two roles that are separated in law, that of the citizen who participates in legislation and that of the private legal person who is subject to the law. The morally free person must be able to understand himself simultaneously as the author of moral commands to which he is subject as addressee. This is possible only if he does not exercise the legislative competence, in which he "participates," in an arbitrary manner (as on a positivistic conception of law) but rather in accordance with the constitution of a political community whose citizens govern themselves. And there only laws can hold sway that could have been agreed upon "by each for all and by all for each."

VII

A law is valid in the moral sense when it could be accepted by everybody from the perspective of each individual. Because only "general" laws fulfill the condition that they regulate matters in the equal interest of all, practical reason finds expression in the generalizability or universalizability of the interests expressed in the law. Thus a person takes the moral point of view when he deliberates *like* a democratic legislator on whether the practice that would result from the general observance of a hypothetically proposed norm could be accepted by all those possibly affected viewed as potential co-legislators. Each person participates in the role of co-legislator in a *cooperative* enterprise and thereby adopts an intersubjectively extended perspective from which it can be determined whether a controversial norm can count as generalizable from the point of view of each participant. Pragmatic and ethical reasons, which retain their internal connection to the interests and self-understanding of individual persons, also play a role in these deliberations; but these agent-relative reasons no longer *count* as rational motives and value-orientations of individual persons but as epistemic contributions to a discourse in which norms are examined with the aim of reaching a communicative agreement. Because a legislative practice can only be undertaken jointly, a monological, egocentric operation of the generalization test in the manner of the Golden Rule will not suffice.

Moral reasons bind the will in a different way than do pragmatic and ethical reasons. Once the self-determination of the will takes the form of self-legislation, reason and the will completely *interpenetrate*. Hence Kant calls only the autonomous, rationally determined will "free." Only someone who lets his will be determined by insight into what all could will acts freely: "Only a rational being has the capacity of acting according to the *conception* of laws (i.e., according to principles). This capacity is the *will*. Since *reason* is required for the derivation of actions from laws, will is nothing other than practical reason."[46] To be sure, *every* act of choice rests on grounds of practical reason; but as long as contingent, subjective determinations are still operative and the will does not act *solely* on grounds of practical reason, not every trace of *compulsion* has been expunged, and the will is not yet truly free.

The normativity that flows from the will's capacity to bind itself *as such* does not as yet have a moral meaning. When an agent adopts technical rules of skill or pragmatic counsels of prudence, he lets his choice be guided by practical reason, but the operative reasons have determining force only in relation to contingent preferences and goals. This holds even for ethical reasons, though in a different way. The authenticity of value-commitments points beyond the subject-centered horizon of instrumental rationality. But strong evaluations acquire objective force for the will only in connection with contingent, though intersubjectively shared, experiences, practices, and forms of life. In both cases the corresponding imperatives and recommendations can claim only conditional validity: they hold under the condition of subjectively given interests or intersubjectively shared traditions.

Moral obligations acquire an unconditional or categorical validity only when they proceed from laws that emancipate the will, assuming it commits itself to them, from all contingent determinations and that in a sense assimilate it to practical reason itself. For the contingent goals, preferences, and value-orientations that otherwise determine the will from without can then be subjected to critical evaluation in light of norms that are justified from the moral point of view. The heteronomous will can also be motivated by reasons to adopt maxims; but its commitment remains bound to preexisting interests and context-dependent value-orientations through pragmatic and ethical reasons. Only when the former are examined as to their compatibility with the interests and values of all others from the moral point of view has the will freed itself from heteronomy.[47]

The abstract opposition between autonomy and heteronomy narrows the theoretical focus onto the individual subject. Kant's transcendental background assumptions lead him to ascribe the free will to an intelligible Ego situated in the realm of ends. Thus he once again attributes self-legislation, which in its original political meaning is a cooperative undertaking in which the individual merely "participates,"[48] to the sole competence of the individual. It is no accident that the categorical imperative is addressed to a second person singular and that it creates the impression that each individual could undertake the required test of norms for himself *in foro interno*. But in fact the reflexive application of the universalization test calls for a form of deliberation in which each participant is compelled to adopt the perspective of all others in order to examine whether a norm could be willed by all *from the perspective of each person*. This is the situation of a *rational discourse* oriented to reaching understanding in which all those concerned participate. This idea of a discursively produced understanding also imposes a greater burden of justification on the isolated judging subject than would a monologically applied universalization test.

Kant may have been so readily inclined to foreshorten an intersubjective concept of autonomy in an individualistic direction because he failed to distinguish ethical questions sufficiently from pragmatic questions.[49] Anyone who takes seriously questions of ethical self-understanding runs up against the stubborn cultural meaning of an individual's or a group's historically changing interpretations of the world and of themselves. As a child of the eighteenth century Kant still thinks in an unhistorical way and consequently overlooks this layer of traditions in which identities are formed. He tacitly assumes that in making moral judgments each individual can project himself sufficiently into the situation of everyone else *through his own imagination*. But when the participants can no longer rely on a transcendental preunderstanding grounded in more or less homogeneous conditions of life and interests, the moral point of view can only be realized under conditions of communication that ensure that *everyone* tests the acceptability of a norm, implemented in a general practice, also from the perspective of his own understanding of himself and of the world. In this way the categorical imperative receives a discourse-theoretical interpretation in which its place is taken by the discourse principle (D), according to which only those norms can claim validity that could meet with the agreement of all those concerned in their capacity as participants in a practical discourse.[50]

I began with the question of whether the cognitive content of a morality of equal respect and solidaristic responsibility for everybody can still be justified after the collapse of its religious foundation. In conclusion, I would like to examine what the intersubjectivistic interpretation of the categorical imperative can contribute to answering this question. Here we must treat two problems separately. First, we must clarify how much of the original intuitions a discourse ethics salvages in the disenchanted universe of postmetaphysical justification and in what sense one can still speak of the cognitive validity of moral judgments and positions (VIII). Second, there is the final question of whether the content of a morality that results from the rational reconstruction of traditional, religious intuitions remains bound, in spite of its procedural character, to its original context (IX).

VIII

With the devaluation of the epistemic authority of the God's eye view, moral commands lose their religious as well as their metaphysical foundation. This development also has implications for discourse ethics; it can neither defend the full moral contents of religious intuitions (1) nor can it represent the validity of moral norms in realist terms (2).

(1) The fact that moral practice is no longer tied to the individual's expectation of salvation and an exemplary conduct of life through the person of a redemptive God and the divine plan for salvation has two unwelcome consequences. On the one hand, moral knowledge becomes detached from moral motivation, and on the other, the concept of morally right action becomes differentiated from the conception of a good or godly life.

Discourse ethics correlates ethical and moral questions with different forms of argumentation, namely, with discourses of self-clarification and discourses of normative justification (and application), respectively. But it does not thereby reduce morality to equal treatment; rather, it takes account of both the aspects of justice and that of solidarity. A discursive agreement depends simultaneously on the nonsubstitutable "yes" or "no" responses of each individual and on overcoming the egocentric perspective, something that all participants are constrained to do by an argumentative practice designed to produce agreement of an epistemic kind. If the pragmatic features of discourse make possible an insightful process of opinion- and will-formation that guarantees both of these conditions, then the rationally motivated "yes" or "no" responses can take the interests of each individual into consideration without breaking the prior social bond that joins all those who are oriented toward reaching understanding in a transsubjective attitude.

However, uncoupling morality from questions of the good life leads to a motivational deficit. Because there is no profane substitute for the hope of personal salvation, we lose the strongest motive for obeying moral commands. Discourse ethics intensifies the intellectualistic separation of moral judgment from action even further by locating the moral point of view in rational discourse. There is no direct route from discursively achieved consensus to action. Certainly, moral judgments tell us what we should do, and good reasons affect our will; this is shown by the bad conscience that "plagues" us when we act against our better judgment. But the problem of weakness of will also shows that moral insight is based on the weak force of epistemic reasons and, in contrast with pragmatic reasons, does not itself constitute a rational motive. When we know what it is morally right for us to do, we know that there are no good (epistemic) reasons to act otherwise. But that does not mean that other motives will not prevail.[51]

With the loss of its foundation in the religious promise of salvation, the meaning of normative obligation also changes. The differentiation between strict duties and less binding values, between what is morally right and what is ethically worth striving for, already sharpens moral validity into a normativity to which impartial judgment alone is adequate. The shift in perspective from God to human beings has a further consequence. "Validity" now signifies that moral norms could win the agreement of all concerned, on the condition that they jointly examine in practical discourse whether a corresponding practice is in the equal interest of all. This agreement expresses two things: the fallible reason of *deliberating* subjects who convince one another that a hypothetically introduced norm is worthy of being recognized, and the freedom of *legislating* subjects who understand themselves as the authors of the norms to which they subject themselves as addressees. The mode of validity of moral norms now bears the traces both of the fallibility of the discovering mind and of the creativity of the constructing mind.

(2) The problem of in which sense moral judgments and attitudes can claim validity reveals another aspect when we reflect on the essentialist statements through which moral commands were previously justified in a metaphysical fashion as elements of a rationally ordered world. As long as the cognitive content of morality could be expressed in assertoric statements, moral judgments could be viewed as true or false. But if moral realism can no longer be defended by appealing to a creationist metaphysics and to natural law (or their surrogates), the validity of moral statements can no longer be assimilated to the truth of assertoric statements. The latter state how things are in the world; the former state what we should do.

If one assumes that, in general, sentences can be valid only in the sense of being "true" or "false" and further that "truth" is to be understood as correspondence between sentences and facts, then every validity claim that is raised for a nondescriptive sentence necessarily appears problematic. In fact, modern moral scepticism is based on the thesis that normative statements cannot be true or false, and hence cannot be justified, because there is no moral order, no such things as moral objects or facts. On this received account, the concept of *the world* as the totality of facts is connected with a correspondence notion of *truth* and a semantic conception of *justification*. I will very briefly discuss these questionable premises in reverse order.[52]

A sentence or proposition is justified on the semantic conception if it can be derived from basic sentences according to valid rules of inference, where a class of basic sentences is distinguished by specific (logical, epistemological, or psychological) criteria. But the foundationalist assumption that there exists such a class of basic sentences whose truth is immediately accessible to perception or to intuition has not withstood linguistic arguments for the holistic character of language and interpretation: every justification must at least *proceed from* a pre-understood context or background understanding.[53] This failure of foundationalism recommends a pragmatic conception of justification as a public practice in which criticizable validity claims can be defended with good reasons. Of course, the criteria of rationality that determine which reasons count as good reasons can themselves be made a matter for discussion. Hence procedural characteristics of the process of argumentation itself must ultimately bear the burden of explaining why results achieved in a procedurally correct manner enjoy the presumption of validity. For example, the communicative structure of rational discourse can ensure that all relevant contributions are heard and that the unforced force of the better argument alone determines the "yes" or "no" responses of the participants.[54]

The pragmatic conception of justification opens the way for an epistemic concept of truth that overcomes the well-known problems with the correspondence theory. The truth predicate refers to the language game of justification, that is, to the public redemption of validity claims. On the other hand, truth cannot be identified with justifiability or warranted assertability. The "cautionary" use of the truth predicate—regardless of how well "p" is justified, it still may not be true—highlights the difference in meaning between "truth" as an irreducible property of statements and "rational acceptability" as a context-dependent property of utterances.[55] This difference can be understood within the horizon of possible justifications in terms of the distinction between "justified in our context" and "justified in every context." This difference can be cashed out in turn through a weak idealization of our processes of argumentation, understood as capable of being extended indefinitely over time. When we assert "*p*" and thereby claim truth for "*p*" we accept the obligation to defend "*p*" in argumentation—in full awareness of its fallibility—against all future objections.[56]

In the present context I am less interested in the complex relation between truth and justification than in the possibility of conceiving truth, purified of all connotations of correspondence, as a special case of validity, where this *general* concept of validity is introduced in connection with the discursive redemption of validity claims.[57] In this way we open up a conceptual space in which the concept of normative, and in particular moral, validity can be situated. The rightness of moral norms (or of general normative statements) and of particular normative injunctions based on them can then be understood as analogous to the truth of descriptive statements. What unites these two concepts of validity is the procedure of discursively redeeming the corresponding validity claims. What separates them is the fact that they refer, respectively, to the social and the objective worlds.

The social world, as the totality of legitimately ordered interpersonal relations, is accessible only from the participant's perspective; it is intrinsically historical and hence has, if you will, an ontological constitution different from that of the objective world which can be described from the observer's perspective.[58] The social world is inextricably interwoven with the intentions and beliefs, the practices and languages of its members. This holds in a similar way for *descriptions* of the objective world but not for this world itself. Hence the discursive redemption of truth claims has a different meaning from that of moral validity claims: in the former case, discursive agreement *signifies* that the truth conditions of an assertoric proposition, interpreted in terms of assertability conditions, are fulfilled; in the latter case, discursive agreement *justifies* the claim that a norm is worthy of recognition and thereby itself contributes to the fulfillment of its conditions of validity. Whereas rational acceptability merely *points to* the truth of assertoric propositions, it makes a *constructive* contribution to the validity of moral norms. The moments of construction and discovery are interwoven in moral insight differently than they are in theoretical knowledge.

What is not at our disposal here is the moral point of view that imposes itself upon us, not an objective moral order assumed to exist independently of our descriptions. It is not the social world as such that is not at our disposal but the structure and procedure of a process of argumentation that facilitates both the production and the discovery of the norms of well-ordered interpersonal relations.

The constructivist meaning of moral judgments, understood on the model of self-legislation, must not be forgotten; but it must not obliterate the epistemic meaning of moral justifications either.[59]

IX

Discourse ethics defends a morality of equal respect and solidaristic responsibility for everybody. But it does this in the first instance through a rational reconstruction of the contents of a moral tradition whose religious foundations have been undermined. If the discourse-theoretical interpretation of the categorical imperative remained bound to the tradition in which it originates, this genealogy would represent an obstacle to the goal of demonstrating the cognitive content of moral judgments *as such*. Thus it remains to provide a theoretical justification of the moral point of view itself.

The discourse principle provides an answer to the predicament in which the members of *any* moral community find themselves when, in making the transition to a modern, pluralistic society, they find themselves faced with the dilemma that though they still argue with reasons about moral judgments and beliefs, their substantive background consensus on the underlying moral norms has been shattered. They find themselves embroiled in global and domestic practical conflicts in need of regulation that they continue to regard as moral, and hence as rationally resolvable, conflicts; but their shared ethos has disintegrated. The following scenario does not depict an "original position" but an ideal-typical development that could have taken place under real conditions.

I proceed on the assumption that the participants do not wish to resolve their conflicts through violence, or even compromise, but through communication. Thus their initial impulse is to engage in deliberation and work out a shared *ethical* self-understanding on a secular basis. But given the differentiated forms of life characteristic of pluralistic societies, such an effort is doomed to failure. The participants will soon realize that the critical appropriation of their strong evaluations leads to competing conceptions of the good. Let us assume that they nevertheless remain resolved to engage in deliberation and not to fall back on a mere modus vivendi as a substitute for the threatened moral way of life.

In the absence of a substantive agreement on particular norms, the participants must now rely on the "neutral" fact that each of them participates in *some* communicative form of life which is structured by linguistically mediated understanding. Since communicative processes and forms of life have certain structural features in common, they could ask themselves whether these features harbor normative contents that could provide a basis for shared orientations. Taking this as a clue, theories in the tradition of Hegel, Humboldt, and G. H. Mead have shown that communicative actions involve shared presuppositions and that communicative forms of life are interwoven with relations of reciprocal recognition, and to this extent, both have a normative content.[60] These analyses demonstrate that morality derives a genuine meaning, independent of the various conceptions of the good, from the form and perspectival structure of unimpaired, intersubjective socialization.[61]

To be sure, structural features of communicative forms of life alone are not sufficient to justify the claim that members of a particular historical community *ought to* transcend their particularistic value-orientations and make the transition to the fully symmetrical and inclusive relations of an egalitarian universalism. On the other hand, a universalistic conception that wants to avoid false abstractions must draw on insights from the theory of communication. From the fact that persons can only be individuated through socialization it follows that moral concern is owed equally to persons both as irreplaceable individuals and as members of the community,[62] and hence it connects justice with solidarity. Equal treatment means equal treatment of unequals who are nonetheless aware of their interdependence. Moral universalism must not take into account the aspect of equality—the fact that persons as such are equal to all other persons—*at the expense of* the aspect of individuality—the fact that as individuals they are at the same time absolutely different from all others.[63] The equal respect for everyone else demanded by a moral universalism sensitive to difference thus takes the form of a *nonleveling* and *nonappropriating* inclusion of the other *in his otherness.*

But how can the transition to a posttraditional morality as such be justified? Traditionally established obligations rooted in communicative action do not *of themselves* reach beyond the limits of the family, the tribe, the city, or the nation.[64] However, the reflexive form of communicative action behaves differently: argumentation of its very nature points beyond all particular forms of life. For in the pragmatic presuppositions of rational discourse or deliberation the normative content of the implicit assumptions of communicative action is *generalized, abstracted, and freed from all limits*—the practice of deliberation is extended to an inclusive community that does not in principle exclude any subject capable of speech and action who can make relevant contributions. This idea points to a way out of the modern dilemma, since the participants have lost their metaphysical guarantees and must so to speak derive their normative orientations from themselves alone. As we have seen, the participants can only draw on those features of a common practice they already *currently* share. Given the failure to identify a shared good, such features shrink to the fund of formal features of the performatively shared situation of deliberation. The bottom line is that the participants have all already entered into the cooperative enterprise of rational discourse.

Although it is a rather meager basis for justification, the neutral content of this common store may provide an opportunity, given the predicament posed by the pluralism of worldviews. A prospect of finding an equivalent for the traditional, substantive grounding of a normative consensus would exist if the *form of communication* in which joint practical deliberation takes place were such that it makes possible a justification of moral norms convincing to all participants because of its impartiality. The missing "transcendent good" can be replaced in an "immanent" fashion only by appeal to the intrinsic constitution of the practice of deliberation. From here, I suggest, three steps lead to a theoretical justification of the moral point of view.

(a) If the practice of deliberation itself is regarded as the only possible resource for a standpoint of impartial justification of moral questions, then the appeal to moral content must be replaced by the self-referential appeal to the form of this practice. This is precisely what is captured by

(D) Only those norms can claim validity that could meet with the acceptance of all concerned in practical discourse.

Here the "acceptance" (*Zustimmung*) achieved under conditions of rational discourse signifies an agreement (*Einverständnis*) motivated by epistemic reasons; it should not be understood as a contract (*Vereinbarung*) that is rationally motivated from the egocentric perspective of each participant. On the other hand, the principle of discourse leaves open the type of argumentation, and hence the route, by which a discursive agreement can be reached. (D) does not by itself state that a justification of moral norms is possible without recourse to a substantive background consensus.

(b) The hypothetically introduced principle (D) specifies the condition that valid norms would fulfill if they *could* be justified. For the moment we are only assuming that the concept of a moral norm is clear. The participants also have an intuitive understanding of how one engages in argumentation. Though they are assumed only to be familiar with the justification of descriptive sentences and not yet to know whether moral validity claims can be judged in a similar way, they can form a conception (without prejudging the issue) of what it *would* mean to justify a norm. But what is still needed for the operationalization of (D) is a rule of argumentation specifying how moral norms can be justified.

The principle of universalization (U) is indeed inspired by (D), but initially it is nothing more than a proposal arrived at abductively.

(U)   A norm is valid when the foreseeable consequences and side effects of its general observance for the interests and value-orientations of *each individual* could be *jointly* accepted by *all* concerned without coercion.

Three aspects of this formulation are in need of clarification. The phrase "interests and value-orientations" points to the role played by the pragmatic and ethical reasons of the individual participants in practical discourse. These inputs are designed to prevent the marginalization of the self-understanding and worldviews of particular individuals or groups and, in general, to foster a hermeneutic sensitivity to a sufficiently broad spectrum of contributions. Second, generalized reciprocal perspective-taking ("of each," "jointly by all") requires not just empathy for, but also interpretive intervention into, the self-understanding of participants who must be willing to revise their descriptions of themselves and others (and the language in which they are formulated). Finally, the goal of "uncoerced joint acceptance" specifies the respect in which the reasons presented in discourse cast off their agent-relative meaning and take on an epistemic meaning from the standpoint of symmetrical consideration.

(c) The participants themselves will perhaps be satisfied with this (or a similar) rule of argumentation as long as it proves useful and does not lead to counterintuitive results. It must turn out that a practice of justification conducted in this manner selects norms that are capable of commanding universal agreement—for example, norms expressing human rights. But from the perspective of the moral theorist there still remains one final justificatory step.

We may assume that the practice of deliberation and justification we call "argumentation" is to be found in all cultures and societies (if not in institutionalized form, then at least as an informal practice) and that there is no functionally equivalent alternative to this mode of problem solving. In view of the universality and nonsubsititutibility of the practice of argumentation, it would be difficult to dispute the neutrality of the discourse principle (D). But ethnocentric assumptions, and hence a specific conception of the good that is not shared by other cultures, may have insinuated themselves into the abduction of (U). The suspicion that the understanding of morality operationalized in (U) reflects eurocentric prejudices could be dispelled through an "immanent" defense of this account of the moral point of view, that is, by appealing to knowledge of what it means to engage in the practice of argumentation as such. Thus the discourse-ethical model of justification consists in the derivation of the basic principle (U) from the implicit content of universal presuppositions of argumentation in conjunction with the conception of normative justification in general expressed in (D).[65]

This is easy to understand in an intuitive way (though any attempt to provide a formal justification would require involved discussions of the meaning and feasibility of "transcendental arguments").[66] Here I will limit myself to the observation that we engage in argumentation with the intention of convincing one another of the validity claims that proponents raise for their statements and are ready to defend against opponents. The practice of argumentation sets in motion a *cooperative* competition for the better argument, where the orientation to the goal of a communicatively reached agreement unites the participants from the outset. The assumption that the competition can lead to "rationally acceptable," hence "convincing," results is based on the rational force of arguments. Of course, what counts as a good or a bad argument can itself become a topic for discussion. Thus the rational acceptability of a statement ultimately rests on reasons in conjunction with specific features of the process of argumentation itself. The four most important features are: (i) that nobody who could make a relevant contribution may be excluded; (ii) that all participants are granted an equal opportunity to make contributions; (iii) that the participants must mean what they say; and (iv) that communication must be freed from external and internal coercion so that the "yes" or "no" stances that participants adopt on criticizable validity claims are motivated solely by the rational force of the better reasons. If everyone who engages in argumentation must make at least these pragmatic presuppositions, then in virtue of (i) the public character of practical discourses and the inclusion of all concerned and (ii) the equal communicative rights of all participants, only reasons that give equal weight to the interests and evaluative orientations of everybody can influence the outcome of practical discourses; and because of the absence of (iii) deception and (iv) coercion, nothing but reasons can tip the balance in favor of the acceptance of a controversial norm. Finally, on the assumption that participants reciprocally impute an orientation to communicative agreement to one another, this "uncoerced" acceptance can only occur "jointly" or collectively.

Against the frequently raised objection that this justification is circular[67] I would note that the content of the universal presuppositions of argumentation is by no means "normative" in the moral sense. For inclusivity only signifies that access to discourse is unrestricted; it does not imply the universality of binding norms of action. The equal distribution of communicative freedoms and the requirement of truthfulness *in* discourse have the status of *argumen-*

tative duties and rights, not of *moral* duties and rights. So too, the absence of coercion refers to the process of argumentation itself, not to interpersonal relations *outside* of this practice. These constitutive rules of the language game of argumentation govern the exchange of arguments and of "yes" or "no" responses; they have the epistemic force of enabling conditions for the justification of statements but do not have any *immediate* practical effects in motivating actions and interactions outside of discourse.

The point of such a justification of the moral point of view is that the normative content of this epistemic language game is transmitted only by a rule of argumentation to the selection of norms of action, which together with their moral validity claim provide the input into practical discourses. A moral obligation cannot follow from the so to speak transcendental constraint of unavoidable presuppositions of argumentation alone; rather it attaches to the specific objects of practical discourse, namely, to the norms *introduced* into discourse to which the reasons mobilized in deliberation refer. I emphasize this when I specify that (U) can be rendered plausible *in connection with a* (weak, hence nonprejudicial) *concept of normative justification.*

This justification strategy, which I have here merely sketched, must be supplemented with genealogical arguments drawing on premises of modernization theory, if (U) is to be rendered plausible.[68] With (U) we reassure ourselves in a reflexive manner of a residual normative substance which is preserved in posttraditional societies by the formal features of argumentation and action oriented to reaching a shared understanding. This is also shown by the procedure of establishing universal presuppositions of argumentation by demonstrating performative self-contradictions, which I cannot go into here.[69]

The question of the application of norms arises as an additional problem. The principle of appropriateness developed by Klaus Günther first brings the moral point of view to bear on singular moral judgments in a *complete* manner.[70] The outcome of successful discourses of justification and application *shows* that practical questions are differentiated by the sharply defined moral point of view; moral questions of well-ordered interpersonal relations are separated from pragmatic questions of rational choice, on the one hand, and from ethical questions of the good or not misspent life on the other. It has become clear to me in retrospect that (U) only operationalized a more comprehensive principle of discourse with reference to a particular subject matter, namely, morality.[71] The principle of discourse can also be operationalized for other kinds of questions, for example, for the deliberations of political legislators or for legal discourses.[72]

II

Political Liberalism: A Debate with John Rawls

2

Reconciliation through the Public Use of Reason

John Rawls's *A Theory of Justice*[1] marks a pivotal turning point in the most recent history of practical philosophy, for he restored long suppressed moral questions to the status of serious objects of philosophical investigation. Immanuel Kant posed the fundamental question of morality in such a way that it admitted a rational answer: we ought to do what is equally good for all persons. Without espousing the background assumptions of Kant's transcendental philosophy, Rawls renewed this theoretical approach with particular reference to the issue of the organization of a just society. In opposition to utilitarianism and value skepticism he proposed an intersubjectivist version of Kant's principle of autonomy: we act autonomously when we obey those laws that could be accepted by all concerned on the basis of a public use of their reason. More recently, in *Political Liberalism,* in which Rawls has concluded a twenty-year process of extension and revision of his theory of justice, he exploits this moral concept of autonomy as the key to explaining the political autonomy of citizens of a democratic society: "Our exercise of political power is fully proper only when it is exercised in accordance with a constitution, the essentials of which all citizens as free and equal may be reasonably expected to endorse in the light of principles and ideals acceptable to their common human reason."[2] Just as previously he took a stand against utilitarian positions, he now responds primarily to contextualist positions that question the presuppositions of a reason common to all human beings.

Because I admire this project, share its intentions, and regard its essential results as correct, the dissent I express here will remain within the bounds of a family quarrel. My doubts are limited to whether Rawls always brings to bear against his critics his important normative intuitions in their most compelling form. But first, let me briefly outline his project in its current state.

Rawls offers a justification of the principles on which a modern society must be constituted if it is to ensure the fair cooperation of its citizens as free and equal persons. His first step is to clarify the standpoint from which fictional representatives of the people could answer this question impartially. Rawls explains why the parties in the so-called original position would agree on two principles: first, on the liberal principle according to which everyone is entitled to an equal system of basic liberties, and, second, on a subordinate principle that establishes equal access to public offices and stipulates that social inequalities are acceptable only when they are also to the advantage of the least privileged. In a second step, Rawls shows that this conception of justice can expect to meet with agreement under the conditions of a pluralistic society which it itself promotes. Political liberalism, as a reasonable construction that does not raise a claim to truth, is neutral toward conflicting worldviews. In a third and final step, Rawls outlines the basic rights and principles of the constitutional state that can be derived from the two principles of justice. Taking these steps in sequence, I will raise objections directed not so much against the project as such but against certain aspects of its execution. I fear that Rawls makes concessions to opposed philosophical positions that impair the cogency of his own project.

My critique is a constructive and immanent one. First, I doubt whether every aspect of the original position is designed to clarify and secure the standpoint of impartial judgment of deontological principles of justice (I). Further, I think that Rawls should make a sharper distinction between questions of justification and questions of acceptance; he seems to want to purchase the neutrality of his conception of justice at the cost of forsaking its cognitive validity claim (II). These two theoretical decisions result in a construction of the constitutional state that accords liberal basic rights primacy over the democratic principle of legitimation. Rawls thereby fails to achieve his goal of bringing the liberties of the moderns into harmony with the liberties of the ancients (III). I conclude my remarks with a thesis on the self-understanding of political philosophy: under conditions of postmetaphysical thought, this should be modest, but not in the wrong way.

The adversarial role assigned me by the editors of the *Journal of Philosophy* compels me to heighten tentative reservations into objections. This intensification is justified by my intention, at once friendly and provocative, of setting the not easily surveyable arguments of a highly complex and well thought-out theory in motion in such a way that the latter can reveal its strengths.[3]

I The Design of the Original Position

Rawls conceives of the original position as a situation in which rationally choosing representatives of the citizens are subject to the specific constraints that guarantee an impartial judgment of practical questions. The concept of full autonomy is reserved for the citizens who already live under the institutions of a well-ordered society. For the construction of the original position, Rawls splits this concept of political autonomy into two elements: the morally neutral characteristics of parties who seek their rational advantage, on the one hand, and the morally substantive situational constraints under which those parties choose principles for a system of fair cooperation, on the other. These normative constraints permit the parties to be endowed with a minimum of properties, in particular, "the capacity for a conception of the good (and thus to be rational)."[4] Regardless of whether the parties entertain exclusively purposive-rational considerations or also address ethical questions of particular plans of life, they always reach their decisions in light of their value-orientations (that is, from the perspective of the groups of citizens they represent). They need not regard matters from the moral point of view, which would require them to take account of what is in the equal interest of all, for this impartiality is exacted by a situation that throws a veil of ignorance over the mutually disinterested though free and equal parties. Because the latter do not know which positions they will occupy in the society that it is their task to order, they find themselves constrained already by their self-interest to reflect on what is equally good for all.

This construction of an original position that *frames* the freedom of choice of rational actors in a reasonable fashion is explained by Rawls's initial intention of representing the theory of justice as part of the general theory of choice. Rawls originally proceeded on the assumption that the range of options open to rationally choosing parties only needed to be limited in an appropriate fashion in order to facilitate the derivation of principles of justice from their enlightened self-interest. But he soon realized that the reason of autonomous citizens cannot be reduced to rational choice conditioned by subjective preferences.[5] Yet even after the revision of the initial goal that the original position was designed to achieve, he has held to the view that the meaning of the moral point of view can be operationalized in this way. This has some unfortunate consequences, three of which I would like to address in what follows: (1) Can the parties in the original position comprehend the highest-order interests of their clients solely on the basis of rational egoism? (2) Can basic rights be assimilated to primary goods? (3) Does the veil of ignorance guarantee the impartiality of judgment?[6]

(1) Rawls cannot consistently follow through on his decision that "fully" autonomous citizens are to be represented by parties who lack this autonomy. Citizens are assumed to be moral persons who possess a sense of justice and the capacity for their own conception of the good, as well as an interest in cultivating these dispositions in a rational manner. But in the case of the parties in the original position, these reasonable characteristics of moral persons are substituted by the constraints of a rational design. At the same time, however, the parties are supposed to be able to understand and take adequate account of the "highest-order interests" of the citizens that follow from these very characteristics. For example, they must take account of the fact that autonomous citizens respect the interests of others on the basis of just principles and not merely from self-interest, that they can be obligated to loyalty, that they can be convinced of the legitimacy of existing arrangements and policies through the public use of their reason, and so forth. Thus, the parties are sup-

posed both to understand and take seriously the implications and consequences of an autonomy that they are themselves denied. This may still be plausible for the advocacy of *self-related* interests and conceptions of the good that are not known in detail. But can the meaning of considerations of justice remain unaffected by the perspective of rational egoists? At any rate, the parties are incapable of achieving, within the bounds set by their rational egoism, the reciprocal perspective taking that the citizens they represent must undertake when they orient themselves in a just manner to what is equally good for all: "in their rational deliberations the parties . . . recognize no standpoint external to their own point of view as rational representatives" (PL 75). But if, despite this, the parties are to understand the meaning of the deontological principles they are seeking and to take sufficient account of their clients' interests in justice, they must be equipped with cognitive competences that extend further than the capacities sufficient for rationally choosing actors who are blind to issues of justice.

Of course, it is open to Rawls to modify the design of the original position accordingly. Already in *A Theory of Justice* he qualified the rationality of the contracting partners in various ways. On the one hand, they take no interest in one another, conducting themselves like players who "strive for as high an absolute score as possible" (TJ 144). On the other hand, they are equipped with a "purely formal" sense of justice, for they are supposed to know that they will conform to whatever principles are agreed upon in their future role as citizens living in a well-ordered society (TJ 145). This can be understood to mean that the parties in the original position are at least cognizant of the kind of binding mutuality that will characterize the life of their clients in the future, although they themselves must for the present conduct their negotiations under different premises. Such stipulations are perfectly admissible. My only question is whether, in being extended in this direction, the design loses its point by becoming too far removed from the original model. For as soon as the parties step outside the boundaries of their rational egoism and assume even a distant likeness to moral persons, the division of labor between the rationality of choice of subjects and appropriate objective constraints is destroyed, a division through which self-interested agents are nonetheless supposed to arrive at morally sound decisions. This consequence may not have any great significance for the rest of the project; but it draws attention to the conceptual constraints imposed by the original (though in the meantime abandoned) intention to provide a decision-theoretical solution to Thomas Hobbes's problem. For another consequence of the rational choice format of the original position is the introduction of basic goods, and this determination is important for the further development of the theory.

(2) For rationally choosing actors bound to the first person perspective, normative issues of whatever kind can be represented solely in terms of interests or values that are satisfied by goods. Goods are what we strive for—indeed, what is good *for us*. Correspondingly, Rawls introduces "primary goods" as generalized means that people may need in order to realize their plans of life. Although the parties know that some of these primary goods assume the form of rights for citizens of a well-ordered society, in the original position they themselves can only describe rights as one category of "goods" among others. For them, the issue of principles of justice can only arise in the guise of the question of the just distribution of primary goods. Rawls thereby adopts a concept of justice that is proper to an ethics of the good, one more consistent with Aristotelian or utilitarian approaches than with a theory of rights, such as his own, that proceeds from the concept of autonomy. Precisely because Rawls adheres to a conception of justice on which the autonomy of citizens is constituted through rights, the paradigm of distribution generates difficulties for him. Rights can be "enjoyed" only by being *exercised*. They cannot be assimilated to distributive goods without forfeiting their deontological meaning. An equal distribution of rights results only if those who enjoy rights recognize one another as free and equal. Of course, there exist rights *to* a fair share of goods or opportunities, but rights in the first instance regulate relations between actors: they cannot be "possessed" like things.[7] If I am correct, the conceptual constraints of the model of rational choice preclude Rawls from construing basic liberties from the outset as basic rights and compel him to interpret them as primary goods. This leads him to assimilate the deontological meaning of obligatory norms to the teleological meaning of preferred values.[8] Rawls thereby blurs cer-

tain distinctions that I shall briefly mention in order to show how this limits his options in the further development of his project.

Norms inform decisions as to what one ought to do, values inform decisions as to what conduct is most desirable. Recognized norms impose equal and exceptionless obligations on their addressees, while values express the preferability of goods that are striven for by particular groups. Whereas norms are observed in the sense of a fulfillment of generalized behavioral expectations, values or goods can be realized or acquired only by purposive action. Furthermore, norms raise a binary validity claim in virtue of which they are said to be either valid or invalid: to ought statements, as to assertoric statements, we can respond only with "yes" or "no"—or refrain from judgment. Values, by contrast, fix relations of preference which signify that certain goods are more attractive than others: hence, we can assent to evaluative statements to a greater or lesser degree. The obligatory force of norms has the absolute meaning of an unconditional and universal duty: what one ought to do is what is equally good for all (that is, for all addressees). The attractiveness of values reflects an evaluation and a transitive ordering of goods that has become established in particular cultures or has been adopted by particular groups: important evaluative decisions or higher-order preferences express what is good for us (or for me), all things considered. Finally, different norms must not contradict each other when they claim validity for the same domain of addressees; they must stand in coherent relations to one another—in other words, they must constitute a system. Different values, by contrast, compete for priority; insofar as they meet with intersubjective recognition within a culture or group, they constitute shifting configurations fraught with tension. To sum up, norms differ from values, first, in their relation to rule-governed as opposed to purposive action; second, in a binary as opposed to a gradual coding of the respective validity claims; third, in their absolute as opposed to relative bindingness; and last, in the criteria that systems of norms as opposed to systems of values must satisfy.

Nevertheless, Rawls wishes to do justice to the deontological intuition that finds expression in these distinctions; hence, he must compensate for the leveling of the deontological dimension which he—as a consequence of the design of the original position—

initially accepts with the concept of primary goods. So he accords the first principle priority over the second. An absolute priority of equal liberties over the primary goods regulated by the second principle is, however, difficult to justify from the first person perspective in which we orient ourselves to our own interests or values. H. L. A. Hart has developed this point clearly in his critique of Rawls.[9] Interestingly, Rawls can meet this criticism only by building a *subsequent* qualification into the primary goods which secures them a relation to basic liberties as basic rights: he acknowledges as primary goods only those that are expedient for the life plans and the development of the moral faculties of citizens *as free and equal persons.*[10] Furthermore, Rawls differentiates the primary goods that are constitutive of the institutional framework of the well-ordered society in the moral sense from the remainder of the primary goods by incorporating the guarantee of the "fair value" of liberty into the first principle.[11]

This additional determination, however, tacitly presupposes a deontological distinction between rights and goods which contradicts the prima facie classification of rights as goods. Since the fair value of equal liberties requires the actual availability of equal opportunities to exercise these rights, only rights, not goods, can be qualified in this manner. Only in the case of rights can we distinguish between legal competence and the actual opportunities to choose and to act. Only between rights, on the one side, and actual chances to exercise rights, on the other, can there exist a chasm that is problematic from the perspective of justice; such a rupture cannot exist between the possession and enjoyment of goods. It would be either redundant or meaningless to speak of the "fair value" of equally distributed goods. The distinction between legal and factual equality has no application to "goods" for grammatical reasons, to put it in Wittgensteinian terms. But if the notion of primary goods is subject to correction in a second step, we may ask whether the first step—the design of the original position that necessitates this conception—is a wise one.

(3) The foregoing reflections show that, for the parties in the original position, the capacity to make rational decisions is not sufficient to comprehend the highest-order interests of their clients or to understand rights (in Ronald Dworkin's[12] sense) as trumps that override collective goals. But why then are the parties deprived of

practical reason in the first place and shrouded in an impenetrable veil of ignorance? Rawls's guiding intuition is clear: the role of the categorical imperative is taken over by an intersubjectively applied procedure which is embodied in participation conditions such as the equality of parties and in situational features such as the veil of ignorance. In my view, however, the potential gains of this turn are dissipated precisely by the systematic deprivation of information. My third question reveals the perspective from which I also pose the two previous questions. I believe that Rawls could avoid the difficulties associated with the design of an original position if he operationalized the moral point of view in a different way, namely, if he kept the procedural conception of practical reason free of substantive connotations by developing it in a strictly procedural manner.

Kant's categorical imperative already goes beyond the egocentric character of the Golden Rule: "Do not do unto others what you would not have them do unto you." Whereas this rule calls for a universalization test from the viewpoint of a given individual, the categorical imperative requires that *all* those possibly affected be able to will a just maxim as a general rule. But as long as we apply this more exacting test in a monological fashion, each of us still considers privately what all could will from individually isolated perspectives. This is inadequate. For only when the self-understanding of each individual reflects a transcendental consciousness, that is, a universally valid view of the world, would what from my point of view is equally good for all actually be in the equal interest of each individual. But this can no longer be assumed under conditions of social and ideological pluralism. If we wish to preserve the intuition underlying the Kantian universalization principle, we can respond to this fact of pluralism in different ways. Rawls imposes a common perspective on the parties in the original position through informational constraints and thereby neutralizes the multiplicity of particular interpretive perspectives from the outset. Discourse ethics, by contrast, views the moral point of view as embodied in an intersubjective praxis of argumentation which enjoins those involved to an idealizing *enlargement* of their interpretive perspectives.

Discourse ethics rests on the intuition that the application of the principle of universalization, properly understood, calls for a joint process of "ideal role taking." It interprets this idea of G. H. Mead in terms of a pragmatic theory of argumentation.[13] Under the pragmatic presuppositions of an inclusive and noncoercive rational discourse between free and equal participants, everyone is required to take the perspective of everyone else and thus to project herself into the understandings of self and world of all others; from this interlocking of perspectives there emerges an ideally extended "we-perspective" from which all can test in common whether they wish to make a controversial norm the basis of their shared practice; and this should include mutual criticism of the appropriateness of the languages in terms of which situations and needs are interpreted. In the course of *successively* undertaken abstractions, the core of generalizable interests can then emerge step by step.[14]

Things are different when the veil of ignorance constrains the field of vision of parties in the original position *from the beginning* to the basic principles on which presumptively free and equal citizens would agree, notwithstanding their divergent understandings of self and world. It is important to see that with this initial abstraction Rawls accepts a *double* burden of proof. The veil of ignorance must extend to all particular viewpoints and interests that could impair an impartial judgment; at the same time, it may extend *only* to such normative matters as can be disqualified without further ado as candidates for the common good to be accepted by free and equal citizens. This second condition places a demand on the theory that is difficult to meet, as is shown by brief reflection. Following the justification of the principles of justice, the veil of ignorance is gradually raised during the successive steps of framing the constitution, of legislation, and of applying law. Since the new information that thereby streams in must harmonize with the basic principles already selected under conditions of informational constraint, unpleasant surprises must be avoided. If we are to ensure that no discrepancies arise, we must construct the original position already with knowledge, and even foresight, of all of the normative contents that could potentially nourish the shared self-understanding of free and equal citizens in the future. In other words, the theoretician himself would have to shoulder the burden of anticipating at least parts of the information of which he previously relieved the parties in the original position! The impartiality of judgment would only be guaranteed in the original position if the basic normative concepts employed in its construction—those of the politically autonomous citizen, of fair cooperation, and of a well-ordered society, in the specific sense Rawls attaches to these terms—could withstand revision in light of morally significant future experiences and learning processes.

If such a heavy burden of proof is generated by the deprivation of information imposed on the parties in the original position by the veil of ignorance, a convenient response would be to lighten this burden by operationalizing the moral point of view in a different way. I have in mind the more open procedure of an argumentative praxis that proceeds under the demanding presuppositions of the "public use of reason" and does not bracket the pluralism of convictions and worldviews from the outset. This procedure can be explicated without recourse to the substantive concepts that Rawls employs in the construction of the original position.

II The Fact of Pluralism and the Idea of an Overlapping Consensus

Since his Dewey Lectures, "Kantian Constructivism in Moral Theory,"[15] Rawls has stressed the *political* character of justice as fairness. This shift is motivated by disquiet concerning the fact of social and, above all, ideological pluralism. In discussing the veil of ignorance, I have already clarified the burden of proof that the theory of justice takes upon itself with its initial theoretical decisions. The decisive issue in the justification of the two highest principles of justice is less the deliberations in the original position than the intuitions and basic concepts that guide the design of the original position itself. Rawls introduces normative contents into the very procedure of justification, above all those ideas he associates with the concept of the moral person: the sense of fairness and the capacity for one's own conception of the good. Thus the concept of the citizen as a moral person, which also underlies the concept of the fair cooperation of politically autonomous citizens, stands in need of a *prior* justification. Further, it needs to be shown that this conception is neutral toward conflicting worldviews and remains uncontroversial after the veil of ignorance has been lifted. This explains Rawls's interest in a "political," as opposed to a metaphysical, conception of justice. I suspect that this terminology indicates a certain unclarity about the precise character of what is in need of justification; from this, in turn, there results an indecisiveness as to how the validity claim of the theory itself should be understood. I will examine whether the overlapping consensus, on which the theory of justice depends, plays a cognitive or merely an instrumental role: whether it primarily contributes to the further justification of the theory or whether it serves, in light of the prior justification of the theory, to explicate a necessary condition of social stability (1). Connected with this is the question of the sense in which Rawls uses the predicate "reasonable": as a predicate for the validity of moral judgments or for the reflective attitude of enlightened tolerance (2).

(1) In order to pin down the underlying normative ideas, Rawls has recourse to the so-called method of reflective equilibrium. The philosopher arrives at the basic concept of the moral person and the adjunct concepts of the politically autonomous citizen, of fair cooperation, of the well-ordered society, and so forth, via a rational reconstruction of proven intuitions, that is, intuitions actually *found* in the practices and traditions of a democratic society. Reflective equilibrium is achieved at the moment when the philosopher has attained the assurance that those involved can no longer reject with good reasons intuitions reconstructed and clarified in this manner. The procedure of rational reconstruction already fulfills Thomas Scanlon's criterion of what it is "not reasonable to reject." Of course, Rawls does not wish to limit himself solely to the fundamental normative convictions of a *particular* political culture: even the present-day Rawls, *pace* Richard Rorty, has not become a contextualist. His aim, as before, is to reconstruct a substratum of intuitive ideas latent in the political culture of his society and its democratic traditions. But if experiences associated with an incipiently successful institutionalization of principles of justice have already become sedimented in the existing political culture—in American political culture, for example—such a reconstructive appropriation can accomplish more than merely the hermeneutic clarification of a contingent tradition. The concept of justice *worked out* on this basis must nonetheless be examined once again as to whether it can expect to

meet with acceptance in a pluralistic society. How is this second step related to the first stage of justification of the two highest principles already examined? Is it even properly a second step of *justification*?

Already in the final chapters of *A Theory of Justice*, Rawls addresses the issue of whether a society constituted in accordance with the principles of justice could stabilize itself: for example, whether it could generate the functionally necessary motivations from its own resources through the requisite political socialization of its citizens (TJ 496ff.). In view of the fact of social and ideological pluralism which he subsequently took more seriously, Rawls now wants to examine in a similar way whether the theoretical conception of justice falls under the "art of the possible" and hence is "practicable."[16] First of all, the central concept of the person on which the theory ultimately rests must be sufficiently neutral to be acceptable from the interpretive perspectives of different worldviews. Hence it must be shown that justice as fairness can form the basis of an "overlapping consensus." So far, so good. What bothers me is Rawls's working assumption that such a test of acceptability is of the same kind as the test of consistency he previously undertook with reference to the well-ordered society's potential for self-stabilization.

This methodological parallel is problematic because the test cannot be undertaken in an immanent manner in the case of acceptability; it is no longer a move within the theory. The test of the neutrality of the basic normative concepts with respect to conflicting worldviews now rests on different premises: it is different from a hypothetical examination of the capacity of a society, already organized in accordance with principles of justice, to reproduce itself. Rawls himself in his present work distinguishes between "two stages" of theory-formation. The principles justified at the first stage must be exposed to public discussion at the second stage. Only when the theoretical design is completed can the fact of pluralism be brought into play and the abstractions of the original position revoked. The theory as a whole must be subjected to criticism by the citizens in the public forum of reason. In this forum it is no longer the fictional citizens of a just society about whom statements are made *within* the theory but real citizens of flesh and blood. The theory, therefore, must leave the outcome of such a test of acceptability undetermined.

For Rawls has in mind real discourses whose outcome is open: "What if it turns out that the principles of justice as fairness cannot gain the support of reasonable doctrines, so that the case for stability fails? . . . We should have to see whether acceptable changes in the principles of justice would achieve stability" (PL 65–66). Clearly, the philosopher can at most attempt to anticipate in reflection the direction of real discourses as they would probably unfold under conditions of a pluralistic society. But such a more or less realistic simulation of real discourses cannot be incorporated into the theory in the same way as can the derivation of possibilities of self-stabilization from the underlying premises of a just society. For now the citizens themselves debate about the premises developed by the parties in the original position.

The misleading parallel would be of no further consequence if it did not cast the "overlapping consensus" with which the principles of justice are supposed to meet in the wrong light. Because Rawls situates the "question of stability" in the foreground, the overlapping consensus merely expresses the functional contribution that the theory of justice can make to the peaceful institutionalization of social cooperation; but in this the intrinsic value of a *justified* theory must already be presupposed. From this functionalist perspective, the question of whether the theory can meet with public agreement— that is, from the perspective of different worldviews in the forum of the public use of reason—would lose an epistemic meaning essential to the theory itself. The overlapping consensus would then be merely an index of the utility, and no longer a confirmation of the correctness of the theory; it would no longer be of interest from the point of view of acceptability, and hence of validity, but only from that of acceptance, that is, of securing social stability. If I understand Rawls correctly, however, he does not wish to distinguish in this way between questions of justification and questions of stability. When he calls his conception of justice "political" his intention appears rather to be to collapse the distinction between its justified acceptability and its actual acceptance: "[T]he aim of justice as fairness as a political conception is practical, and not metaphysical or epistemological. That is, it presents itself not as a conception of justice that is true, but one that can serve as a basis of informed and willing political agreement between citizens viewed as free and equal persons."[17]

In my view, Rawls must make a sharper distinction between acceptability and acceptance. A purely instrumental understanding of the theory is already invalidated by the fact that the citizens must first be *convinced* by the proposed conception of justice before such a consensus can come about. The conception of justice must not be political in the wrong sense and should not merely lead to a modus vivendi. The theory itself must furnish the premises that "we and others recognize as true, or as reasonable for the purpose of reaching a working agreement on the fundamentals of political justice."[18] But if Rawls rules out a functionalist interpretation of justice as fairness, he must allow some *epistemic* relation between the validity of his theory and the prospect of its neutrality toward competing worldviews being confirmed in public discourses. The stabilizing effect of an overlapping consensus would then be explained in cognitive terms, that is, in terms of the confirmation of the assumption that justice as fairness is neutral toward "comprehensive doctrines." I don't mean to say that Rawls accepts premises that would prevent him from drawing this consequence; I mean only that he hesitates to assert it because he associates with the characterization "political" the proviso that the theory of justice should not be burdened with an epistemic claim and that its anticipated practical effect should not be made contingent on the rational acceptability of its assertions. Thus we have reason to ask why Rawls does not think his theory admits of truth and *in what sense* he here uses the predicate "reasonable" in place of the predicate "true."

(2) On a weak interpretation, the claim that a theory of justice cannot be true or false has merely the unproblematic sense that normative statements do not describe an independent order of moral facts. On a strong interpretation, this thesis has the value-skeptical sense that behind the validity claim of normative statements there lurks something purely subjective: feelings, desires, or decisions, expressed in a grammatically misleading fashion. But for Rawls both value skepticism and moral realism are equally unacceptable. He wants to secure for normative statements—and for the theory of justice as a whole—a form of rational obligation founded on justified

intersubjective recognition, but without according them an epistemic meaning. For this reason he introduces the predicate "reasonable" as a complementary concept to "true." The difficulty here is in specifying in what sense the one is a "complementary concept" to the other. Two alternative interpretations suggest themselves. Either we understand "reasonable" in the sense of practical reason as synonymous with "morally true," that is, as a validity concept analogous to truth and on the same plane as propositional truth; this reading is supported by at least one line of argumentation (a). Or we understand "reasonable" in more or less the same sense as "thoughtfulness" in dealing with debatable views whose truth is for the present undecided; then "reasonable" is employed as a higher-level predicate concerned more with "reasonable disagreements," and hence with the fallibilistic outlook and civil demeanor of persons, than with the validity of their assertions. In general, Rawls seems to favor this latter reading (b).

(a) Rawls first introduces the "reasonable" as a property of moral persons. People count as reasonable who possess a sense of justice and thus are both willing and able to take account of fair conditions of cooperation, but who are also aware of the fallibility of knowledge and—in recognition of these "burdens of reason"—are willing to justify their conception of political justice publicly. By contrast, persons act merely "rationally" as long as they are prudently guided by their conception of the good.[19] What it means to be "reasonable" can indeed be explicated in terms of such qualities of moral persons. But the concept of a person itself already presupposes the concept of practical reason.

Ultimately Rawls explains the meaning of practical reason by reference to two dimensions: on the one hand, the deontological dimension of normative validity (which I here leave to one side as unproblematic) and, on the other, the pragmatic dimension of a public sphere and the process of public reasoning (which is of particular interest in the present context). The public use is in a sense inscribed in reason. "Publicity" is the common perspective from which the citizens *mutually* convince one another of what is just and unjust by the force of the better argument. This perspective of the public use of reason, in which all participate, first lends moral convictions their objectivity. Rawls calls valid normative statements "objective" and he explains "objectivity" in a procedural manner with reference to a public use of reason that satisfies certain counterfactual conditions: "Political convictions (which are also, of course, moral convictions) are objective—actually founded on an order of reasons—if reasonable and rational persons, who are sufficiently intelligent and conscientious in exercising their powers of practical reason . . . would eventually endorse those convictions . . . provided that these persons know the relevant facts and have sufficiently surveyed the grounds that bear on the matter under conditions favorable to due reflection" (PL 119). Rawls does add in this passage that grounds are only specified as good grounds in the light of a recognized concept of justice; but this concept must in turn meet with agreement under the same ideal conditions (PL 137). Hence Rawls must be understood to mean that, on his view too, the procedure of the public use of reason remains the final court of appeal for normative statements.

In light of this reflection, it could be said that the predicate "reasonable" points to the discursive redemption of a validity claim. By analogy with a nonsemantic concept of truth purified of all connotations of correspondence, one could understand "reasonable" as a predicate for the validity of normative statements.[20] Clearly Rawls does not want to draw this—in my view, correct—conclusion; otherwise he would have to avoid the perplexing usage according to which worldviews need not be true even when they are reasonable, and vice versa. The problem is not Rawls's rejection of moral realism or the consequent rejection of a semantic truth predicate for normative statements, but the fact that he does attach such a truth predicate to worldviews (comprehensive doctrines). He thereby denies himself the possibility of exploiting the epistemic connotations of the expression "reasonable," connotations that he must nevertheless attribute to his own conception of justice if it is to be able to claim some sort of normative binding force.

(b) On Rawls's conception, metaphysical doctrines and religious world-interpretations admit of truth and falsity. As a consequence, a political conception of justice could only be true if it were not merely compatible with such doctrines but also *derivable* from a true doctrine. Yet from the point of view of a political philosophy that is neutral toward worldviews we cannot determine whether and when this is the case. From this secular viewpoint, the truth claims of all reasonable worldviews have equal weight, where those worldviews count as "reasonable" that compete with one another in a reflexive attitude, that is, on the assumption that one's own truth claim could prevail in public discourse in the long run only through the force of better reasons. "Reasonable comprehensive doctrines" are ultimately distinguished by their recognition of the burdens of proof, which enables groups with competing ideologies to accept—for the time being—a "reasonable disagreement" as the basis of their peaceful coexistence.

Since disputes concerning metaphysical and religious truths remain unresolved under conditions of enduring pluralism, only the reasonableness of this kind of reflexive consciousness can be transferred as a validity predicate to a political conception of justice compatible with all reasonable doctrines. By way of this transference, a reasonable conception of justice preserves an oblique relation to a truth claim projected into the future. But it cannot be certain that one of the reasonable doctrines from which it is derivable is also the true one. A political conception of justice is reasonable in the sense that it can afford a kind of tolerance toward not unreasonable worldviews, in the sense advocated by Gottfried Lessing. What remains is an act of faith in reason, "reasonable faith in the real possibility of a just constitutional regime."[21] This view may appeal to some of our better intuitions, but how can it be harmonized with Rawls's reasons for accepting the priority of the right over the good in the first place?

Questions of justice or moral questions admit of justifiable answers—justifiable in the sense of rational acceptability—because they are concerned with what, from an ideally expanded perspective, is in the equal interest of all. "Ethical" questions, by contrast, do not admit of such impartial treatment because they refer to what, from the first person perspective, is in the long run good for me or for us—even if this is not equally good for all. Now, metaphysical or religious worldviews are at the very least permeated with answers to basic ethical questions; they articulate in an exemplary fashion collective identities and guide individual plans of life. Hence, worldviews are measured more by the authenticity of the lifestyles they shape than by the truth of the statements they admit. Because such doctrines are "comprehensive" in precisely the sense that they offer interpretations of the world as a whole, they cannot merely be understood as an ordered set of statements of fact; their contents cannot be expressed completely in sentences that admit of truth and they do not form a symbolic system that can be true or false as such. So, at least, it appears under the conditions of postmetaphysical thinking in which justice as fairness is to be justified.

But then it is impossible to make the validity of a conception of justice contingent on the truth of a worldview, however "reasonable" it may be. Rather, under these premises it makes sense to analyze the different validity claims that we associate, respectively, with descriptive, evaluative, and normative statements (of various kinds) independently of the characteristic complex of validity claims that are obscurely fused together in religious and metaphysical interpretations of reality.[22]

Why does Rawls nevertheless think that identity-stabilizing worldviews admit of truth? A possible motive might be the conviction that a profane, freestanding morality is untenable, that moral convictions must be embedded in metaphysical or religious doctrines. That, at any rate, would cohere with Rawls's way of posing the problem of an overlapping consensus: he takes as his model that political institutionalization of freedom of belief and conscience which brought the religious civil wars of the modern period to an end. But could the religious conflicts have been brought to an end if the principle of tolerance and freedom of belief and conscience had not been able to appeal, with good reasons, to a moral validity *independent* of religion and metaphysics?

III Private and Public Autonomy

The objections I raised in the first part against the design of the original position and in the second against the assimilation of questions of validity to those of acceptance point in the same direction. By subjecting rationally choosing parties to reasonable procedural constraints, Rawls remains dependent on substantive normative assumptions; at the same time, by tailoring a universalistic theory of justice to questions of political stability through an overlapping consensus, he compromises its epistemic status. Both strategies are pursued at the cost of a strict proceduralist program. In contrast with this approach, Rawls could satisfy more elegantly the burdens of proof he incurs with his strong and presumptively neutral concept of the moral person if he developed his substantive concepts and assumptions out of the procedure of the public use of reason.

In my view, the moral point of view is already implicit in the socio-ontological constitution of the public practice of argumentation, comprising the complex relations of mutual recognition that participants in rational discourse "must" accept (in the sense of weak transcendental necessity). Rawls believes that a theory of justice developed in such exclusively procedural terms could not be "sufficiently structured." Since I subscribe to a division of labor between moral theory and the theory of action, I do not regard this as a serious reservation: the conceptual structuring of the contexts of interaction to which questions of political justice refer is not within the province of moral theory. Together with the content of action-conflicts in need of resolution, a whole conceptual frame for normatively regulated interaction is forced upon us—a network of concepts in which persons and interpersonal relations, actors and actions, norm-conforming and deviant behavior, responsibility and autonomy, and even intersubjectively structured moral feelings all find their place. Each of these concepts deserves a prior analysis. If we then take the concept of practical reason in the procedural sense that Rawls himself intimates with his notion of the public use of reason, we could say that precisely those principles are valid that meet with uncoerced intersubjective recognition under conditions of rational discourse. It remains as a further, and primarily empirical, question whether and when such valid principles ensure political stability under conditions of pluralism. In what follows, I am interested in the execution of the proceduralist program only with reference to an implication it has for the explanation of the constitutional state.

Liberals have stressed the "liberties of the moderns": liberty of belief and conscience, the protection of life, personal liberty, and

property—in sum, the core of subjective private rights. Republicanism, by contrast, has defended the "liberties of the ancients": the
political rights of participation and communication that make possible the citizens' exercise of self-determination. Jean-Jacques Rousseau and Kant shared the aspiration of deriving both elements from
the same root, namely, from moral and political autonomy: the
liberal rights may neither be merely foisted on the practice of self-
determination as extrinsic constraints nor be made merely instrumental to its exercise. Rawls, too, subscribes to this intuition;
nevertheless, the two-stage character of his theory generates a priority of liberal rights that demotes the democratic process to an infe-
rior status.

Rawls certainly proceeds from the idea of political autonomy and
models it at the level of the original position: it is represented by the
interplay between the rationally choosing parties and the framework
conditions that guarantee impartiality of judgment. But this idea is
brought to bear only selectively at the institutional level of the democratic procedure for the political will-formation of free and equal
citizens from which it is nonetheless borrowed. The form of political
autonomy granted virtual existence in the original position, and thus
on the first level of theory formation, does not fully unfold in the
heart of the justly constituted society. For the higher the veil of
ignorance is raised and the more Rawls's citizens themselves take on
real flesh and blood, the more deeply they find themselves subject
to principles and norms that have been anticipated in theory and
have already become institutionalized beyond their control. In this
way, the theory deprives the citizens of too many of the insights that
they would have to assimilate anew in each generation.

From the perspective of the theory of justice, the act of founding
the democratic constitution cannot be repeated under the institutional conditions of an already constituted just society, and the process of realizing the system of basic rights cannot be assured on an
ongoing basis. It is not possible for the citizens to experience this
process as open and incomplete, as the shifting historical circumstances nonetheless demand. They cannot reignite the radical
democratic embers of the original position in the civic life of their
society, for from their perspective all of the *essential* discourses of

legitimation have already taken place within the theory; and they find the results of the theory already sedimented in the constitution. Because the citizens cannot conceive of the constitution as a *project,* the public use of reason does not actually have the significance of a present exercise of political autonomy but merely promotes the nonviolent *preservation of political stability.* Granted, this reading does not reflect Rawls's intention in formulating his theory,[23] but if I am correct it uncovers one of its undesired consequences. This is shown, for example, by the rigid boundary between the political and the nonpublic identities of the citizens. According to Rawls, this boundary is set by basic liberal rights which constrain democratic self-legislation, and with it the sphere of the political, *from the beginning,* that is, prior to all political will-formation.

Rawls uses the term "political" in a threefold sense. Thus far we have become acquainted with the theoretical meaning: a conception of justice is political and not metaphysical when it is neutral toward conflicting worldviews. Further, Rawls uses the term "political" in the usual sense to classify matters of public interest, so that political philosophy limits itself to the justification of the institutional framework and the basic structure of society. Both meanings are ultimately combined in an interesting way in Rawls's treatment of "political values." "Political" in this third sense constitutes a fund both for shared convictions of citizens and for the purpose of delimiting an object-domain. Rawls treats the political value sphere, which is distinguished in modern societies from other cultural value spheres, as something given, almost in the manner of a neo-Kantian like Max Weber. For only with reference to political values, whatever they may be, can he split the moral person into the public identity of a citizen and the nonpublic identity of a private person shaped by his or her individual conception of the good. These two identities then constitute the reference points for two domains, the one constituted by rights of political participation and communication, the other protected by basic liberal rights. The constitutional protection of the private sphere in this way enjoys priority while the "role of the political liberties is . . . largely instrumental in preserving the other liberties."[24] Thus with reference to the political value sphere a prepolitical domain of liberties is delimited which is withdrawn from the reach of democratic self-legislation.

But such an a priori boundary between private and public autonomy not only contradicts the republican intuition that popular sovereignty and human rights are nourished by the same root; it also conflicts with historical experience, above all with the fact that the historically shifting boundary between the private and public spheres has always been problematic from a normative point of view.[25] In addition, the development of the welfare state shows that the boundaries between the private and public autonomy of citizens are in flux and that such differentiations must be subjected to the political will-formation of the citizens if the latter are to have the opportunity to press a legal claim to the "fair value" of their liberties.

A theory of justice can take better account of this circumstance if it differentiates the "political" in accordance with the criterion of "legal regulation" (mentioned only in passing by Rawls). It is ultimately by means of positive and coercive law that the life of a political community is legitimately regulated (PL 215). The basic question then is: Which rights must free and equal persons mutually accord one another if they wish to regulate their coexistence by the legitimate means of positive and coercive law?

According to Kant's conception of legality, *coercive law* extends only to the external relations between persons and addresses the freedom of choice of subjects who are allowed to follow their own conception of the good. Hence modern law, on the one hand, constitutes the status of legal subjects in terms of actionable subjective liberties that may be exercised by each according to her own preferences. Since it must also be *possible* to obey a legal order for moral reasons, the status of private legal subjects is legitimately determined by the right to *equal* subjective liberties.[26] As *positive* or codified law, on the other hand, this medium calls for a political legislator, where the legitimacy of legislation is accounted for by a democratic procedure that secures the autonomy of the citizens. Citizens are politically autonomous only if they can view themselves as the joint authors of the laws to which they are subject as individual addressees.

The dialectical relation between private and public autonomy becomes clear in light of the fact that the status of such democratic citizens equipped with lawmaking competences can be institutionalized in turn only by means of coercive law. But because this law is directed to persons who could not even assume the status of legal

subjects without subjective private rights, private and public autonomy of citizens *mutually* presuppose each other. As we have seen,
both elements are already interwoven in the concept of positive and
coercive law: there can be no law at all without actionable subjective
liberties that guarantee the private autonomy of individual legal
subjects, and no legitimate law without collective democratic lawmaking by citizens who, as free and equal, are entitled to participate
in this process. Once the concept of law has been clarified in this
way it becomes clear that the normative substance of basic liberal
rights is already contained in the indispensable medium for the legal
institutionalization of the public use of reason of sovereign citizens.
The main objects of further analysis are then the communicative
presuppositions and the procedure of a discursive process of opin-
ion- and will-formation in which the public use of reason is manifested. I cannot discuss this alternative in greater detail in the
present context.[27]

Such a procedural moral and legal theory is at the same time both
more and less modest than Rawls's theory. It is more modest in that
it focuses exclusively on the procedural aspects of the public use of
reason and derives the system of rights from the idea of its legal
institutionalization. It can leave more questions open because it
entrusts more to the *process* of rational opinion- and will-formation.
Philosophy shoulders different theoretical burdens when, as on
Rawls's conception, it claims to elaborate the idea of a just society,
while the citizens then use this idea as a platform from which to
judge existing arrangements and policies. By contrast, I propose that
philosophy limit itself to the clarification of the moral point of view
and the procedure of democratic legitimation, to the analysis of the
conditions of rational discourses and negotiations. In this more
modest role, philosophy need not proceed in a constructive, but
only in a *reconstructive* fashion. It leaves substantial questions that
must be answered here and now to the more or less enlightened
engagement of participants, which does not mean that philosophers
may not also participate in the public debate, though in the role of
intellectuals, not of experts.

But Rawls insists on a modesty of a different kind. He wants to
extend the "method of avoidance," which is intended to lead to an

overlapping consensus on questions of political justice, to the philosophical enterprise. He hopes to develop political philosophy into a sharply focused discipline and thereby avoid most of the controversial questions of a more general nature. This avoidance strategy can lead to an impressively self-contained theory, as we can see from the wonderful example before us. But even Rawls cannot develop his theory in as "freestanding" a fashion as he would like. As we have seen, his "political constructivism" draws him willy-nilly into a dispute concerning concepts of rationality and truth. His concept of the person as well oversteps the boundaries of political philosophy. These and other preliminary theoretical decisions involve him in as many long-running and still unresolved debates. The subject matter itself, it seems to me, makes a presumptuous encroachment on neighboring fields often unavoidable and at times even fruitful.

3

"Reasonable" versus "True," or the Morality of Worldviews

John Rawls claims that his idea of "justice as fairness" is a "freestanding" conception: it is supposed to "move entirely within the domain of the political" and "leave philosophy as it is." The goal and feasibility of this strategy of avoidance depend on how we understand the term "political." Rawls uses it in the first place to specify the object domain of a political theory that deals with the institutional frame and basic structure of a (modern) society. The conventional element in the choice of basic concepts is never beyond controversy; but once a theory demonstrates its utility such discussions lose their point. However, a second and less trivial use of the term—"political" in contrast with "metaphysical"—leads to controversies that cannot be so easily resolved.[1]

Rawls uses the term "political" in contrast with "metaphysical" to characterize those conceptions of justice that satisfy an essential requirement of liberalism: neutrality toward competing worldviews or "comprehensive doctrines." With the term "political" Rawls here associates a particular interpretation of neutrality: "it means that we must distinguish between how a political conception is presented and its being part of, or derivable within, a comprehensive doctrine."[2] The kind of neutrality that defines the "political" character of "justice as fairness" is explained by its being able to be presented as "freestanding." And this status is explained in turn by one of the most striking assumptions of Rawls's theory: "I assume all citizens to affirm a comprehensive doctrine to which the political conception they accept is in some way related. But a distinguishing feature of a political conception is that it is . . . expounded apart from, or without reference to, any such wider background. . . . [T]he political conception is a module . . . that fits into and can be supported by various reasonable comprehensive doctrines that endure in the society regulated by it" (PL 12).

In this second meaning, the term "political" does not refer to a specific subject matter but to the peculiar epistemic status to which political conceptions of justice should aspire: they should be able to form a coherent part of various comprehensive doctrines. In addition they can be justified only within a comprehensive doctrine, although they can be conceived and "expounded"—that is, introduced in a plausible manner—independently of any worldview. Rawls's "political liberalism" also aspires to the status of a freestanding theory. Since this status itself requires explanation within the theory, "freestanding" in this context has a double reference. On the one hand, it specifies a necessary condition of all conceptions of justice that qualify as candidates for inclusion in an "overlapping consensus." At the same time the predicate "freestanding" is supposed to apply to the very theory that explains it: "justice as fairness" is one of the most promising among those candidates. This self-referential use of "freestanding" can be understood as a political claim: Rawls assumes that his own theory—under conditions of "general and wide reflective equilibrium"[3]—provides a basis on which the members of contemporary American (or any other modern) civil society could achieve a basic political agreement.

Less plausible, however, is Rawls's burdening of the self-referential use of "freestanding" with a further claim of a different, theoretical kind. He seems to think that a theory that is freestanding in the political domain will be freestanding in the philosophical domain as well and will steer clear of all controversial metaphysical problems—"leaving philosophy as it is." But it is hard to see how Rawls can explain the epistemic status of a freestanding political conception, without taking a position on philosophical questions which, while not falling under the category of the metaphysical, nevertheless reach well beyond the domain of the political.

The term "metaphysical" acquires its special meaning within the theory from its opposition to the term "political." In modern societies a consensus on principles of justice that is neutral with respect to worldviews, and hence inclusive, is required in view of religious and cultural pluralism. A theory that aims even to foster such a consensus must certainly be "political and not metaphysical" in this sense. But it does not follow that political theory can itself move entirely within the domain of the political (R 133) and steer clear of stubborn philosophical controversies. Philosophy can move beyond the domain of the political in different directions. The philosophical enterprise is institutionally framed in terms of a cooperative search for the truth and is not necessarily internally related to metaphysics (as conceived in *Political Liberalism*). If the explanation of the epistemic status of a freestanding conception involves us in nonpolitical questions concerning reason and truth, this does not necessarily mean that we must engage with metaphysical problems and controversies. The following investigation seeks to illustrate this point in an indirect, so to speak, performative way. It will attempt to clarify explicitly the epistemic status of a freestanding conception of justice (where "freestanding" is understood in an unproblematic, political sense).

I want to examine how Rawls's division of labor between the political and the metaphysical, which is reflected in a peculiar dependence of the "reasonable" on the "true," actually works. It is far from obvious why publicly defensible and actor-independent reasons should only support the "reasonableness" of a political conception, while nonpublic and actor-relative reasons should be sufficient to establish the strong and autochthonous claim to moral "truth." Rawls's generous and detailed reply to my tentative remarks[4] clarifies among other things the "kinds of justification" that are supposed to lead to an overlapping consensus. In the light of these elucidations I will argue that reasonable citizens cannot be expected to develop an overlapping consensus so long as they are prevented from jointly adopting a moral point of view independent of, and prior to, the various perspectives they individually adopt from within each of their comprehensive doctrines. The notion of reasonableness is either so etiolated that it is too weak to characterize the mode of validity of an intersubjectively recognized conception of political justice, or it is defined in sufficiently strong terms, in which case what is practically reasonable is indistinguishable from what is morally right. I will try to show why Rawls cannot ultimately avoid giving full weight to requirements of practical reason that *constrain* rational comprehensive doctrines rather than merely *reflect* their felicitous overlapping.[5]

Before I enter *medias in res* I will characterize the challenge of the modern condition to which theories of justice cannot avoid responding (1). Then I will offer a necessarily brief sketch of the philosophical move from Hobbes to Kant (2), for this forms the background for Rawls's alternative approach (3). In the main part of the essay I will analyze the division of the burdens of justification between the "reasonable" conceptions of justice and the "morally true" worldviews (4), before discussing difficulties that this poses for the justification of an overlapping consensus (5). Finally, I will offer arguments in support of a proceduralist conception of the "public use of reason" which is closer to Kant (6). If political justice is understood in this way, democratic self-legislation assumes the position occupied by the negative liberties in Political Liberalism. With this the accent shifts in favor of Kantian Republicanism (7).

1 The Modern Condition

Political liberalism provides a response to the challenge posed by the fact of pluralism. It is primarily concerned with the possibility of achieving a consensus on political essentials which grants equal freedoms to all citizens without regard to their cultural heritage, their religious convictions, or their individual lifestyles. The required consensus on issues of political justice can no longer be based on a settled traditional ethos that encompasses the whole of society. Yet members of modern societies still share the expectation that they can live together under conditions of fair and peaceful cooperation. In spite of the lack of a substantive consensus on values rooted in a socially accepted worldview, they continue to appeal to moral convictions and norms that each of them thinks everyone else should accept. People continue to debate moral questions with reasons they take to be compelling, regardless of whether a mere modus vivendi would be sufficient for cooperation. They engage in moral discourses in everyday life as well as in politics, most especially in disputes concerning constitutional principles. These discourses persist, even though it is not clear whether moral disputes can still be settled by arguments. Citizens tacitly attribute to each other a moral sense or a sense of justice operating across the boundaries between different worldviews, while at the same time they learn to tolerate these differences in outlook as sources of reasonable ethical disagreements.

Rawls responds to these features of the modern condition with a constructivist proposal to develop a sufficiently neutral conception of justice around which a constitutional consensus among citizens with different religious or metaphysical outlooks can crystallize. In general, moral philosophers and political theorists have felt that their task is to provide a convincing substitute for traditional justifications of norms and principles. In traditional societies morality was an integral component of ontological or soteriological worldviews that could command public acceptance. Moral norms and principles were viewed as elements of a rational "order of things" imbued with value or as part of an exemplary way of life leading to salvation. Of particular interest in the present context is that these "realistic" explanations were presented in the assertoric mode of statements expressing truth claims. However, with the public devaluation of religious or metaphysical explanations and with the rise of the epistemic authority of the empirical sciences, normative statements have become more sharply differentiated from descriptive statements, on the one hand, and from value judgments and expressive utterances on the other. Notwithstanding one's position on the issue of "is" and "ought," with the transition to modernity the "objective" reason embodied in nature or sacred history was displaced by the "subjective" reason of the human mind. With this there arose the question of whether normative statements retain any cognitive content and, if so, how they can be justified.

This question poses a particular challenge for those who (like Rawls and myself) reject both moral realism and modern value-skepticism. The mutual attribution of a capacity for moral judgment which we observe in everyday life calls for a kind of explanation that does not flatly deny the reasonable character of moral arguments. That moral disputes persist says something about the underlying structure of a social life that is shot through with trivial validity claims. The social integration of everyday life depends largely on communicative practices oriented toward mutual understanding and based on the recognition of fallible claims to validity.[6]

Against this background, the premise with which Hobbes sought to lead practical philosophy out of its dead end does not appear especially plausible. He wanted to reduce practical reason to instrumental reason. Indeed, to this very day there are sophisticated approaches in the Hobbesian contractualist tradition that conceive of moral reasons as rational motives and reduce moral judgment to rational choice. The social contract is supposed to provide a procedure for reaching agreement based solely on the enlightened self-interest of the participants. The contracting parties need only consider whether it is advantageous or rational for them in light of their desires and preferences to adopt a rule of action or a system of such rules. But it is well known that this strategy misses the specific *obligatory* force of binding norms and valid moral statements, as is shown by the problem of the free rider. I will simply cite in passing Thomas Scanlon's argument against utilitarianism: "The right-making force of a person's desires is specified by what might be called a conception of morally legitimate interests. Such a conception is a product of moral argument; it is not given, as the notion of individual well-being may be, simply by the idea of what it is rational for an individual to desire."[7] But if the cognitive content of normative statements cannot be explained in terms of instrumental rationality, to what conception of practical reason must we then appeal?

2   From Hobbes to Kant

Here we are faced with the alternative that provided the decisive impulse for Rawls's theoretical innovation: we can either follow the path leading from Hobbes to Kant and develop a notion of practical reason that in some way preserves the cognitive content of moral statements, or we can fall back once again on the "strong" traditions and "comprehensive" doctrines that ground the truth of the moral conceptions embedded in them. Whichever route we take we encounter obstacles. If we take the former, we have to distinguish practical reason clearly from theoretical reason, but in such a way that it does not completely lose its cognitive force; if we take the latter, we have to cope with the irreducible plurality of worldviews that are held to be true within each of the corresponding communities of believers, although everyone knows that only one of them can be true.

In the Kantian tradition, practical reason provides the perspective from which moral norms and principles can be judged in an impartial manner. This "moral point of view" has been explained in terms of various principles or procedures, be it the categorical imperative or G. H. Mead's ideal role-taking, Scanlon's rule of argumentation or Rawls's construction of an original position that imposes suitable constraints on the rational choice of participants. Each of these different designs is intended to yield an agreement or an understanding that satisfies our intuitions concerning equal respect and mutual solidarity with everybody. Since the principles and norms selected in this way claim universal recognition, a procedurally correct agreement must be "rationally motivated" in an epistemic sense. The reasons that bear on the outcome must carry an epistemic weight and may not simply express what it is rational for a particular person to do in light of her existing preferences.

One way to capture the epistemic character of practical deliberations is through a precise description of how, from a moral point of view, individual interests that provide the input for deliberation in the form of rational motives change their role and meaning in the course of argumentation. In practical discourses, only those interests "count" for the outcome that are presented as intersubjectively recognized values and hence are *candidates* for inclusion in the semantic content of valid norms. Only *generalizable* value-orientations, which all participants (and all those affected) can accept with good reasons as appropriate for regulating the subject matter at hand, and which can thereby acquire binding normative force, pass this threshold. An "interest" can be described as a "value-orientation" when it is shared by other members of a community in similar situations. Thus an interest only deserves consideration from the moral point of view once it is stripped of its intrinsic relation to a first person perspective. Once it is translated into an intersubjectively shared evaluative vocabulary, it is no longer tied to contingent desires and preferences and can achieve, as a candidate for value-generalization in moral justification, the epistemic status of an argument. What enters discourse as a desire or preference survives the generalization test only under the description of a value that appears to be generally acceptable to all participants as a basis for regulating the relevant matter.

Let us assume that practical deliberation can be analyzed as a form of argumentation different from both rational choice and fact-stating discourse. A pragmatic theory of argumentation would then provide a suitable basis for developing a conception of practical reason distinct from both instrumental and theoretical reason. We would thereby preserve an epistemic meaning for ought sentences without assimilating them to assertoric sentences or reducing their validity to instrumental rationality. However, the *analogy* between truth and normative rightness that remains intact would certainly give rise to further questions. We could no more avoid being drawn into the familiar debates concerning semantic and pragmatic conceptions of truth and justification than into the discussions about the relation between meaning and validity, the structure and role of arguments, the logic, procedure, and communicative structure of argumentation, and so forth. We would have to deal with the problem of the relation between the social world and the objective and subjective worlds and would unavoidably be drawn into long-running debates about rationality. Hence Rawls has good reasons to try to avoid discussions of this kind—even if one does not classify these controversies immediately as "metaphysical."

On the other hand, whether the avoidance strategy of making a clean separation of the political from the metaphysical can meet with success is a different question. Rawls initially followed the straightforward Kantian strategy; in *A Theory of Justice* he set himself the task of explicating the "moral point of view" in terms of the original position. However, the construction of "justice as fairness" was informed by a conception of practical reason embodied in the two "higher capacities" of moral persons. Rawls developed this "Kantian constructivism" further in the Dewey Lectures[8] and this approach still leaves its traces in the third chapter of *Political Liberalism*. But this book represents a shift to an entirely new framework within which reason loses its central position. Practical reason is robbed of its moral core and is deflated to a reasonableness that becomes dependent on moral truths justified otherwise. The moral validity of conceptions of justice is now no longer grounded in a universally binding practical reason but in the lucky convergence of reasonable worldviews whose moral components overlap to a sufficient degree. However, the remnants of the original conception cannot be seamlessly integrated into the current theory.

Two conflicting justification programs clash in *Political Liberalism*. The idea of the overlapping consensus involves a decisive weakening of the rational claim of the Kantian conception of justice. In what follows, I will first outline the new division of the burdens of justification between the "reasonableness" of political justice and the "truth" of worldviews and will then examine certain inconsistencies which suggest that Rawls hesitates to subordinate practical reason to the morality of worldviews to the extent called for by his favored alternative to Kantian approaches.

3 The Alternative to Kantian Proceduralism

An overlapping consensus occurs "when all the reasonable members of political society carry out a justification of the shared political conception by embedding it in their several reasonable comprehensive views" (R 143). Thus Rawls advocates a division of labor between the political and the metaphysical that leads to a distinction between *what* all citizens can agree upon and *the reasons for* their individually accepting it as true. This construction presupposes precisely two perspectives: each citizen combines the perspective of a participant with that of an observer. Observers can describe what happens in the political realm, for example, that an overlapping consensus has occurred. They can see that this agreement is the result of the successful overlapping of the moral components of different religious or metaphysical worldviews and that it contributes to the stability of the community. But in the objectifying attitude of observers, citizens cannot penetrate each others' worldviews and judge their truth content from the internal perspective peculiar to each. Bound by the constraints of factual discourse, they cannot take a stand on what committed participants claim to be true, right, and valuable from their first person perspectives. If citizens want to raise claims about what is morally true or, more generally, about "conceptions of what is of value in human life" (PL 175), they have to shift to the participant's perspective inscribed in their own comprehensive doctrine. For thick comprehensive worldviews are the only source of reasons for justifying moral statements and value judgments. Moral reasons for a presumptively shared conception of justice are by definition nonpublic.

A citizen can convince herself of the truth of a conception of justice suitable for everybody only from within her own interpretive framework. Such a conception demonstrates its suitability to serve as a shared platform for a *public* justification of constitutional essentials by the fact that it meets with the agreement of all participants on the basis of *nonpublic* reasons. Only the lucky convergence of the differently motivated nonpublic reasons can generate the public validity or "reasonableness" of the content of this "overlapping consensus" that everyone accepts. Agreement in conclusions *results* from premises rooted in different outlooks. It is significant for the design of the theory as a whole that the participants can only register this convergence as a social fact: "The express contents of these doctrines have no normative role in public justification" (R 144). At this stage Rawls does not allow his citizens a third perspective in addition to that of the observer and participants. Before an overlapping consensus is established there is no public, intersubjectively shared perspective from which the citizens could make inherently impartial judgments. The citizens are denied the "moral point of view" from which they could develop and justify a political conception *in joint public deliberation*. What Rawls calls the "public use of reason" presupposes the shared platform of an already achieved political consensus on fundamentals. The citizens can avail themselves of this platform only *post festum,* that is, *as a consequence of* the emerging "overlap" of their different background convictions: "Only when there is a reasonable overlapping consensus can political society's political conception of justice be *publicly* . . . justified" (R 144, my emphasis).

The model for the complementary relation between the political and the metaphysical is provided by a description of the modern condition from a "believer's" point of view, that is, from the "metaphysical" side. The division of labor between the political and the metaphysical reflects the complementary relation between *public* agnosticism and *privatized* religious faith, between the color blindness of the neutral state toward religious confessions and the illuminating force of worldviews that compete for the "Truth" in the emphatic sense. The moral truths that are still embedded in religious or metaphysical worldviews share this strong claim to truth, whereas the fact of pluralism reveals at the same time that the comprehensive doctrines no longer admit of public justification.

The ingenious division of the burdens of justification relieves political philosophy of the troubling task of providing a substitute for the metaphysical justification of moral truths. Though struck from the public agenda, the metaphysical nevertheless remains the ultimate ground of the validity of what is morally right and ethically good. The political sphere, by contrast, is deprived of any source of validity of its own. The innovative idea of an "overlapping consensus" preserves an internal connection between political justice and the moral components of worldviews, though with the proviso that this relation can only be grasped by the morality of worldviews and hence remains *publicly inaccessible:* "it is up to each comprehensive doctrine to say how its idea of the reasonable connects with its concept of truth" (PL 94). The overlapping consensus rests on the converging moral segments of the diverging totalities of what each citizen holds to be true. From an observer's perspective nobody can know which of the competing belief systems, if any, is actually true. Yet the truth of any single one of them would guarantee that "all the reasonable doctrines yield the right conception of justice, even though they do not do so for the right reasons as specified by the one true doctrine" (PL 128).

Like Hobbes, Rawls concentrates on questions of political justice, and he borrows from the Hobbesian tradition the idea that the sought-for public agreement must be supported by private, nonpublic reasons. But in contrast with Hobbes, for Rawls the rational acceptability of proposals that admit of agreement is now based not on the complementary preferences of different persons but on the moral substance of different, though convergent, worldviews. Rawls shares with the Kantian tradition the idea of a moral foundation of political justice. The morally convincing reasons support a consensus that goes beyond a mere modus vivendi. But these reasons cannot be publicly inspected by everyone in common, given that the public use of reason depends on a platform that can only be constructed on the basis of nonpublic reasons. Like a compromise, the overlapping consensus rests on the each party's *different* reasons; but unlike a compromise, these reasons are of a moral kind.

4 A Third Perspective for the Reasonable

The idea of an overlapping consensus calls for an explanation of the term "reasonable." Although the acceptance of a freestanding conception of justice is parasitic on complementary metaphysical truths, this political conception is nevertheless supposed to exhibit a reasonableness that *adds* the aspect of public recognition to those idiosyncratic and mutually nontransparent truths. From the point of view of validity, an uneasy asymmetry prevails between the public conception of justice that raises a weak claim to reasonableness and the nonpublic doctrines with their strong claims to truth. That a public conception of justice should ultimately derive its moral authority from nonpublic reasons is counterintuitive. Anything valid should also be capable of public justification. Valid statements deserve the acceptance of everyone for the same reasons. The expression "agreement" is ambiguous in this respect. Whereas parties who negotiate a compromise might accept the result for different reasons, participants in argumentation must reach a rationally motivated agreement, if at all, for the same reasons. Such practices of justification depend on a *jointly and publicly reached* consensus.

Even outside of the political domain, arguments call for a public use of reason (in a sense). Rational discourses merely make a topic of what functions in everyday life as a resource for the binding force of speech acts, namely, validity claims that demand intersubjective recognition and offer the prospect of public justification when they are questioned. The same holds for normative validity claims. The practice of reason-giving in moral disputes would break down if participants had to assume that moral judgments depend essentially on personal background beliefs and could no longer count on the acceptance of those who do not share these beliefs.[9] Of course, this cannot be applied immediately to politics, for political disputes are of a mixed nature. But the more they focus on constitutional essentials and underlying conceptions of justice, the more they *resemble* moral discourses. Moreover, basic political questions are linked to questions of legal implementation. And *coercive* regulations make a basic political consensus among citizens absolutely necessary.

The demand itself is not controversial, only *how* it is to be fulfilled. The question is whether citizens can grasp something as reasonable if it is not open to them to adopt a third standpoint besides that of an observer or a participant. Can the plurality of reasons rooted in worldviews, whose nonpublic character is mutually recognized, lead to a consensus that can serve as the basis for a public use of reason for citizens of a political community? I wonder whether Rawls can account for the possibility of an overlapping consensus without tacitly assuming such a third perspective from which "we," the citizens, can publicly examine in common what is in the equal interest of everybody.

The perspective of an adherent of a community of true believers is different from that of a participant in public discourse. The existential resolve of an inalienable individual reflecting in the first person singular on how she should live her life is quite different from the fallibilistic consciousness of a citizen participating in processes of political opinion- and will-formation. But, as we have seen, Rawls cannot conceive of the process of reaching an understanding on a shared conception of justice in such a way that the citizens adopt a shared perspective. Because such a perspective is lacking, the conception that emerges as "reasonable" must fit into the context of the different worldviews in each case taken to be true by the corresponding parties. But how can the fact that the nonpublic truth of religious or metaphysical doctrines enjoys priority over the reasonableness of a political conception fail to affect the universalistic meaning of "reasonable"?

Rawls introduces the predicate "reasonable" in the following manner. Citizens who are willing and able to live in a "well-ordered" society are reasonable; as reasonable people they also have reasonable views of the world as a whole. If the expected consensus results from reasonable comprehensive doctrines, its content also counts as reasonable. Hence "reasonable" refers in the first instance to the attitude of people who are (a) willing to propose, agree upon, and abide by fair terms of social cooperation between free and equal citizens, and (b) capable of recognizing the burdens of argument and willing to accept their consequences. The predicate is then extended from the *attitudes* to the *beliefs* of reasonable persons. Reasonable worldviews reinforce an attitude of tolerance among their adherents because they exhibit a certain reflexivity and are subject to certain constraints with regard to their practical consequences. A "reflexive" consciousness results from the fact that an expectation of reasonable disagreement exists between competing doctrines. And such subjective belief systems can only compete with one another on fair terms under conditions of a pluralism of worldviews if their adherents renounce the use of political violence to enforce their doctrines.

In the present context what is of primary importance is that the reasonableness alone of citizens and worldviews, thus specified, by no means requires the adoption of the perspective from which the fundamental questions of political justice could be jointly and publicly discussed. The moral point of view is neither implied by "reasonable" attitudes nor is it made possible by "reasonable" worldviews. Such a perspective is first opened up when an overlapping consensus on a conception of justice has emerged. However, Rawls cannot avoid making at least an unofficial use of this third perspective even in the "basic case of public justification" (R 144). I have the impression that he is torn between the original strategy pursued in *A Theory of Justice,* which relied more heavily on Kant, and the more recently developed alternative which is intended to take seriously the fact of pluralism. Here the philosopher again adopts the perspective of impartial judgment; but this "professional" standpoint does not correspond to a moral point of view that citizens could share by their own lights.

Rawls has in the meantime addressed the problem of the justification of the overlapping consensus at greater length (R 142ff.). If we examine closely the three kinds of justification he lays out there we run up against the interesting question of how "reasonable" worldviews can even be identified as such if standards rooted in a practical reason independent of worldviews are not available. Winnowing out reasonable worldviews calls for "thin" normative decisions which must be justifiable independently of "thick" metaphysical background assumptions.

5 The Last Stage of Justification

According to Rawls, the justification of a political conception of justice[10] must be situated in "the place among citizens in civil society—the viewpoint of you and me." Here every citizen starts from the context of her own worldview and the moral notion of justice embedded therein, for the participant's perspective is at first the only one available for normative reasoning. So to begin with there is no relevant difference between the position of the philosopher and that of any other citizen. Whether or not she is a philosopher, a reasonable person will employ her sense of justice to develop a freestanding political conception which she hopes can be accepted by all reasonable persons in their role as free and equal citizens. The first constructive step then requires her to abstract from comprehensive doctrines. For the purposes of this "*pro tanto* justification" the citizens may also consider various duly reflected upon and elaborated philosophical doctrines. Such theories offer guidelines for the required kind of abstraction. For example, the "original position" offers one scheme for such a universalization test: principles that pass the test appear to be acceptable to everyone.

But nobody will be able to abstract completely from her own preunderstanding in applying the procedure. "You and I" cannot perform the test in a presuppositionless manner; each of us must undertake it from the perspective shaped by her own background beliefs. In particular, background assumptions concerning the political sphere and what should count as a matter of politics enter in here. Hence there can hardly be any surprise at the next stage when each citizen embeds in her own comprehensive doctrine the concept that seems promising to her. The universalization test does indeed demand that all reasonable citizens abstract from the specifics of their respective comprehensive doctrines; but this operation of universalization must nevertheless be carried out against the background of their own conceptions of the world. For nobody can give up her participant's perspective without losing sight of the normative dimension as such in taking on the objectivating attitude of an observer.

This is why the universalization test functions at the first stage in a way roughly similar to the Golden Rule: it filters out anything that does not appear *from my viewpoint* to qualify for equal acceptance by all reasonable persons. Precisely those principles and practices and those regulations and institutions pass the test which, assuming that they can be universally established, are in the equal interest of everybody *given my understanding of the political sphere.* In this way the application of the test is conditioned by preconceptions peculiar to my comprehensive doctrine, for otherwise the third stage of justification—analogous to the move from the Golden Rule to the categorical imperative[11]—would be superfluous. Rawls regards this step as necessary because "you and I" cannot know whether we succeeded in abstracting from every comprehensive doctrine when, each proceeding from *her own* best understanding of the political sphere, we subjected our normative convictions to the constraints of the original position. Only at the final stage, which Rawls calls the stage of "wide and general reflective equilibrium" (R 141, n.16), do we take the other citizens into account: "reasonable citizens take one another into account as having reasonable comprehensive doctrines that endorse that political conception" (R 143).

This step, which is supposed to lead finally to an overlapping consensus, can be understood as the radicalization of an as yet incomplete, still egocentric universalization procedure. Only a *recursive* application of the procedure can yield the anticipated result: all citizens, not just you and I, have to decide, from their own perspectives and understandings of the political world, whether there is a proposal that can meet with universal acceptance. Rawls speaks of "mutual accounting;" but what is meant is a mutual *observation* through which participants establish whether an agreement occurs. The consensus is an event that happens: "Public justification *happens* when all the reasonable members of political society carry out a justification of the shared political conception by embedding it in their several reasonable comprehensive views" (R 143, my emphasis). The terms "public" and "shared" are somewhat misleading in this context. The overlapping consensus results from everybody's deciding simultaneously, but each individually and for herself, whether the proposed conception fits into her own comprehensive doctrine. If it is to work, everyone must accept the same conception, though each for her own, nonpublic reasons, and each must at the same time satisfy herself that all others also accept it: "the express contents of these doctrines have no normative role in public justification; citizens do not look into the content of others' doctrines. . . . Rather, they take into account and give some weight to only the fact—the existence—of the reasonable overlapping consensus itself" (R 144). Hence the overlapping consensus rests on what Rainer Forst has called a "private use of reason with public-political intent."[12] Again, this design of "three kinds" of justification lacks a perspective of impartial judgment and a public use of reason in the strict sense, which would not be contingent on the overlapping consensus but would be shared *from the beginning*.

Moreover, it is doubtful whether "reasonable" citizens in the sense outlined would ever reach an overlapping consensus if they could only convince themselves from within their own individual comprehensive doctrines of the validity of a conception of justice.[13] The prospect of reaching a consensus depends essentially on what kinds of revisions are permitted at the last stage of a decentered justification. A *pro tanto* justified conception that "you or I" judge to be valid from our respective points of view may be overridden by the veto of others "once all values are tallied up." Our conception must be revised before it can be endorsed by everyone. The disagreements that motivate such adaptations concern in the first instance differences in the understanding of the political that you or I did not anticipate at the first or second stages. Following Rawls, I distinguish between three kinds of disagreements: those concerning (a) the definition of the domain of political matters, (b) the ranking and reasonable balancing of political values, and finally and most importantly (c) the priority of political over nonpolitical values.

(a)–(b) Different interpretations of the principle of the separation of church and state, for example, touch on the extent and scope of the political domain; for they lead to different normative guidelines, in this case guidelines concerning the status and the role of religious communities and organizations. Other controversies concern the ranking of political values, for example, whether one accords intrinsic or merely instrumental value to political participation in cases where political rights must be balanced against negative liberties. These disputes are normally settled by courts—in the final instance by the Federal Constitutional Court[14]—and hence on the basis of an already accepted conception of justice. This is also how Rawls deals with such issues. But in some cases conflicts can be so deep that the differences in opinion place in question the underlying political consensus. Such conflicts undermine the overlapping consensus itself. But we would like to think that most of these disagreements can be resolved in a consensual manner, if necessary by revising the currently accepted constitutional principles. Successful adaptations of this type would confirm that citizens could learn from one another at the third stage of justification, if only in an indirect way. The veto of others can lead each of us to realize that the conceptions of justice we initially proposed were not yet sufficiently *decentered*.

(c) There is a kind of conflict, however, that has an impact on the definition of "reasonable" doctrines. Such conflicts expose the concept of the "reasonable" itself to contestation. The abortion debate, on a certain description, is a case in point. Catholics, for example, who insist on a general legal prohibition, assert that their religious conviction concerning the inviolability of life is more important than any political value in whose name other citizens urge them to accept, say, a moderately liberal regulation. Rawls deals with this issue in passing, but he shifts the conflict from the level of the *priority* of political values to that of a reasonable *balancing* of political values (PL 243f.). For he presupposes that the principle of the public use of reason requires citizens to *translate* their ethical-existential views into the language of political justice. But on Rawls's own premises "public reason" can impose such constraints on citizens only if a consensus concerning political essentials has already been reached. While an overlapping consensus is still being worked out there is no equivalent for the neutral authority of a Supreme Court (which in any case only understands the language of law). Nor is it possible at this stage to appeal to the priority of the right over the good, for this again presupposes the priority of political over nonpolitical values.[15] Now Rawls recognizes that an overlapping consensus is possible only among citizens who assume in cases of conflict that political values outweigh all other values (PL 139). But this does not follow from the "reasonableness" of citizens and their convictions. Rawls simply asserts that political values are "very great" ones (PL 139, 155). Elsewhere he restricts himself to the "hope" that this priority will ultimately be recognized by adherents of reasonable comprehensive doctrines.[16]

These cautious formulations suggest that deep-seated conflicts of the third kind could only be resolved if the tolerance of reasonable citizens and the reasonableness of their comprehensive views *imply* that everyone shares the same view of the political world and that political values have priority. But such a rational requirement does not simply highlight qualities that reasonable comprehensive doctrines possess in any case; that expectation of reasonableness has to be *imposed* on the competing worldviews. The priority of political values is a requirement of practical reason: the requirement of a form of impartiality that elsewhere finds expression in the moral point of view. But the latter is not contained in the concept of the reasonable introduced by Rawls. The attitude of "reasonable" people who wish to treat each other fairly while recognizing that they do not agree in their religious and metaphysical convictions does not imply a moral point of view shared by all, any more than does the reflexivity and the renunciation of force of "reasonable" worldviews. Clearly a requirement of practical reason to which comprehensive doctrines must *submit* if an overlapping consensus is to be possible can only be justified by appeal to an epistemic authority that is itself independent of worldviews.[17]

With practical reason liberated from dependence on the morality of comprehensive doctrines, the internal relation between the true and the reasonable would also become publicly accessible. This connection need remain opaque only as long as the justification of a political conception can only be grasped within the context of a particular comprehensive view. However, this approach is turned on its head once the priority of political values has to be justified on the basis of a conception of practical reason that first determines which comprehensive doctrines can count as reasonable.

6 Philosophers and Citizens

There remains an unresolved tension between the reasonableness of a political conception acceptable to all citizens with reasonable comprehensive doctrines and the truth that individuals ascribe to this conception from within their respective comprehensive views. On the one hand, the validity of the political conception ultimately depends on the validity-generating resources of the different comprehensive doctrines insofar as they are reasonable; on the other, reasonable doctrines must in turn satisfy standards prescribed to them by practical reason. What makes them reasonable cannot be defined by standards internal to any one of them. Can Rawls ground these constraints in practical reason without falling back on the Kantian standpoint of *A Theory of Justice,* or must he abandon the liberal device of the division of labor between the political and the metaphysical? To be sure, Rawls also takes the constraints of "public reason"—"the general ones of theoretical and practical reason"—into consideration in *Political Liberalism.* But they only take effect once "justice as fairness" has been accepted by the citizens; only then can they determine the priority of the right over the good (PL 210) and the form of the public use of reason (PL 216ff.).

But if the reasonableness of comprehensive doctrines finds expression in restrictions that are not self-imposed, what should count as reasonable must be determined by a standard of impartiality that is already operative prior to the emergence of a basic political agreement. *A Theory of Justice* claimed validity in the name of practical reason; it did not depend on affirmation by reasonable comprehensive doctrines. Over time Rawls came to realize that the basic design of this theory, rather than its content, failed to give sufficient weight to the "fact of reasonable pluralism" (R 144, n. 21). This is why he now presents the essential content of the original theory as a first constructive step in need of supplementation. A further step is supposed to lead from the academic arena into the political public sphere and allow the philosophical investigation to issue in an actual agreement between all citizens on basic political questions. The distribution of the burdens of justification between the two steps is reflected in the relation between the reasonable and the true. The citizens, not the philosopher, are to have the final word. While Rawls does not completely shift the burden of justification onto the reasonable comprehensive doctrines, they are the *ultimate* arbiters. For the theory would violate its own liberal spirit if it prejudged the political will-formation of the citizens by anticipating its results: "students of philosophy take part in formulating these ideas but always as citizens among others" (R 175).

However, only a theory that lays down the complete design of a well-ordered society for the citizens creates the danger of political paternalism. Rawls does not consider that a consistently worked-out proceduralism could defuse the whole issue of whether philosophy undermines the political autonomy of the citizens.[18] A theory that restricts itself to clarifying the implications of the legal institutionalization of procedures of democratic self-legislation does not prejudge the results that the citizens themselves must first reach within an institutional framework shaped by these procedures. Once a post-metaphysical authority independent of comprehensive doctrines is restored to a practical reason that is embodied in processes rather than in contents, it cannot itself play a paternalistic role. I favor this approach and there is at least some support for it in Rawls.

But first let me bring together the results of the discussion thus far. Reasonable political conceptions that take account of the priority of political values, and thereby also define which religious and metaphysical worldviews can count as reasonable, must not only be worked out but must also be *accepted* from an impartial standpoint. This standpoint transcends the participant's perspective, occupied by citizens who are constrained by their respective comprehensive doctrines. Hence the citizens can have the last word only when they already participate in the "formulation of these ideas" from a more comprehensive, intersubjectively shared perspective, or, what amounts to the same thing, from the moral point of view. The recursive universalization test that Rawls reserves for the third stage of justification would instead become an integral component of a process of public deliberation on proposed conceptions of justice capable of commanding public agreement. The rational acceptability of the outcome—be it "justice as fairness" or some other conception—would not be established by the mutual observation of an *established* consensus; instead authorizing force would devolve to conditions of discourse, formal features of discursive processes, which compel participants to adopt the standpoint of impartial judgment.

We find a similar conception in *Political Liberalism* but at a different systematic level—that of the professional elaboration of a freestanding conception of justice. The philosopher first projects a *pro tanto* justification of his conception and then tests whether the basic concepts of his theory—such as those of the moral person, of the citizen as a member of an association of free and equal persons, and of society as a system of fair cooperation—cohere with the normative background intuitions that are actually widely shared in the political traditions of a democratic society (conceived as a "complete and closed social system"). Both of these operations, (a) the construction of a conception of justice and (b) the reflexive testing of its conceptual foundations, have interesting implications for the relation between the philosopher and the citizens.

(a) A philosopher who, like Rawls, adheres to the principles of "political constructivism" commits himself to objectivity, that is, he accepts the "essentials of the objective point of view" and the "requirements of objectivity" (PL III, sections 5–7). These are procedural features of practical reason: "it is by the reasonable that we enter the public world of others and stand ready to propose, or accept, as the case may be, reasonable principles to specify fair terms of cooperation. These principles issue from a procedure of construction that expresses the principles of practical reason. . . ." (PL 114). Thus the philosopher observes standards of rationality that have a moral-practical content though they are independent of any comprehensive doctrine. Whether these standards at the same time impose limitations on the comprehensive doctrines of reasonable citizens depends on how one understands the philosopher's task. Sometimes Rawls seems to suggest that his professionally worked-out proposal should have a *structuring* influence on the citizens' worldviews. At any rate Rawls expresses the hope that "in fact [the philosophical offer] will have the capacity to *shape* those doctrines toward itself" (R 145, my emphasis). On this conception the philosopher would administer an objective point of view to which the citizens have to *adapt* their comprehensive doctrines. This would indeed involve only a procedural prejudgment, not a substantive one; but not even this reading is fully compatible with the egalitarian status of the philosopher as one citizen among others.

(b) The method of reflective equilibrium accords the philosopher a more modest role in any case by referring him to the intersubjectively shared background knowledge of a liberal political culture. Of course, this knowledge can only serve as a control on the choice of basic theoretical concepts if it has already been shaped by the perspective of an impartial judgment of questions of political justice. Otherwise the philosopher could learn nothing from the citizens and their political convictions. If the method of reflective equilibrium is to get off the ground, philosophy must "find" its own perspective already operating in civil society. This is not to imply that philosophy could rely on the basic consensus which—according to the premises—already exists in liberal societies and thereby offers a platform for the public use of reason (as institutionalized, e.g., in the constitutional court). Not every culture that calls itself liberal is in fact liberal. A hermeneutic philosophy that limited itself to clarifying what already exists would lose all critical force.[19] Philosophy should not merely accept established convictions but must also be able to *judge* them by the standards of a rational conception of justice. On the other hand, it may not construct such a conception out of whole cloth and hold it up to a society as a norm. It must avoid equally the uncritical affirmation of the status quo and the assumption of a paternalistic role. It should neither simply accept established traditions nor construct a detailed design for a well-ordered society.

The method of reflective equilibrium itself, properly understood, shows us a way out of the dead end, because it calls for a *critical* appropriation of traditions. This succeeds with traditions that can be understood as the expression of learning processes. A prior standpoint of critical evaluation is necessary in order to identify learning processes as such. Philosophy finds such a standpoint in its aspiration to objectivity and impartiality. But insofar as it draws on procedural properties of practical reason, it can find *confirmation* in a perspective that it encounters in society itself: by the moral point of view from which modern societies are criticized by their own social movements. Philosophy adopts an affirmative stance only toward the negatory potential embodied in the social tendencies to unstinting self-criticism.

7 The Point of Liberalism

If political justice is conceived in this way, that is, in procedural terms, the relations between the political and the moral and between the moral and the ethical appear in a different light. A political justice that stands on its own moral feet no longer needs the support of the truth of religious or metaphysical comprehensive doctrines. Moral statements can satisfy the conditions of postmetaphysical thinking no less than descriptive statements, though in a different way. Thanks to the moral point of view, which also finds expression in what Rawls calls "the procedural requirements for a public use of reason" and "standards of reasonableness," moral judgments gain independence from metaphysical contexts. Like the truth of descriptive statements, the rightness of moral statements can be explained in terms of the discursive redemption of validity claims. (Of course, even together descriptive and moral statements cannot exhaust the meaning of metaphysical truths.) Since moral judgments are only concerned with questions of justice in general, questions of *political* justice must be specified in terms of the medium of law. This need not concern us further here.

But once moral and political reasoning draw on an independent source of validity, comprehensive doctrines take on a different cognitive role. They reveal their essentially ethical content and provide the context for what Rawls calls the "substantive content of comprehensive conceptions of the good." These "visions of the good life" form the core of an individual or collective self-understanding. Ethical questions are questions of identity. They have an existential significance and they do admit of rational criticism within certain limits. Ethical discourses obey standards of hermeneutical reflection on what "is good" for me or for us, all things considered. Ethical recommendations claim a kind of validity distinct from both truth and moral rightness. They are measured by the authenticity of the self-understandings of individuals or collectives that were formed in the context of life-histories or intersubjectively shared traditions. Consequently, ethical reasons are context-dependent in a specific way—they are "nonpublic" in the Rawlsian sense. To be sure, we accept the usual burdens of proof and argumentative obligations— in Rawls's terms, "burdens of judgment"—with every statement. But strong evaluations are not merely subject to general reservations concerning fallibilism. We cannot reasonably expect ethical disputes over the value of competing lifestyles and forms of life to lead to anything other than reasonable disagreements.[20] By contrast, we expect that moral questions and questions of political justice admit in principle of universally valid answers.

Kantian conceptions claim neutrality vis-à-vis comprehensive doctrines, that is, a "freestanding" status in the sense of ethical, though not of philosophical, neutrality. Our discussion of the epistemological underpinnings of *Political Liberalism* should have made clear that Rawls cannot avoid philosophical controversies either. The problematic relation between the reasonable and the true calls for an explanation that raises questions concerning Rawls's strategy of avoidance. The concept of practical reason cannot be drained of moral substance and morality cannot be relegated to the black box of comprehensive doctrines. I cannot see any plausible alternative to the straightforward Kantian strategy. There seems to be no way around the explanation of the moral point of view in terms of a procedure that claims to be context-independent. Such a procedure is by no means free of normative implications, as Rawls correctly emphasizes (R 170ff.), for it is intertwined with a concept of autonomy that integrates "reason" and "free will;" *to that extent* it cannot be normatively neutral. An autonomous will is one that is guided by practical reason. Freedom in general consists in the capacity to choose in accordance with maxims; but autonomy is the self-binding of the will by maxims we adopt on the basis of *insight*. Because it is mediated by reason, autonomy is not just one value alongside others.

This explains why *this* normative content does not impair the neutrality of a procedure. A procedure that operationalizes the moral point of view of impartial judgment is neutral with respect to arbitrary constellations of values but not with respect to practical reason itself.

Rawls's construction of an overlapping consensus shifts the accent from the Kantian concept of autonomy to something like ethical-existential self-determination: a person is free when he accepts authorship for his own life. This approach also has something to recommend it. The division of labor between the political and the metaphysical draws attention to the ethical dimension neglected by Kant. Rawls salvages a valuable insight of Hegel's critique of Kant;[21] moral norms may not be imposed in an abstract manner on the life-histories of individual persons, even if these norms appeal to a practical reason all individuals have in common or to a universal sense of justice. Moral commands must be *internally* related to the life-plans and lifestyles of affected persons in a way they can grasp for themselves.

The different weights accorded moral freedom and ethical-existential self-determination provide an occasion for a final remark. The differences in design, if not in substance, between theories of political justice reveal differences in the underlying intuitions that inform them.

Political or constitutional liberalism starts from the intuition that the person and her individual way of life must be protected from the intrusion of state power: "political liberalism allows . . . that our political institutions contain sufficient space for worthy ways of life, and that in this sense our political society is just and good" (PL 210). Consequently, the distinction between the private and public spheres takes on fundamental importance. It sets the standards for the authoritative interpretation of freedom: the legally guaranteed freedom of choice of private legal subjects creates the free space for pursuing a plan of life informed by one's own conception of the good. Rights are *liberties,* protective barriers for private autonomy. At the heart of this approach lies a concern for the equal freedom of every person to lead a self-determined, authentic life. From this perspective the public autonomy of citizens who participate in the practice of political self-legislation is supposed to make possible the personal self-determination of private persons. While it may also have an intrinsic value for many people, public autonomy appears in the first instance as a means for realizing private autonomy.

Kantian Republicanism, as I understand it, starts from a different intuition. Nobody can be free at the expense of anybody else's freedom. Because persons are individuated only by way of socialization, the freedom of one individual cannot be tied to the freedom of everyone else in a purely negative way, through reciprocal restrictions. Rather, correct restrictions are the result of a process of self-legislation conducted jointly. In an association of free and equal persons, all members must be able to understand themselves as joint authors of laws to which they feel themselves bound individually as addressees. Hence the public use of reason, legally institutionalized in the democratic process, provides the key for guaranteeing equal freedoms.

Once moral principles must be embodied in the medium of coercive and positive law, the freedom of the moral person splits into the public autonomy of co-legislators and the private autonomy of addressees of the law, in such a way that they reciprocally presuppose one another. This complementary relationship between the public and the private does not refer to anything given or natural but is conceptually generated by the very structure of the legal medium. Hence it is left to the democratic process continually to define and redefine the precarious boundaries between the private and the public so as to secure equal freedoms for all citizens in the form of both private and public autonomy.[22]

III

Is There a Future for the Nation-State?

4

The European Nation-State: On the Past and Future of Sovereignty and Citizenship

As even the name of the United Nations reveals, world society today is composed politically of nation-states. The historical type of state that emerged from the French and American revolutions has achieved global dominance. This fact is by no means trivial.

The classical nation-states in Northern and Western Europe evolved within the boundaries of existing territorial states. They were part of the European state system which already took on a recognizable shape with the Peace of Westphalia of 1648. By contrast, the "belated" nations—beginning with Italy and Germany—followed a different course, one which was also typical for the formation of nation-states in Central and Eastern Europe; here the formation of the state followed the trail blazed by an anticipatory national consciousness disseminated by propaganda. The difference between these two paths (from state to nation vs. from nation to state) is reflected in the backgrounds of the actors who formed the vanguard of nation and state builders. Along the first path, these were lawyers, diplomats, and military officers who belonged to the king's administrative staff and together constructed a "rational state bureaucracy" (in Max Weber's sense); along the second, they were writers and historians, and scholars and intellectuals in general, who laid the groundwork for Cavour's and Bismarck's subsequent diplomatic and military unification of the state by propagating the more or less imaginary unity of the "cultural nation." After the Second World War, a third generation of very different nation-states emerged from the process of decolonization, primarily in Africa and Asia. Often these states, which were founded within the frontiers established by the former colonial regimes, acquired sovereignty before the imported forms of state organization could take root in a national identity that transcended tribal differences. In these cases, artificial states had to be first "filled" by nations that coalesced only later. Finally, with the collapse of the Soviet Empire, the trend toward the formation of independent nation-states in Eastern and Southern Europe has followed the path of more or less violent secessions; in the socially and economically precarious situation in which these countries found themselves, the old ethnonational slogans had the power to mobilize distraught populations for independence.

Thus today the nation-state has definitively superseded older political formations.[1] To be sure, the classical city-states also had successors in modern Europe, for a certain period, in the cities of Northern Italy and—in the territory of the old Lotharingia (Lorraine)—in the belt of cities out of which Switzerland and the Netherlands emerged. The structures of the old empires also reemerged, first in the form of the Holy Roman Empire and later in the multination-states of the Russian, Ottoman, and Austro-Hungarian Empires. But in the meantime the nation-state has displaced these remnants of premodern states. We are at present witnessing the fundamental transformation of China, the last of the old empires.

Hegel took the view that every historical formation is condemned to decline once it has reached maturity. One need not accept Hegel's philosophy of history to recognize that the triumphal procession of the nation-state also has an ironical, obverse side. The nation-state at one time represented a cogent response to the historical challenge to find a functional equivalent for the early modern form of social integration which was in the process of disintegrating. Today we are confronting an analogous challenge. The globalization of commerce and communication, of economic production and finance, of the spread of technology and weapons, and above all of ecological and military risks, poses problems that can no longer be solved within the framework of nation-states or by the traditional method of agreements between sovereign states. If current trends continue, the progressive undermining of national sovereignty will necessitate the founding and expansion of political institutions on the supranational level, a process whose beginnings can already be observed. In Europe, North America, and Asia, new forms of organization for continental "regimes" are gradually emerging above the level of the state, regimes which could one day provide the requisite infrastructure for the currently rather inefficient United Nations.

This unprecedented increase in abstraction is merely the continuation of a process the first major example of which is the integration achieved by the nation-state. Hence I think that we can take our orientation on the precarious path toward postnational societies from the very historical model we are on the point of superseding. First I would like to review the accomplishments of the nation-state by clarifying the concepts "state" and "nation" (I) and explaining the two problems to which the nation-state provided a solution (II). Then I will examine the potential for conflict built into this form of national state, namely the tension between republicanism and nationalism (III). Finally, I would like to deal with two current challenges that overburden the nation-state's capacity for action: the differentiation of society along multicultural lines (IV) and the processes of globalization that are undermining both the internal (V) and the external (VI) sovereignty of the existing nation-states.

I "State" and "Nation"

The "state" on the modern conception is a legally defined term which refers, at the level of substance, to a state power that possesses both internal and external sovereignty, at the spatial level over a clearly delimited terrain (the state territory) and at the social level over the totality of members (the body of citizens or the people). State power constitutes itself in the forms of positive law, and the people is the bearer of the legal order whose jurisdiction is restricted to the state territory. In political usage, the concepts "nation" and "people" have the same extension. But in addition to its legal definition, the term "nation" has the connotation of a political community shaped by common descent, or at least by a common language, culture, and history. A people becomes a "nation" in this historical sense only in the concrete form of a particular form of life. The two components, which are yoked together in such concepts as "nation-state" and "nation of citizens," can be traced back to two far-from-parallel processes of historical development—the formation of states on the one hand (1), and of nations on the other (2).

(1) The historical success of the nation-state is due in large part to the advantages of the modern state apparatus as such. Evidently, the territorial state, with its monopoly on the legitimate use of violence and its differentiated administrative apparatus financed by taxation, was better able to cope with the functional imperatives of social, cultural, and, above all, economic modernization than were older political formations. For our purposes it will suffice to recall the ideal-typical model worked out by Marx and Weber.

(a) The executive branch of the state which became detached from the royal household consisted of a functionally specialized bureaucratic organization which was run by legally trained officials and which could draw on the reserve force of a standing army, the police, and the penal system. The imposition of "civil peace" (*Land-frieden*) was the necessary precondition for monopolizing these legitimate means of violence. A state is sovereign only if it can both maintain law and order internally and protect its borders against external threats. It must be capable of prevailing over all competing powers within its borders and of asserting itself in the international arena as a competitor with equal standing. The status of a subject of international law is contingent upon achieving international recognition as an "equal" and "independent" member of the system of states. Internal sovereignty presupposes the ability to maintain law and order, external sovereignty the ability to assert oneself in the "anarchistic" competition for power among states.

(b) Even more important for the modernization process is the separation of the state from "civil society" (in Hegel's sense of "*bür-gerliche Gesellschaft*"); hence the functional specification of the state apparatus. The modern state is both an administrative and a tax-based state, which means that it limits itself to essentially administrative tasks. It leaves the productive tasks, which were formerly accomplished *within the framework* of political power, to a market economy differentiated from the state. To this extent, it secures the "general conditions of production"; hence the legal framework and infrastructure that are necessary for capitalistic commodity exchange and for the corresponding organization of the labor force. The financial needs of the state are met by a privately generated tax income. The price the administrative system pays for the benefits of this functional specialization is its dependence on the performance of an economy regulated by markets. Although markets can be established and regulated by political means, they obey a logic of their own that escapes state control.

The differentiation of the state from the economy is reflected in the differentiation between public and private law. Insofar as the modern state makes use of positive law as a means of organization and implementation, it binds itself to a medium that instantiates, through the concept of law and the derivative concepts of subjective right and of the legal person (as the bearer of rights), a new principle made explicit by Hobbes: within an order of modern law that is set free from immediate moral expectations (though only in certain respects), the citizens are permitted to do anything that is not prohibited. Regardless of whether state power has already been domesticated by the rule of law and the crown has become "subject to the law," the state cannot make use of the medium of law without organizing social intercourse in the separate sphere of civil society in such a way that private persons enjoy—at first unequally distributed—individual liberties. With the separation of private from public law, the individual citizen, in her role as "subject" ("*Untertan*" in Kant's terminology), first acquires at least a core of private autonomy.[2]

(2) Today we all live in national societies that owe their unity to an organization of this type. Of course, such states existed long before there were "nations" in the modern sense. State and nation have fused into the nation-state only since the revolutions of the late eighteenth century. Before I examine the specific nature of this connection I would like to review, in a brief digression on conceptual history, the genesis of the modern consciousness that underlies the interpretation of the citizen body as a nation in something other than a merely legal sense.

In the classical Roman usage, "natio" like "gens" functions as a contrasting concept to "civitas." Nations were originally communities of shared descent which were integrated geographically through settlements and neighborhoods and culturally through their common language, customs, and traditions; but they were not yet integrated politically through the organizational form of a state. This root meaning persisted through the Middle Ages into early modern times whenever "natio" and "lingua" were treated as equivalent. Thus, for example, students at medieval universities were divided into "nationes" according to their country of origin. In an era of increasing geographical mobility, the concept served primarily as a means of internal differentiation of orders of knights, of universities, monasteries, ecclesiastical councils, merchant settlements, etc. Thus it happened that a national origin *ascribed by others* was from the very beginning linked in a conspicuous way with the negative demarcation of foreigners from one's own people.[3]

Around this time, the term "nation" acquired a meaning opposed to the nonpolitical usage in a different context. The feudal system of the old German Empire had been superseded by corporative states (*Ständestaaten*) based on contracts in which the king or emperor, whose power depended on taxes and military support, granted the nobility, the Church, and the towns certain privileges, and therewith limited participation in the exercise of political power. These ruling estates, which met in "parliaments" or "diets," represented the country or "the nation" vis-à-vis the court. As the "nation," the aristocracy acquired a political existence that was still denied the "people" as the mass of the subjects. This explains the revolutionary implications of the slogan "the King in Parliament" in England and, especially, of the identification of the "Third Estate" with the "nation" in France.

The democratic transformation of the *Adelsnation,* the nation of the nobility, into a *Volksnation,* the nation of the people, which has been in progress since the late eighteenth century, presupposes a deep transformation in consciousness inspired by intellectuals, a transformation first accomplished by the urban, and above all formally educated, middle classes before it found a resonance in the wider population and gradually brought about a political mobilization of the masses. Popular national consciousness crystallized into the "imagined communities" (Benedict Anderson) propagated in national histories, which became the catalysts of a new form of collective self-identification: "Thus nations arose in the final decades of the eighteenth century and in the course of the nineteenth century . . .: conceived by a small number of scholars, publicists, and poets—*Volksnationen* in concept but far from it in reality."[4] To the extent that this idea took root, however, it became apparent that, with its transformation from the concept of an aristocratic nation into that of a nation of the people, the political concept had inherited the power to generate stereotypes from the older, prepolitical concept of the nation as an index of descent and origin. The positive self-understanding of one's own nation now became an efficient mechanism for repudiating everything regarded as foreign, for devaluing other nations, and for excluding national, ethnic, and religious minorities, especially the Jews. In Europe nationalism became allied with antisemitism, with disastrous consequences.

II   The New Form of Social Integration

Interpreted in light of their results, the complex and long-running processes of the "invention of the nation" (Schulze) played the role of a catalyst in the transformation of the early modern state into a democratic republic. Popular national self-consciousness provided the cultural background against which "subjects" could become politically active "citizens." Belonging to the "nation" made possible for the first time a relation of solidarity between persons who had previously been strangers to one another. Thus the achievement of the nation-state consisted in solving two problems at once: it made possible a new *mode of legitimation* based on a new, more abstract form of *social integration*.

Briefly stated, the legitimation problem resulted from the fact that the pluralism of worldviews that followed the schism of the religious confessions gradually stripped political authority of its religious grounding in "divine right." The secularized state now had to derive its legitimation from different sources. The second problem, that of social integration, was connected, simplifying once again, with urbanization and economic modernization, with the increasing scope and acceleration of the circulation of people, goods, and news. Populations became unmoored from the corporative social ties of early modern societies, thereby becoming at the same time both geographically mobilized and isolated. The nation-state responded to both of these challenges by *politically* mobilizing its citizens. For the emerging national identity made it possible to combine a more abstract form of social integration with new structures of political decision making. Democratic participation, as it slowly became established, generated a new level of legally mediated *solidarity* via the status of citizenship while providing the state with a secular source of *legitimation*. Of course, there was no modern state that had not defined its social boundaries in terms of citizenship rights. But belonging to a particular state at first meant nothing more than being subject to a state power. Only with the transition to the democratic state was this ascriptive, organizational membership transformed into an acquired membership—based on (at least implicit) consent—of citizens who were expected to participate actively in the exercise of political power. However, we must distinguish between the legal-political and the properly cultural aspects of the new meaning that membership acquired with the shift from the status of a subject to that of a *citizen*.

As we have seen, the two defining characteristics of the modern state were the sovereignty of state power embodied in the prince and the differentiation of the state from society through which a core of individual liberties was conferred (in a paternalistic manner) on the private citizens. With the shift from royal to popular sovereignty, the rights of subjects were transformed into human rights and civil rights, that is, into basic liberal and political rights of citizens. Viewed as ideal types, they guaranteed political as well as private autonomy, and in principle, even equal political autonomy for everyone. The democratic constitutional state is, ideally speaking, a voluntary political order established by the people themselves and legitimated by their free will-formation. According to Rousseau and Kant, the addressees of the law should be able to conceive of themselves at the same time as its authors.

But such a legal-political transformation would have lacked driving force, and formally established republics would have lacked staying power, if a nation of more or less self-conscious citizens had not emerged from a people defined by its subjection to state power.

This political mobilization called for an idea that was vivid and powerful enough to shape people's convictions and appealed more strongly to their hearts and minds than the dry ideas of popular sovereignty and human rights. This gap was filled by the modern idea of the nation, which first inspired in the inhabitants of state territories an awareness of the new, legally and politically mediated form of community. Only a national consciousness, crystallized around the notion of a common ancestry, language, and history, only the consciousness of belonging to "the same" people, makes subjects into citizens of a single political community—into members who can feel responsible *for one another.* The nation or the *Volksgeist,* the unique spirit of the people—the first truly *modern* form of collective identity—provided the cultural basis for the constitutional state. As described by historians, this thoroughly artificial fusion of older loyalties into a new national consciousness, which was also steered by bureaucratic imperatives, is a long, drawn-out process.

This leads to a double coding of citizenship, with the result that the legal status defined in terms of civil rights also implies membership in a culturally defined community. Without this cultural interpretation of political membership rights, the nation-state in its emergent phase would scarcely have had sufficient strength to establish a new, more abstract level of social integration through the legal implementation of democratic citizenship. The counterexample of the United States does demonstrate that the nation-state can assume and maintain a republican form even without the support of such a culturally homogeneous population. However, in this case a civil religion rooted in the majority culture took the place of nationalism.

Thus far I have focused exclusively on the *achievements* of the nation-state. But the connection between republicanism and nationalism also engenders dangerous *ambivalences.* With the rise of the nation-state, the meaning of state sovereignty also changes, as we have seen. This not only has an impact on the shift from royal to popular sovereignty; it also changes the perception of external sovereignty. The idea of the nation is inextricably bound up with the Machiavellian will to self-assertion by which the conduct of sovereign states in the arena of the "great powers" had been guided from the beginning. Now the strategic self-assertion of the modern state against external enemies is transformed into the existential self-assertion of "the nation." With this a third concept of "freedom" is introduced. The collective concept of national freedom competes with the two individualistic concepts of freedom, that of the private liberties of members of civil society and that of the political autonomy of citizens. More important is the question of *how* the freedom of the nation is to be construed: whether on an analogy with the liberty of private persons who differentiate themselves from, and compete with, one another, or on the model of the cooperative self-legislation of autonomous citizens.

The model of public autonomy takes precedence if the nation is primarily conceived as a legally constituted entity, that is, as a nation of citizens. These citizens may indeed be patriots who understand and uphold their constitution as an achievement in the context of the history of their country. But they construe the freedom of the nation—following Kant—in cosmopolitan terms, namely, as the authorization and obligation to enter into cooperative agreements or to establish a balance of interests with other nations within the framework of a peaceful federation (*Völkerbund*). The naturalistic conception of the nation as a prepolitical entity, by contrast, suggests a different interpretation, according to which the freedom of the nation consists essentially in its ability to assert its independence by military means if necessary. Like private persons in the market, peoples pursue their respective interests in the free-for-all of international power politics. The traditional image of external sovereignty is dressed up in national colors and in this guise awakens new energies.

III The Tension between Nationalism and Republicanism

In contrast to the republican freedoms of individuals, the independence of one's nation, which must if necessary be defended with the "blood of its sons," designates the place where the secularized state preserves a residue of nonsecular transcendence. In times of war the nation-state imposes on its citizens the duty to risk their lives for the collective. Since the French Revolution, general conscription has gone hand-in-hand with civil rights; the willingness to fight and die for one's country is supposed to express both national consciousness and republican virtue. Thus the inscriptions of French national history reflect a double memory-trace: political milestones in the fight for republican freedom are united with the death-symbolism of memorials for soldiers killed in action.

The nation is Janus-faced. Whereas the voluntary nation of citizens is the source of democratic legitimation, it is the inherited or ascribed nation founded on ethnic membership (*die geborene Nation der Volksgenossen*) that secures social integration. *Staatsbürger* or citizens constitute themselves as a political association of free and equal persons by their own initiative; *Volksgenossen* or nationals already find themselves in a community shaped by a shared language and history. The tension between the universalism of an egalitarian legal community and the particularism of a community united by historical destiny is built into the very concept of the national state.

This ambivalence remains harmless as long as a cosmopolitan understanding of the nation of citizens is accorded priority over an ethnocentric interpretation of the nation as in a permanent state of war. Only a nonnaturalistic concept of the nation can be combined seamlessly with the universalistic self-understanding of the democratic constitutional state. Then the republican idea can take the lead in penetrating socially integrating forms of life and structuring them in accordance with universalistic patterns. The nation-state owes its historical success to the fact that it substituted relations of solidarity between the citizens for the disintegrating corporative ties of early modern society. But this republican achievement is endangered when, conversely, the integrative force of the nation of citizens is traced back to the prepolitical fact of a quasi-natural people, that is, to something independent of and prior to the political opinion- and will-formation of the citizens themselves. Of course, many reasons could be given for the lurch into nationalism. I will mention just two, one conceptual, the other empirical.

There is a conceptual gap in the legal construction of the constitutional state, a gap that is tempting to fill with a naturalistic conception of the people. One cannot explain in purely normative terms how the universe of those who come together to regulate their common life by means of positive law should be composed. From a normative point of view, the social boundaries of an association of free and equal consociates under law are perfectly contingent. Since the voluntariness of the decision to engage in a law-giving praxis is a fiction of the contractualist tradition, in the real world who gains the power to define the boundaries of a political community is settled by historical chance and the actual course of events—normally, by the arbitrary outcomes of wars or civil wars. It is a theoretical mistake with grave practical consequences, one dating back to the nineteenth century, to assume that this question can also be answered in normative terms with reference to a "right to national self-determination."[5]

Nationalism has found its own solution to the problem of boundaries. While national consciousness itself may very well be an artifact, it projects the imaginary reality of the nation as an organic development which, in contrast with the artificial order of enacted law and the construction of the constitutional state, needs no justification beyond its sheer existence. For this reason, recourse to the "organic" nation can conceal the contingency of the historically more or less arbitrary boundaries of the political community and can lend them an aura of imitated substance and "inherited" legitimacy.

The other reason for the lurch into nationalism is more trivial. Precisely the artificiality of national myths, both in their learned origins and their dissemination through propaganda, makes nationalism intrinsically susceptible to misuse by political elites. That domestic conflicts can be neutralized by foreign military successes rests on a socio-psychological mechanism that governments have repeatedly exploited. But how the class conflicts generated by accelerated capitalist industrialization can be diverted was prefigured for a belligerent nation-state striving for world prominence: the collective freedom of the nation could be interpreted in terms of an imperial expansion of power. The history of European imperialism between 1871 and 1914, and the integral nationalism of the twentieth century (not to speak of the racist policies of the Nazis), illustrate the sad fact that the idea of the nation did not so much reinforce the loyalty of the population to the constitutional state but more often served as an instrument to mobilize the masses for political goals that can scarcely be reconciled with republican principles.[6]

The lesson to be learned from this sad history is obvious. The nation-state must renounce the ambivalent potential that once propelled it. Though the national state is today running up against its limits, we can still learn from its example. In its heyday, the nation-state founded a domain of political communication that made it possible to absorb the advances in abstraction of societal modernization and to re-embed a population uprooted from traditional forms of life in an extended and rationalized lifeworld through the cultivation of national consciousness. It could play this integrative role all the better in that democratic citizenship was connected with cultural membership in the nation. Today, as the nation-state finds itself challenged from within by the explosive potential of multiculturalism and from without by the pressure of globalization, the question arises of whether there exists a functional equivalent for the fusion of the nation of citizens with the ethnic nation.

IV   The Unity of Political Culture in the Multiplicity of Subcultures

Originally, the suggestive unity of a more or less homogenous nation could ensure the cultural embedding of a legally defined citizenship status. In this context, democratic citizenship could form the focal point of social ties of mutual responsibility. But today we live in pluralistic societies that are moving further and further away from the model of a nation-state based on a culturally homogeneous population. The diversity of cultural forms of life, ethnic groups, religions, and worldviews is constantly growing. There is no alternative to this development, except at the normatively intolerable cost of ethnic cleansing. Hence republicanism must learn to stand on its own feet. The central idea of republicanism is that the democratic process can serve at the same time as a guarantor for the social integration of an increasingly differentiated society. In a society characterized by cultural and religious pluralism, this task cannot be displaced from the level of political will-formation and public communication onto the seemingly natural substrate of a supposedly homogeneous nation. The latter would merely serve as a façade for a hegemonic majority culture. For historical reasons, in many countries the majority culture is fused with the general political culture which claims to be recognized by *all* citizens regardless of their cultural background. This fusion must be dissolved if it is to be possible for different cultural, ethnic, and religious forms of life to coexist and interact on equal terms within *the same* political community. The level of the shared political culture must be uncoupled from the level of subcultures and their prepolitical identities. Of course, the claim to coexist with equal rights is subject to the proviso that the protected faiths and practices must not contradict the reigning constitutional principles (as they are interpreted by the political culture).

The political culture of a country crystallizes around its constitution. Each national culture develops a distinctive interpretation of those constitutional principles that are equally embodied in other republican constitutions—such as popular sovereignty and human rights—in light of its own national history. A "constitutional patriotism" based on these interpretations can take the place originally occupied by nationalism. This notion of constitutional patriotism appears to many observers to represent too weak a bond to hold together complex societies. The question then becomes even more urgent: under what conditions can a liberal political culture provide a sufficient cushion to prevent a nation of citizens, which can no longer rely on ethnic associations, from dissolving into fragments?

Today this problem has arisen even for classical immigrant countries like the United States. The political culture of the United States provides more space than other countries for the peaceful coexistence of citizens from widely divergent cultural backgrounds; it enables everyone to maintain two identities simultaneously, to be both a member and a stranger in her own land. But the rising tide of fundamentalism and even terrorism (as witnessed by the Oklahoma bombing) represent a warning signal that even here the safety net of a civil religion, which interprets an impressively continuous constitutional history of more than two centuries, could be torn apart. My sense is that multicultural societies can be held together by a political culture, however much it has proven itself, only if democratic citizenship pays off not only in terms of liberal individual rights and rights of political participation, but also in the enjoyment of social and cultural rights. The citizens must be able to experience *the fair value of their rights* also in the form of social security and the reciprocal recognition of different cultural forms of life. Democratic citizenship can only realize its integrative potential—that is, it can only found solidarity between strangers—if it proves itself as a mechanism that actually realizes the material conditions of preferred forms of life.

This perspective is suggested at any rate by the type of welfare state that developed in Europe under the favorable—though, of course, no longer obtaining—conditions of the postwar period. After the hiatus of the Second World War, an over-heated nationalism had exhausted its reserves of energy. Under the umbrella of a nuclear balance between the superpowers, the European countries—and not just the divided Germany—could not conduct a foreign policy of their own. Territorial disputes ceased to be an issue. Internal social conflicts could not be diverted outward but had to be dealt with in accordance with the primacy of domestic politics. Under these conditions it became possible to uncouple the universalistic understanding of the democratic constitutional state to a large extent from the imperatives of a power politics guided by national interests and oriented to geopolitical goals. In spite of a then prevailing mood of global civil war and anticommunist propaganda, the traditional linkage of the constitutional state with the ambitions of national self-assertion was loosened also throughout the broader population.

The trend toward what might be termed a "postnational" self-understanding of the political community may have been more pronounced in the former Federal Republic of Germany than in other European states, given its peculiar situation and the fact that it had, after all, been deprived of fundamental sovereignty rights. But in most of the Western and Northern European countries, the welfare-state pacification of class antagonisms had given rise to a new situation. Over time, social security systems were instituted and expanded, reforms in areas such as schooling, the family, criminal law and the penal system, data protection, etc., were implemented, and policies of equal opportunity for women were at least initiated. Within a single generation the status of citizens, however imperfect, was markedly improved in its legal and material substance. What is important in the present context is that this made the citizens themselves more keenly aware of the *priority* of the issue of the implementation of basic rights—of the priority that the real nation of citizens must maintain over the imagined ethnic-cultural nation.

The system of rights was extended under the economically favorable conditions of a comparatively long period of economic growth. Each individual could come to recognize and appreciate citizenship status as that which links her with the other members of the political community and makes her at the same time dependent upon and co-responsible for them. It became clear to all that private and public autonomy presuppose one another in the circuit of reproduction and improvement of the conditions of preferred ways of life. At any rate, the citizens intuitively realized that they could succeed in regulating their private autonomy fairly only by making an appropriate use of their civic autonomy, and that an intact private sphere is in turn a necessary precondition of such political participation. The constitution confirmed itself as the institutional framework for a dialectic of legal and factual equality that simultaneously reinforces the private and the civic autonomy of the citizens.[7]

But this dialectic has in the interim ground to a halt quite independently of local causes. If we are to explain this fact, we must turn our attention to the trends that are currently receiving attention under the heading of "globalization."

V   Limits of the Nation-State: Restrictions of Internal Sovereignty

The nation-state at one time guarded its territorial and social boundaries with a zeal bordering on the neurotic. Today these defenses have long since been penetrated by inexorable transnational developments. Anthony Giddens defines "globalization" as the intensification of worldwide relations resulting in reciprocal interconnections between local happenings and distant events.[8] Global communication takes place either in natural languages (usually via electronic media) or in special codes (principally, money and law). Since "communication" has a double meaning here, these processes give rise to two opposed tendencies. On the one hand they promote the expansion of actors' consciousness, on the other the differentiation, extension, and interconnection of systems, networks (such as markets), or organizations. Whereas the growth of systems and networks multiplies possible contacts and exchanges of information, it does not lead per se to the expansion of an intersubjectively shared world and to the discursive interweaving of conceptions of relevance, themes, and contributions from which political public spheres arise. The consciousness of planning, communicating, and acting subjects seems to have simultaneously expanded and fragmented. The publics produced by the internet remain closed off from one another like global villages. For the present it remains unclear whether an expanding public consciousness, though centered in the lifeworld, nevertheless has the ability to span systemically differentiated contexts, or whether the systemic processes, having become independent, have long since severed their ties with all contexts produced by political communication.

The nation-state at one time provided the framework within which the republican idea of a society that consciously shapes itself was articulated and even institutionalized to a certain extent. Typical of the nation-state, as we have seen, was a complementary relationship between state and economy on the one hand, and between domestic politics and power struggles between states on the other. Of course, this schema only applied under conditions in which national politics could still exert effective influence on the corresponding "national economy" (*Volkswirtschaft*). Thus in the era of Keynesian economic policies, for example, growth depended on factors that were by no means only favorable to capital investment but also benefited the population as a whole—factors such as the stimulation of mass consumption (under pressure from independent trade unions) and improvements in production techniques (based on independent research) which also led to the shortening of the working day, or such as the training of workers within the framework of an expanding education system (which improved the general level of education of the population as a whole), and so forth. At any rate, national economies provided a range of opportunities for redistribution that could be exploited, through wage policies and—on the side of the state—welfare and social policies, to satisfy the aspirations of a demanding and intelligent population.

Although capitalism from its inception was a global development,[9] the economic dynamic was fostered by the modern state system and in turn had the effect of reinforcing the nation-state. But today these two developments no longer reinforce one another. To be sure, "the territorial restriction of capital never corresponded to its structural mobility. It was due rather to the peculiar historical conditions of European civil society."[10] But these conditions have undergone a fundamental transformation with the denationalization of economic production. Nowadays all industrial countries are affected by the orientation of the investment strategies of ever more enterprises to globally interconnected financial *and labor* markets.

The current debates over economic competitiveness highlight the ever-widening gap between the limited room for nation-states to maneuver and global economic imperatives that are less and less susceptible to political influence. The most important variables are, first, the accelerated development and diffusion of new productivity-enhancing technologies and, second, the sharp increase in the reserves of comparatively cheap labor. The dramatic employment problems in the former First World stem not from classical international trade relations but from globally interconnected relations of production. Sovereign states can benefit from their economic systems only as long as "national economies" to which their interventionist policies are tailored still exist. But with the recent trend toward the denationalization of the economy, national politics is gradually losing its influence over the conditions of production under which *taxable* income and profits are generated. Governments have less and less influence over enterprises that orient their investment decisions within a global horizon. They are caught in the dilemma of having to avoid two equally unreasonable reactions. A policy of protectionistic isolationism and the formation of defensive cartels is hopeless; but balancing the budget through cutbacks in the domain of social policy is no less dangerous in view of its likely social consequences.

The social consequences of an abdication of politics, which tacitly accepts a chronically high level of unemployment and the dismantling of the welfare state as the price to be paid for international competitiveness, are already discernible in the OECD countries. The sources of social solidarity are drying up, with the result that social conditions of the former Third World are becoming commonplace in the urban centers of the First World. These trends are crystallizing in the phenomenon of a new "underclass." Under this misleading singular term sociologists unite the diffuse varieties of marginalized groups who are to a large extent segmented off from the rest of society. The underclass comprises those pauperized groups who are left to fend for themselves, although they are no longer in a position to improve their social lot through their own initiative. They no longer possess any veto power, any more than do the impoverished regions over the developed regions of the world. However, this kind of segmentation does not mean that fragmented societies could simply abandon part of their population to their fate *without political consequences*. In the long term at least three consequences are unavoidable. An underclass produces social tensions that discharge in aimless, self-destructive revolts and can only be controlled by repressive means, with the result that the construction of prisons and the organization of internal security in general becomes a growth industry. In addition, social destitution and physical immiseration cannot be locally contained; the poison of the ghettos infects the infrastructure of the inner cities, even of whole regions, and penetrates the pores of the society as a whole. This leads finally to a moral erosion of the society, which inevitably undermines the universalistic core of any republican polity. Formally correct majority decisions that merely reflect the status anxieties and self-assertive reflexes of a middle class threatened by the prospect of social decline undermine the legitimacy of the procedures and institutions of the democratic constitutional state. In this way the great achievement of the nation-state in integrating society through the political participation of its citizens is squandered.

While this scenario is by no means unrealistic, it illustrates just one among several possible future developments. There are no laws of history in the strict sense, and human beings, even whole societies, are capable of learning. An alternative to the abdication of politics would be if politics were to follow the lead of the markets by constructing supranational political agencies. Europe in transition toward the European Union provides a suitable example. Unfortunately, more than one lesson can be drawn from it. At present the European states are lingering on the threshold of a monetary union which would require the national governments to renounce their sovereignty in currency matters. A denationalization of money and monetary policy would necessitate a common financial, economic, and social policy. Since the Maastricht Treaty, opposition has been growing in the member states to a vertical expansion of the European Union that would confer essential characteristics of a state on the Union, thereby relativizing the sovereignty of the member states. The nation-state, conscious of its historical achievements, stubbornly asserts its identity at the very moment when it is being overwhelmed, and its power eroded, by processes of globalization. For the present, a politics still operating within the framework of the nation-state limits itself to adapting its own society in the least costly way to the systemic imperatives and side-effects of a global economic dynamic that operates largely free from political constraints. But instead it should make the heroic effort to overcome its own limitations and construct political institutions capable of acting at the supranational level. Moreover, the latter would have to be connected to processes of democratic will-formation if the normative heritage of the democratic constitutional state is to function as a break on the at present unfettered dynamic of globalized capitalist production.

VI "Overcoming" the Nation-State: Abolition or Transformation?

Talk of overcoming the nation-state is ambiguous. On one reading—let us call it the postmodern—the end of the nation-state also marks the end of the project of civic autonomy, which, on this view, has in any case hopelessly overdrawn its credit. According to the other, nondefeatist reading, the project of a society that is capable of learning and of consciously shaping itself through its political will is still viable even after the demise of a world of nation-states. The dispute concerns the normative self-understanding of the democratic constitutional state. Can we still identify with it in an era of globalization or must we renounce it as a cherished, though obsolete, relic of the old Europe?

If not only the nation-state has run its course but along with it all forms of *political* integration, then individual citizens are abandoned to a world of anonymously interconnected networks in which they must choose between systemically generated options in accordance with their preferences. In this *postpolitical* world the multinational corporation becomes the model for all conduct. The impotence of a normatively guided politics in the face of an increasingly independent global economic system appears, from a systems-theoretical perspective at any rate, only as a special case of a more general development. Its vanishing point is a completely decentered world society that splinters into a disordered mass of self-reproducing and self-steering functional systems. Like Hobbesian individuals in the state of nature, these systems form environments for one another. They no longer speak a common language. Lacking a universe of intersubjectively shared meanings, they merely observe one another and behave toward one another in accordance with imperatives of self-preservation.

J. M. Guéhenno depicts this anonymous world from the perspective of individual citizens who have become detached from the obsolete solidarity of democratic communities and must now orient themselves in the chaotic bustle of mutually adapting functional systems. These "new" human beings have sloughed off the illusory self-understanding of modernity. The neoliberal inspiration of this Hellenistic vision is all too clear. The autonomy of the citizen is unceremoniously stripped of the moral components of democratic self-determination and pared back to private autonomy: "Like the Roman citizen of the time of Caracalla, the citizen of the imperial age of the networks defines himself less and less by his participation in the exercise of sovereignty and more and more by the possibility he has to act in a framework in which the procedures obey clear and predictable rules. . . . It matters little whether a norm is imposed by a private enterprise or by a committee of bureaucrats. It is no longer the expression of sovereignty but simply something that reduces uncertainties, a means of lowering the cost of transactions, of increasing transparenc[y]."[11] Through a perverse play on Hegel's polemic against the administrative state (*Not- und Verstandesstaat*), the democratic state is replaced by a "state of law deprived of all philosophical reference to natural law, reduced to an ensemble of rules with no other basis than the daily administered proof of its smooth functioning."[12] Norms that are both effective *and* responsive to expectations of popular sovereignty and human rights are replaced—

under the guise of a "logic of networks"—by the invisible hand of supposedly spontaneously regulated processes of the global economy. However, these mechanisms which are insensitive to external costs do not exactly inspire confidence. This is true at any rate of the two best-known examples of global self-regulation.

The "balance of powers" on which the international system was based for three hundred years collapsed some time between the First and Second World Wars, if not before. Without an international court and a supranational sanctioning power, international law could not be invoked and enforced like state law. However, conventional morality and the "ethics" of dynastic relations ensured a certain level of normative regulation of warfare. In the twentieth century, total war has destroyed even this weak normative framework. The advanced state of weapons technology, the arms build-up, and the spread of weapons of mass destruction[13] have made abundantly clear the risks inherent in this anarchy of powers unregulated by any invisible hand. The founding of the League of Nations was the first attempt at least to domesticate the unpredictable dynamic of power relations within a collective security system. With the foundation of the United Nations, a second attempt was made to set up supranational political agencies responsible for instituting peace on a global scale. With the end of the bipolar balance of terror, the prospect of a "global domestic politics" (C. F. von Weizsäcker) seems to have opened up, in spite of all the set-backs in the field of international human rights and security policy. The failure of the anarchistic balance of power has at least made evident the desirability of political interventions and arrangements.

Similar observations hold true for the other prime example of spontaneous self-regulation. Obviously even the global market cannot be managed exclusively by the World Bank and the International Monetary Fund if the asymmetrical interdependence between the OECD countries and the marginalized countries that have not yet developed self-sustaining economies is ever to be overcome. The conclusion reached by the recent UN global summit on social problems in Copenhagen is unsettling. There is a lack of competent agencies at the international level with the power to agree on the necessary arrangements, procedures, and political frameworks. Not only the disparities between North and South call for such cooperation but also the drop in standards of living in the wealthy North Atlantic countries, where social policies restricted to the nation-state are powerless to deal with the effects of lower wages on globalized and rapidly expanding labor markets. The lack of supranational agencies is especially acute when it comes to dealing with the ecological problems addressed from a global perspective at the Earth Summit in Rio. A more peaceful and just political and economic world order is unthinkable without international institutions that are capable of taking initiatives, and above all without a harmonization between the continental regimes that are today just emerging, and without the kind of policies that could only be carried out under pressure from a mobilized global civil society.

This lends support to the competing reading according to which the nation-state should be "transformed" rather than abolished. But could its normative content also be preserved? The optimistic vision of supranational agencies which would empower the United Nations and its regional organizations to institute a new political and economic world order is clouded by the troubling question of whether democratic opinion- and will-formation could ever achieve a binding force that extends beyond the level of the nation-state.

5

On the Relation between the Nation, the Rule of Law, and Democracy

For Hans-Ulrich Wehler on his sixty-fifth birthday

As in the period of decolonization following the Second World War, the collapse of the Soviet empire has been marked by a series of rapid dissociative state-formations. The Dayton and Paris peace accords mark the provisional end of successful secessions leading to the foundation of new nation-states or to the restoration of states that had been destroyed, had become dependent, or had been divided up. These, it would seem, are merely the most manifest symptoms of the enduring vitality of a phenomenon that has been largely forgotten not just by the social sciences: "With the collapse of imperial spheres of influence, the world of states reconstitutes itself within traditional boundaries which are explained in terms of national history."[1] Today the political future seems to belong once again to the "hereditary powers" among which Hermann Lübbe numbers "religion or ecclesiastical confessions on the one hand, and nation on the other." Other authors speak of "ethnonationalism" in order to underline the unconditional relation to the past, whether in the physical sense of common descent or in the broader sense of a shared cultural inheritance.

Terminologies are far from innocent; they imply a particular point of view. The neologism "ethnonationalism" blurs the traditional distinction between "ethnos" and "demos."[2] This expression emphasizes the proximity between an "ethnos," a prepolitical community of shared descent organized around kinship ties, on the one hand, and a nation constituted as a state that at least aspires to political independence, on the other. In this way the assumption that ethnic communities are more "natural" and evolutionarily "more primitive" than nations is implicitly contradicted.[3] The "we-consciousness," founded on an imagined blood relation or on cultural identity, of people who share a belief in a common origin, identify one another as "members" of the same community, and thereby set themselves apart from their environment, is supposed to constitute the *common* core of ethnic *and* of national social formations. In view of this commonality, nations would differ from other ethnic communities only in their degree of complexity and scope: "It is the largest group that can command a person's loyalty because of felt kinship ties; it is, from this perspective, the fully extended family."[4]

This ethnological concept of the nation conflicts with the concept as it is usually employed by historians. It glosses over the specific connections to the legal order of the constitutional state, to political historiography, and to the dynamics of mass communication to which the national consciousness that arose in Europe in the nineteenth century owes its reflexive and distinctively artificial character.[5] If the national, as previously the ethnic, community appears from the perspective of a *generalized* constructivism as a "believed" or "imagined commonality" (Max Weber), the "invention of the ethnic nation (*Volksnation*)" (H. Schulze) can be given a surprisingly affirmative twist. As a specific manifestation of a universal form of social integration, the quasi-natural character of the nation once again takes on an almost natural aspect even for the scientist who assumes that it is constructed. For once we recognize that the nation is merely a variant of a social universal, the resurgence of the national no longer needs to be explained. When the presumption of normality shifts in favor of ethnonationalism it no longer makes any sense to describe the conflicts that today once again command our attention as symptoms of regression and alienation in need of explanation and to conceive of them, for example, as compensations for the loss of an international power status or as attempts to come to terms with a condition of social and economic deprivation.

Modern states which are functionally integrated by market and administrative power still delimit themselves from one another as "nations" as they always have done. But this says nothing about the specific character of national self-understanding. It remains an empirical question when and to what extent modern populations understand themselves as a nation based on ethnic membership or as a nation of citizens. This double coding has a bearing on the issue of exclusion and inclusion. National consciousness vacillates in a peculiar fashion between more extensive inclusion and renewed exclusion.

As a modern form of consciousness, national identity is distinguished on the one hand by its tendency to transcend particularistic, regional ties. In nineteenth century Europe the nation founded new bonds of solidarity between persons who had previously been strangers to one another. This universalistic transformation of hereditary loyalties to village and family, locality and dynasty, is a difficult and in any case a protracted process. Even in the classical nation-states of the West it did not encompass the whole population before the beginning of the twentieth century.[6] On the other hand, it is no accident that this more abstract form of integration found expression in the readiness to fight and in the spirit of self-sacrifice of military draftees who were mobilized against the "enemies of the fatherland." In an emergency the solidarity of the citizens was supposed to prove itself in the solidarity of those who risk their lives for people and fatherland. On the romantically inspired concept of a people who assert their existence and distinctive identity in the struggle against other nations, the quasi-natural moment of an imagined community of shared language and ancestry is fused with the contingent moment of a narratively constructed community of shared destiny. But this national identity rooted in fictional pasts also prefigures the future realization of republican liberty rights.

The Janus face of the nation, which opens itself internally but shuts itself off from the outside, is already implicit in the ambivalent meaning of the concept of freedom. The particularistic freedom of an externally asserted collective national independence seems to be merely the protective shield for the internally realized individual liberties of the citizens—their private autonomy as members of civil society (*Gesellschaftsbürger*) no less than their political autonomy as citizens (*Staatsbürger*). The conceptual opposition between a compulsory, ascriptive ethnic membership viewed as an inalienable property, on the one hand, and a freely chosen membership guaranteed by subjective rights in a voluntary political community that grants its citizens the option of emigrating, on the other, is dissolved in this syndrome. This double coding still inspires competing interpretations and contradictory political diagnoses.

The idea of the ethnic nation suggests that the *demos* of citizens must be rooted in the *ethnos* of nationals (*Volksgenossen*) if it is to stabilize itself as a political association of free and equal legal consociates. The binding force of citizenship is supposedly not adequate to this task. The loyalty of citizens has to be anchored in the quasi-natural, historically fateful sense of togetherness of the people. The "anodyne" academic idea of "constitutional patriotism" is no substitute for a "healthy national consciousness": "This concept (of constitutional patriotism) hangs in the air without support . . . . Hence appeal to the nation . . . [and] to the emotionally binding we-consciousness it contains, is unavoidable."[7] Seen from another perspective, however, the symbiotic relation between nationalism and republicanism reveals itself as merely a transitional, historical constellation. A national consciousness propagated by intellectuals and scholars that slowly spread outward from the urban bourgeoisie—a consciousness that crystallized around the fiction of a common ancestry, the construction of a shared history, and a grammatically standardized written language—did indeed transform subjects for the first time into politically aware citizens who identify with the republican constitution and its declared goals. But notwithstanding this catalyzing role, nationalism is not a necessary or permanent precondition of a democratic process. The progressive extension of the status of citizenship to the whole population does not just provide the state with a new source of secular legitimation; it also produces a new level of abstract, legally mediated social integration.

Both interpretations assume that the nation-state was a response to the problem of the disintegration of a populace that had become uprooted from the corporative social ties of early modern society. But the one side situates the solution to the problem at the cultural level, whereas the other looks for a solution at the level of democratic procedures and institutions. Ernst-Wolfgang Bökenförde emphasizes the aspect of collective identity: "A relative homogenization in a shared culture is needed by way of compensation . . . if the society which tends to become atomized is to be reunited into a unity capable of concerted action, in spite of being differentiated into a multiplicity of parts. This task is performed by the nation and its attendant national consciousness along with, and in succession to, religion . . . . Thus the ultimate goal cannot be to overtake national identity and replace it with something else, not even with a universalism of human rights."[8] The opposing view is based on the conviction that the democratic process itself can provide the necessary guarantees for the social integration of an increasingly differentiated society.[9] Indeed, in pluralistic societies this burden cannot be shifted from the level of political will-formation and public communication onto the seemingly natural cultural substrate of a supposedly homogeneous people. From these premises Hans-Ulrich Wehler concludes that "federal unions bound together by a sense of loyalty based primarily on the achievements of the constitutional and welfare states represent an incomparably more attractive utopian ideal than the regression to the supposed normality of the German . . . nation-state."[10]

I am not competent to engage in this debate at the level of historical arguments. Instead I am interested in the constitutional models of the relation between the nation, the rule of law, and democracy in terms of which the conflict is fought out at the normative level. Jurists and political theorists intervene in the public processes of the self-understanding of citizens with different, but no less effective, means than historians; they can even influence the decisions of the Federal Constitutional Court. On the classical, late eighteenth-century conception, "nation" refers to the people who constitute themselves as a state by giving themselves a democratic constitution. Opposed to this view is the conception that arose in the nineteenth century according to which popular sovereignty presupposes a nation that projects itself into the past as an organically evolving entity in contrast with the artificial order of positive law: "The 'people,' . . . which is the subject of constitutional authority in democracies, does not first acquire its identity from the constitution that it gives itself. This identity is rather a preconstitutional, historical fact: thoroughly contingent, but not for that reason arbitrary . . .

it is unavoidable for those who find that they belong to a particular people."[11]

Carl Schmitt played an important role in the history of this idea. I will begin by contrasting Schmitt's account of the relation between nation, rule of law, and democracy with the classical conception (I). These approaches have different consequences for a number of current, interconnected problems: the right of national self-determination (II), equal rights in multicultural societies (III), the right of humanitarian intervention (IV), and the transfer of sovereign rights to supranational institutions (V). Taking these problems as my guide, I will argue that the ethnonational conception of popular sovereignty is misguided.

I Constitutional Constructions of Popular Sovereignty

(1) In his interpretation of the Weimar constitution, Carl Schmitt accords a constructivist notion of ethnonationalism a constitutional status. The Weimar Republic stood in the tradition of the rule of law—already exemplified by constitutional monarchy—which is supposed to protect the citizens from the abuse of state power; but for the first time in German history it combined the rule of law with the constitutional form and the political content of democracy. This starting point, which is peculiar to German legal history, is reflected in the architectonic of Schmitt's "constitutional theory." There Schmitt makes a strict distinction between the "legal" and the "political" components of the constitution and treats the "nation" as a hinge between the traditional principles of the bourgeois constitutional state and the democratic principle of the self-determination of the people. He argues that national homogeneity is a necessary precondition for the democratic exercise of political authority: "A democratic state in which democracy is founded on the national homogeneity of its citizens conforms to the so-called nationality principle according to which each nation forms a state and each state a nation."[12]

With this principle, Schmitt adopts the formulation of Johann Caspar Bluntschli; he also consciously aligns himself with the principles—accepted by both Wilson and Lenin—that informed the European postwar political order laid down in the Versailles peace settlement. But the specific conceptualization is more important than historical agreements. Schmitt conceives of the citizens' equal political participation in political will-formation as a matter of a spontaneous harmony between the expressions of will of like-minded members of a more or less homogeneous people.[13] Democracy must take the form of a national democracy because the "self" of the self-determination of the people is conceived as a macrosubject capable of action and because the ethnic nation seems to be the appropriate entity to fill this conceptual gap—it is viewed as the quasi-natural substrate of the state organization. This collectivistic interpretation of the Rousseauean model of self-legislation prejudices all further considerations.

It is true that democracy can only be exercised as a joint practice. But Schmitt does not construe this commonality in terms of the higher-level intersubjectivity of a discursive agreement between citizens who reciprocally recognize one another as free and equal; instead he reifies it into the *homogeneity* of members of a single people. He makes the norm of equal treatment contingent on the fact of a uniform national origin: "Democratic equality is a substantive equality. Because all citizens share in this substance, they can be treated as equal, they have equal electoral and voting rights, etc."[14] This substantialist understanding of the citizenry is related to an existentialist conception of the democratic decision-making process. Schmitt conceives of political will-formation as the collective self-affirmation of a people: "What the people want is good just because the people want (it)."[15] Severing democracy from the rule of law here reveals a hidden meaning: given that the guiding political will has no rational content but is exhausted by the expressive content of a naturalized *Volksgeist*, it does not need to be generated through a public discussion, participation in which is guaranteed by civic rights.

Aside from any consideration of its rationality or irrationality, the authenticity of the people's will is attested exclusively by the plebiscitary proclamation of the will of an actually present people. Even before the self-determination of the people becomes solidified into the competences of state organs, it finds expression in the spontaneous "yes" and "no" responses of the people to predetermined alternatives: "Only the actually assembled people is the people . . . and can perform the activity that specifically pertains to this people: it can acclaim—in other words, signal its acceptance or rejection by a simple act of acclamation."[16] The principle of majority rule merely operationalizes the accord between individual expressions of will: "all will the same thing." This convergence only brings to the fore the substantive a priori of a shared national form of life. The a priori preunderstanding is granted by the substantive homogeneity of nationals who set themselves apart as a separate nation from all others: "The democratic concept of equality is a political concept that is predicated on the possibility of differentiation. Hence political democracy cannot rest on the undifferentiatedness of all human beings but only on membership of a particular people. . . . Thus the equality that is essential to democracy applies only internally, not externally."[17]

In this way, Schmitt sets up a polemical contrast between the "people," on the one hand, and a humanistically conceived "humanity" connected with the moral concept of equal respect for everyone, on the other: "The central concept of democracy is the people, not humanity. If democracy is indeed a political form, it can only be a democracy of the people, not of humanity."[18] Insofar as the "idea of the equality of all human beings," in the sense of equal consideration of the interests of everybody, has any relevance for the constitution, it finds expression in a rule of law that applies to private citizens. The meaning of human rights is exhausted by the private enjoyment of equal liberties, whereas the exercise of political freedoms by citizens is supposed to obey a completely different logic. The meaning of democratic self-determination based on ethnic homogeneity is not the political autonomy of individual citizens but rather national independence—the self-assertion, self-affirmation, and self-realization of a nation in its specificity. This nation mediates between the rule of law and democracy: only the citizens, who have been transformed from private persons into members of a politically self-conscious nation, can participate in democratic rule.

(2) By uncoupling the basic rights regulating private interactions within civil society from a substantialized "*Volksdemokratie*"[19] in this

way, Schmitt sets himself in stark opposition to a republicanism grounded in social contract theory. On this tradition, "people" and "nation" are interchangeable concepts for a citizenry that is co-original with the political community. The people who make up the state are viewed not as a prepolitical datum but as the product of the social contract. The participants form an association of free and equal consociates under law through their joint decision to make use of their original right "to live under public laws of freedom." The decision to live in political freedom is synonymous with the undertaking to engage in a constitution-founding praxis. In contrast with Carl Schmitt's account, on this conception popular sovereignty and human rights, democracy and the constitutional state, are conceptually intertwined. For the initial decision to engage in democratic self-legislation can only be carried out by realizing the rights that the participants must mutually grant one another if they want to legitimately regulate their life in common by means of positive law. This calls in turn for a legitimacy-guaranteeing procedure of lawmaking that gives permanent form to the further elaboration of the system of rights.[20] Following the Rousseauean formula, in this procedure all must reach the same decisions for all. Thus the basic rights *spring from* the very idea of the legal institutionalization of the procedure of democratic self-legislation.

The idea of a procedural, future-oriented popular sovereignty along these lines renders meaningless the demand to tie political will-formation to the substantive a priori of a past, prepolitically established consensus among homogeneous members of a nation: "Positive law is not legitimate because it corresponds to substantive principles of justice but because it is enacted in accordance with procedures that are formally just, that is, democratic. That all decide the same thing for all in the legislative process is a demanding normative presupposition that is no longer defined in a substantive manner but is intended to prevent arbitrary decisions and minimize domination through the self-legislation of the addressees of the law, through equal procedural positions, and through the universality of legal regulation."[21] A prior background consensus based on a homogeneous culture is not necessary, because democratically structured opinion- and will-formation make possible rational agreement even between strangers. Because the democratic process guarantees legitimacy in virtue of its procedural characteristics, it can if necessary bridge gaps in social integration. Insofar as it secures the fair value of individual liberties for all, it ensures that the network of civic solidarity remains intact.

Criticism of this classical conception is primarily directed against its "liberalistic" interpretation. Schmitt disputes the capacity of the constitutional state founded on democratic procedures to secure social integration under the two headings that informed Hegel's critique of the "Not- und Verstandesstaat" [literally, "state of necessity and of the understanding"] of social contract theory and have been taken up again by the "communitarians" in their controversy with "liberals."[22] The principal targets of this critique are the atomistic conception of the individual as an "unencumbered self" and the instrumentalist concept of political will-formation as a matter of aggregating social interests. From the point of view of these critics, the parties to the social contract are conceived as isolated, enlightened rational egoists who are not shaped by common traditions and hence do not share any cultural value-orientations, and whose actions are not oriented to reaching understanding. Political will-formation on this description must take the form of negotiations concerning a modus vivendi without any possibility of reaching a mutual understanding from ethical or moral points of view. Indeed, it is difficult to see how such parties could produce an intersubjectively recognized legal order that can be expected to forge a nation of citizens from strangers—in other words, generate civic solidarity between strangers. Against such a Hobbesian backdrop, the shared ethnic or cultural inheritance of a more or less homogeneous people recommends itself as the source and guarantor of the kind of normative bonds to which possessive individualism is blind.

However, the well-founded criticism of this extreme version of natural law does not apply to the *intersubjectivistic* understanding of procedural popular sovereignty, which is in any case more congenial to the republican tradition. On this interpretation, the practice of deliberation between participants in communication who want to arrive at rationally motivated decisions takes the place of the private law model of a contract between market players. Political opinion-

and will-formation is not limited to the formation of compromises but also conforms to the model of public discourses oriented to the rational acceptability of regulations in the light of generalized interests, shared evaluative orientations, and justified principles. This noninstrumental conception of politics is based on the idea of the communicatively acting person. Nor should the autonomy of legal persons be conceived in terms of self-ownership. The social character of natural persons is such that they develop into individuals in the context of intersubjectively shared forms of life and stabilize their identities through relations of reciprocal recognition. Hence, also from a legal point of view, individual persons can be protected only by *simultaneously* protecting the context in which their formation processes unfold, that is, only by assuring themselves access to supportive interpersonal relations, social networks, and cultural forms of life. A discursively instituted process of legislation and political decision-making that keeps this in view must take account of values and norms as well as existing preferences. As such, it is well qualified to fulfill the task of providing a political substitute for processes of integration that fail at other levels.

From the point of view of Kant and of Rousseau (properly understood[23]), democratic self-determination does not have the collectivistic and at the same time *exclusionary* meaning of the assertion of national independence and of the realization of a unique national character. Rather, it has the inclusive meaning of self-legislation which involves all citizens equally. It is inclusive in that such a political order keeps itself open to the equal protection of those who suffer discrimination and to the *integration* of the marginalized, but without *imprisoning* them in the uniformity of a homogenized ethnic community. In this connection the principle of voluntariness is crucial; that citizens belong to a state is a function at least of their implicit agreement. Whereas the substantive understanding of popular sovereignty assumes an essential interconnection between "freedom" and the *external* independence of a people, the procedural understanding connects sovereignty with the private and public autonomy granted everybody equally *within* an association of free and equal legal subjects. Given the challenges that confront us today, I want to argue, the communicative account of republicanism is more appropriate than either an ethnonational or even a communitarian conception of the nation, the rule of law, and democracy.

II On the Meaning and Limits of National Self-determination

The nationality principle implies a right of national self-determination. According to this principle, every nation that wishes to govern itself has the right to exist as an independent state. The ethnonational understanding of popular sovereignty seems to provide a solution to a problem that republicanism cannot solve: How are we to define the totality of those to whom citizens' rights should legitimately apply?

Kant ascribes to every human being as such the right to have rights and to regulate his life in common with others in such a way that everyone can enjoy equal liberties in accordance with public, coercive laws. But this does not settle who may actually make use of this right with whom and when; nor does it settle who may unite into a self-determining commonwealth on the basis of a social contract. The question of the *legitimate composition* of the citizen body remains open as long as democratic self-determination only affects the mode of organization of the common life of legal consociates in general. Of course, the self-legislation of a nation with a democratic constitution can be traced back to the decision of a founding generation to give themselves a constitution; but with this act the participants qualify themselves only *retroactively* as a sovereign people (*Staatsvolk*). It is through the shared will to found a state and, as a consequence of this resolution, through the constitution-founding practice itself that the participants constitute themselves as a nation of citizens.

This approach remains unproblematic as long as borders are not in fact disputed, as for example in the French or even the American Revolution when the citizens struggled for republican freedoms either against their own government, and hence within the boundaries of an already existing state, or against a colonial power which had itself already defined the boundaries of unequal treatment. But in other cases the circular answer that the citizens constitute themselves as a people, and thereby delimit themselves both socially and territorially from their environment, is not sufficient: "To say that all people . . . are entitled to the democratic process begs a prior question. When does a collection of persons constitute an entity—'a people'—entitled to govern itself democratically?"[24] In the real world, who in each instance acquires the power to define the disputed borders of a state is settled by historical contingencies, usually by the quasi-natural outcome of violent conflicts, wars, and civil wars. Whereas republicanism reinforces our awareness of the contingency of these borders, this contingency can be dispelled by appeal to the idea of a grown nation that imbues the borders with the aura of imitated substantiality and legitimates them through fictitious links with the past. Nationalism bridges the normative gap by appealing to a so-called right of national self-determination.

In contrast with social contract theory which grounds the legal order in relations of mutual recognition between individual citizens, Carl Schmitt seems to be in a position to justify such a collective right. For if democratic self-determination is understood on the model of collective self-assertion and self-realization, no single person can realize his fundamental right to equal citizens' rights outside the context of an ethnic nation that enjoys the organizational independence of a state. On this view the collective right of every people to form an independent state is a necessary condition for the effective guarantee of equal individual rights. This justification of the principle of nationality also yields the possibility of endowing the actual success of a national independence movement with retrospective normative force. A particular group of people qualifies for the right of national self-determination by the fact that it defines itself as a homogeneous people *and* at the same time has the power to control the territorial boundaries that derive from such ascriptive characteristics.

On the other hand, the assumption of a homogeneous people contradicts the principle of voluntariness and has certain normatively undesirable consequences which Schmitt makes no attempt to conceal: "A nationally homogeneous state then appears normal; a state that lacks this homogeneity is abnormal, a threat to peace."[25] The assumption of a compulsory, collective identity necessitates repressive policies, whether it be the forced assimilation of alien elements or the purification of the people through apartheid and ethnic cleansing, for, as Schmitt puts it, "a democratic state (would) rob itself of its substance by consistently recognizing the universal equality of human beings in the domain of public life and of public law."[26] In addition to suggesting preventive measures limiting the admission of aliens, Schmitt recommends the "suppression and expulsion of heterogeneous elements of the population" as well as their geographical segregation, hence the establishment of protectorates, colonies, reservations, homelands, etc.

Of course, the republican conception does not preclude ethnic communities' giving themselves democratic constitutions and establishing themselves as sovereign states so long as this independence is legitimated by the individual right of citizens to live in freedom under laws. But as a general rule nation-states do not develop peacefully from separate peoples living in isolation; rather they typically encroach on neighboring regions, tribes, subcultures, and linguistic or religious communities. For the most part new nation-states emerge at the expense of assimilated, suppressed, or marginalized "subaltern" peoples. The formation of nation-states under the banner of ethnonationalism has almost always been accompanied by bloody purification rituals, and it has generally exposed new minorities to new waves of repression. In late nineteenth- and twentieth-century Europe it left in its wake a horrific legacy of emigration and expulsion, of forced resettlement, disenfranchisement, and physical extermination, up to and including genocide. Often enough the persecuted themselves mutated into persecutors once they succeeded in emancipating themselves. In the prevailing practice concerning recognition in international law, the emergence of the nationality principle coincided with a shift to the "principle of effectiveness" according to which every new government—regardless of its legitimacy—can count on recognition only if it succeeds in stabilizing its sovereignty both externally and internally.

But as in the salient cases of colonialism and domination by a foreign power, the injustices against which legitimate resistance is directed do not result from the violation of a supposed collective right of national self-determination but from the violation of the basic rights of individuals. The demand for self-determination can only have as its immediate content the implementation of equal civil rights. The abolition of discrimination against minorities does not per se call into question the territorial boundaries of an unjust regime. A demand to secede is legitimate only when the central state power violates the rights of a portion of the population concentrated in a particular territory; in this case the demand for inclusion can be realized via national independence. From this standpoint, the independence of the United States was already recognized by Spain and France in 1778. Since the defection of the Spanish colonies in South and Central America, and contrary to the practice that prevailed until that time,[27] the view has gained general acceptance that international recognition of a secession from the mother country is permissible even without the assent of the former sovereign.[28]

So long as national independence movements appeal to democratic self-determination in the republican sense, a secession (or the annexation of a seceded portion of a territory by another state) cannot be justified without taking account of the legitimacy of the status quo. For so long as all citizens enjoy equal rights and nobody suffers discrimination, there is no compelling normative reason to secede from the larger political community. Under these circumstances, issues of repression or of "foreign domination" (*Fremdherrschaft*) which would give minorities the right to secede cannot arise. This view fits the resolution of the UN General Assembly which, in accordance with the UN Charter, guarantees all peoples a right of self-determination, but does so without employing the concept "people" in the ethnic sense.[29] The resolution rejects explicitly the right to secede from "states that conduct themselves in accordance with the principles of equal treatment and of the right of self-determination of peoples and therefore possess a government which represents the whole people, without discrimination on the basis of race, religion or sex."[30]

III A Model of Inclusion Sensitive to Difference

To be sure, the liberal interpretation of democratic self-determination obscures the problem of "born" minorities, which comes into sharper focus from the communitarian perspective[31] and from the intersubjective point of view of discourse theory.[32] The problem also occurs in democratic societies when a politically dominant, majority culture imposes its way of life on minorities and thereby denies effective equality of rights to citizens from other cultural backgrounds. This problem concerns political issues that bear on the ethical self-understanding and the identity of citizens. In these matters minorities should not be simply outvoted by a majority. Here the principle of majority rule runs up against its limits as the contingent composition of the citizenry prejudices the outcomes of a seemingly neutral procedure: "The majority principle itself depends on prior assumptions about the unit: that the unit within which it is to operate is itself legitimate and that the matters on which it is employed properly fall within the jurisdiction of that unit. In other words, whether the scope and domain of majority rule are appropriate in a particular unit depends on assumptions that the majority principle itself can do nothing to justify. The justification for the unit lies beyond the reach of the majority principle and, for that matter, mostly beyond the reach of democratic theory itself."[33]

The problem of "born" minorities can be explained by the fact that citizens, even when viewed as legal subjects, are not abstract individuals who are cut off from their origins. By intervening in ethical-political issues, the law affects the integrity of the forms of life in which each person's conduct of life is embedded. In addition to moral considerations, pragmatic deliberations, and negotiable interests, this aspect of the law brings *strong evaluations* into play that depend on intersubjectively shared, but culturally specific, traditions. Legal orders as wholes are also "ethically imbued" in that they interpret the universalistic content of the same constitutional principles in different ways, namely, against the background of the experiences that make up a national history and in light of a historically prevailing tradition, culture, and form of life. Often the regulation of culturally sensitive matters, such as the official language, the public school curriculum, the status of churches and religious communities, and the norms of criminal law (e.g., those regulating abortion), but also of less obvious matters such as the status of the family and marriage-like partnerships, the acceptance of security standards, or the demarcation of the private from the public realm, is merely a reflection of the ethical-political self-understanding of a majority culture that has achieved dominance for contingent, historical reasons. Such implicitly overwhelming regulations can also spark a cultural struggle by disrespected minorities against the majority culture even within a republican polity that guarantees formally equal civil rights, as is shown by numerous examples such as the Francophones in Canada, the Walloons in Belgium, and the Basques and Catalans in Spain.

A nation of citizens is composed of persons who, as a result of socialization processes, also embody the forms of life in which they formed their identities, even if as adults they renounce the traditions in which they were brought up. In virtue of the constitution of their character, persons are so to speak nodal points in an ascriptive network of cultures and traditions. The contingent composition of the citizen body—in Dahl's terminology, the "political unit"—also implicitly determines the evaluative horizon within which cultural conflicts and ethical-political discourses of self-interpretation are played out. This evaluative horizon also changes with shifts in the social composition of the citizenry. For example, political questions that depend on a culture-specific background are not necessarily treated differently after a secession, though the outcomes of votes are different; new majorities are not always the result of new arguments.

Of course, a minority that suffers discrimination can achieve equal rights through secession only on the improbable condition that its members are geographically concentrated. Otherwise the old problems merely recur under new banners. In general, discrimination can be eliminated not through national independence but only through a process of inclusion that is sufficiently sensitive to the cultural background of individual and group-specific differences. The problem of born minorities, endemic to all pluralistic societies, becomes more acute in multicultural societies. But when the latter are organized as democratic constitutional states, several different routes to the elusive goal of a "difference-sensitive" inclusion are at any rate available: federalist delegation of powers, a functionally specified transfer or decentralization of state competences, above all guarantees of cultural autonomy, group-specific rights, compensatory policies, and other arrangements for effectively protecting minorities. In this way the body of citizens who participate in the democratic process in a particular territory or in particular policy domains changes without affecting its principles.

To be sure, the coexistence with equal rights of different ethnic communities, language groups, religious faiths, and forms of life should not be purchased at the cost of the fragmentation of society. The painful process of uncoupling must not rend the society asunder into a multiplicity of subcultures closed off from one another.[34] On the one hand, the majority culture must detach itself from its fusion with the general political culture in which all citizens share equally; otherwise it dictates the parameters of political discourses from the outset. As just one part, it may no longer form the façade of the whole without prejudicing the democratic procedure in specific questions of existential relevance for minorities. On the other hand, the binding force of the common political culture, which becomes progressively more abstract as subcultures reduce it to a common denominator, must remain strong enough to prevent the nation of citizens from falling apart: "Multiculturalism, while endorsing the perpetuation of several cultural groups in a single political society, also requires the existence of a common culture. . . . Members of all cultural groups . . . will have to acquire a common political language and conventions of conduct to be able to participate effectively in the competition for resources and the protection of group as well as individual interests in a shared political arena."[35]

IV Democracy and State Sovereignty: The Case of Humanitarian Intervention

The substantive and procedural understandings of democracy not only entail different conceptions of national self-determination and multiculturalism; they also have different consequences for the conceptualization of state sovereignty. The state that developed in modern Europe depended from the beginning on the reserve force of a standing army, the police, and the penal system, and it exercised a monopoly over the legitimate means of violence. Internal sovereignty meant the enforcement of the laws of the state, external sovereignty the ability to assert oneself in the competition among the major powers (as this became consolidated in the European state system after the Peace of Westphalia). From this standpoint the process of democratization which was set in motion by the formation of nation-states appears as the transfer of sovereign power from the prince to the people. But this formula lacks precision in comparison with the alternative that concerns us here.

If democratic self-determination means the equal participation of free and equal citizens in the process of decision making and legislation, then democracy in the first place changes the nature and mode of exercising internal sovereignty. The constitutional state revolutionizes the basis on which political rule is legitimated. If, by contrast, democratic self-determination means the collective self-assertion and self-realization of a homogeneous people, the issue of external sovereignty moves into the foreground. For the preservation of state power in the international system thereby acquires the additional significance that a nation secures, together with its existence, its unique character over and against other nations. Thus, in the first case, the connection between democracy and state sovereignty lays down stringent conditions for the legitimacy of the internal order but leaves the question of external sovereignty open; in the second case it interprets the place of the nation-state in the international arena, but the only criterion of legitimacy it requires for the internal exercise of power is civil peace, the maintenance of "law and order."

The conception of sovereignty in classical international law entails a prohibition on interference in the internal affairs of an internationally recognized state. This prohibition of intervention is indeed reaffirmed by the UN Charter; but from the beginning it stood in tension with the development of the international protection of human rights. The erosion of the principle of nonintervention in recent decades has been due primarily to the politics of human rights.[36] It is hardly surprising that Schmitt categorically repudiated this development. His rejection of intervention grounded in appeals to human rights can already be accounted for by his belligerent conception of international relations, indeed of politics in general.[37] It was not only the introduction of crimes against humanity after the Second World War that elicited his scornful protest. The condemnation of offensive wars[38] had already struck him as incompatible with the status and range of action of nations that can assert their existence and unique identity only in the antagonistic role of sovereign subjects of international law.

Michael Walzer, who could not be further from the militant ethnonationalism of a Schmitt, defends a similar position. Without wishing to suggest false parallels, I would like to examine his communitarian reservations concerning humanitarian intervention,[39] for they throw light on the internal connection between conceptions of democracy and the treatment of sovereignty rights. In his book on just wars,[40] Walzer proceeds from the assumption that any community has a right of national self-determination if it possesses its own collective identity and, inspired by an awareness of its cultural heritage, has the will and determination to carve out a state existence for itself and to assert its political independence. A group of people enjoys the right of national self-determination if it succeeds in laying claim to it.

To be sure, Walzer does not understand the candidate for political independence as an ethnic community of descent but rather as a cultural community of inheritance. However, the historically evolving cultural nation, like the community of shared ancestry, is also understood as a prepolitical entity that has the right to preserve its integrity in the form of a sovereign state: "The idea of communal integrity derives its moral and political force from the rights of contemporary men and women to live as members of a historic community and to express their inherited culture through political forms worked out among themselves."[41] Walzer also deduces three exceptions to the principle of nonintervention from this right of self-determination. He regards interventions as permissible (a) to lend support to a national liberation movement that manifests the identity of an independent community by the very act of resistance and (b) to defend the integrity of a political community under attack when it can only be protected by an opposing intervention. Walzer also justifies the third exception, not on the basis of violations of human rights per se, but on the grounds that (c) in cases of enslavement, massacre, or genocide a criminal government deprives its own citizens of the possibility of giving expression to their forms of life and thereby of preserving their collective identity.

The Nation, the Rule of Law, and Democracy

The communitarian interpretation of popular sovereignty emphasizes the aspect of external sovereignty in such a way that the question of the legitimacy of the internal order gets pushed into the background. The point of Walzer's reflections is that a humanitarian intervention against violations of human rights by a dictatorial regime can only be justified when the affected citizens themselves take up the cudgels against political repression and, by a recognizable act of rebellion, provide concrete proof that the government is opposed to the true aspirations of the people and threatens the integrity of the community. Accordingly, the legitimacy of a political order is measured in the first instance by the accord between the political leadership and the cultural form of life that is constitutive of the identity of the people: "A state is legitimate or not, depending upon the 'fit' of government and community, that is, the degree to which the government actually represents the political life of its people. When it doesn't do that, the people have a right to rebel. But if they are free to rebel then they are also free not to rebel . . . because they still believe the government to be tolerable, or they are accustomed to it, or they are personally loyal to its leaders . . . . Anyone can make such arguments, but only subjects or citizens can act on them."[42]

Walzer's critics proceed from a different understanding of democratic self-determination; they reject the view that internal sovereignty is simply a matter of the effective preservation of civil peace. On this reading the key to judging the legitimacy of the internal order is not common cultural inheritance but the realization of civil rights: "The mere fact that the multitude shares *some* form of common life—common traditions, customs, interests, history, institutions, and boundaries—is not sufficient to generate a genuine, independent, legitimate political community."[43] The critics dispute the principle of nonintervention and advocate, as far as possible, the expansion of the international protection of human rights. Here, of course, that a state is illegitimate according to the standards of the constitutional state is not a *sufficient* condition for intervening in its internal affairs. Otherwise the UN General Assembly would have to be composed along completely different lines. Walzer rightly points out that from a moral point of view every decision to act on behalf of citizens of another country is dubious. Proposals for a case-by-case treatment of intervention[44] also take into account the limits and the extreme dangers of a politics of human rights.[45] But the decisions and strategies of the world organization, and especially the interventions of forces carrying out UN mandates since 1989, indicate the direction along which international law (*Völkerrecht*) is gradually being transformed into a cosmopolitan law (*Weltbürgerrecht*).[46]

These political and legal developments are reactions to an objectively changed situation. The unprecedented nature and scale of the government criminality that spread in the wake of the technologically unfettered and ideologically unrestrained Second World War makes a mockery of the classical presumption of the innocence of the sovereign subjects of international law. A prescient politics of peacekeeping must take into account the complex social and political causes of war. What is urgently needed are strategies designed to influence—where possible, in a nonviolent manner—the internal order of formally sovereign states whose goal is to foster self-sustaining economies and tolerable social conditions, equal democratic participation, the rule of law, and a culture of tolerance. Such interventions in support of internal democratization are, however, irreconcilable with a conception of democratic self-determination that grounds a right of national independence for the sake of the collective self-realization of a cultural form of life.

V Only a Europe of Fatherlands?

In view of the subversive forces and imperatives of the world market and of the increasing density of worldwide networks of communication and commerce, the external sovereignty of states, however it may be grounded, is by now in any case an anachronism. Also the increasing global dangers which have long since united the nations of the world unwittingly into an involuntary risk society render a practical necessity the creation of politically competent organizations on the supranational level. For the time being there is a lack of collective actors who could pursue a "domestic" politics on a global scale and would have the power to agree on the requisite parameters, arrangements, and procedures. Yet these circumstances have in the meantime compelled nation-states to unite into larger units. This process gives rise to dangerous legitimation deficiencies, as is shown by the example of the European Union. As new organizations emerge even further removed from the political base, such as the Brussels bureaucracy, the gap between self-programming administrations and systemic networks, on the one hand, and democratic processes, on the other, grows constantly. The helpless defensive reactions to these challenges again demonstrate the inappropriateness of a substantive conception of popular sovereignty.

Although the verdict of the Federal Constitutional Court of Germany concerning the Maastricht Treaty effectively ratifies the proposed expansion of the competences of the European Union, the justification it provides reaffirms the assumption that the principle of democracy would be unacceptably "emptied of content" if the exercise of state functions could not be tied once more to a "relatively homogeneous" citizen body. The Court, which takes its orientation from Hermann Heller (rather than Carl Schmitt), apparently wants to reject an ethnonationalist conception of the people. Nevertheless, it takes the view that a democratically legitimated state authority must flow from a political will-formation through which a people gives sufficient expression to its prepolitically given "national identity." If a democratic process is to take root at all, it must be possible for the citizen body to express legally "what unites them socially and politically in a relatively homogeneous manner."[47]

Given this basic assumption, the Court explains why the Maastricht Treaty will not found a European federal state into which the Federal Republic would be subsumed, thereby stripping it of its standing as a subject of international law (with the right to conduct independent judicial, domestic, and foreign policies, and to maintain its own defense forces).[48] In essence the argument of the Court aims to prove that the treaty does not establish the supreme constitutional authority (*Kompetenz-Kompetenz*) of an independent supranational legal subject (on an analogy with the United States, for example). The "alliance of states"[49] is supposed to owe its existence only to the "authorization of states which *remain* sovereign": "The Maastricht Treaty takes account of the independence and sovereignty of the member states by obligating the Union to respect the national identity of its member states."[50] Formulations such as these betray the *conceptual* barriers that the substantive concept of popular sovereignty erects to the transfer of sovereignty rights to supranational bodies. Moreover, they lead to astonishing conclusions that cannot be reconciled with earlier verdicts of the court on the primacy of European Community law.[51]

One would not be mistaken if one discerned in the tenor of the Court's justification a certain level of agreement with the conclusion that Hermann Lübbe draws from his philippic against the "United States of Europe;" as he confidently asserts in the subtitle, this union is "not to be": "The legitimacy of the future European Union . . . rests on the shared interests of its member countries, not on the self-determining will of a European citizenry. A European people has no political existence and, while there is no reason to think that an experience of mutual belonging among Europeans analogous to that which unites a people is inconceivable, at the present time there are no foreseeable circumstances under which a legitimacy-founding European will could take shape."[52] Against this skepticism one could point to the decisive historical experiences that undeniably unite the European peoples. For the catastrophes of two world wars have taught Europeans that they must abandon the mind-sets on which nationalistic, exclusionary mechanisms feed. Why should a sense of belonging together culturally and politically not grow out of these experiences—especially against the rich background of shared traditions which have long since achieved world-historical significance, as well as on the basis of the overlapping interests and dense networks of communication which have more recently developed in the decades of economic success of the European Community? Clearly Lübbe's euroskepticism is motivated by the artificial demand for a mutual belonging, "analogous to that of a people." But the "homogeneous people," which is again proving an impediment to reflection, is the wrong analogy.

The conflict-ridden history of state formation in the postcolonial period in Asia and especially in Africa does not offer a convincing counterexample. When the erstwhile colonies were "granted" independence by the withdrawal of the colonial powers, the problem was that these artificial territories achieved external sovereignty without already having an effective state power at their disposal. After the withdrawal of the colonial administration the new governments in many instances could assert their sovereignty internally only with great difficulty. Nor could this be achieved by means of repression: "The problem was everywhere to 'fill in' ready-made states with national content. This poses the interesting question, why postcolonial states had to be nations. . . . Nation-building as development means the extension of an active sense of membership to the entire populace, the secure acceptance of state authority, the redistribution of resources to further the equality of members, and the extension of effective state operation to the periphery."[53] The continuing tribal conflicts in formally independent postcolonial states serve as a reminder that nations only arise once they have traversed the difficult road from ethnically based commonalities among people who know one another to a legally mediated solidarity among citizens who are strangers to one another. In the West, this process of nation-state formation, which interconnects and mixes tribes and regions, took more than a century.

This process of integration itself demonstrates the true functional requirements for democratic will-formation, namely, the communicative circuits of a political public sphere that developed out of bourgeois associations and through the medium of the mass press. This enabled the same themes to acquire simultaneously the same relevance for a large public that remained anonymous and to spur citizens separated by great distances to make spontaneous contributions. This process gives rise to public opinions that aggregate themes and attitudes to the point where they exercise political influence. The correct analogy is obvious: the initial impetus to integration in the direction of a postnational society is not provided by the substrate of a supposed "European people" but by the communicative network of a European-wide political public sphere embedded in a shared political culture. The latter is founded on a civil society composed of interest groups, nongovernmental organizations, and citizen initiatives and movements, and will be occupied by arenas in which the political parties can directly address the decisions of European institutions and go beyond mere tactical alliance to form a European party system.[54]

6

Does Europe Need a Constitution? Response to Dieter Grimm

I basically agree with Dieter Grimm's diagnosis [of the current constitutional status of the European Union][1]—however, an analysis of its presuppositions leads me to draw a different political conclusion.

The Diagnosis

From a constitutional perspective, one can discern a contradiction in the European Union's present situation. On the one hand, the EU is a supranational organization established by international treaties and without a constitution of its own. In this respect it is not a state (in the modern sense of a constitutional state characterized by a monopoly on violence and a domestically and internationally recognized sovereignty). On the other hand, Community institutions create European law that binds the member states—thus the EU exercises a supreme authority previously claimed only by individual states. From this results the oft-bemoaned democratic deficit. Commission and Council pronouncements, as well as decisions by the European Court, are intervening ever more profoundly into the member states' internal affairs. Within the framework of the sovereignty rights conferred upon the Union, the European executive may enforce its pronouncements over and against the opposition of the national governments. At the same time, as long as the European Parliament is only equipped with weak competences, these pronouncements and enactments lack direct democratic legitimation.

The executive institutions of the community derive their legitimacy from that of the member governments. They are not institutions of a state that is itself constituted by the act of will on the part of the united citizens of Europe. The European passport does not as yet confer rights constitutive for democratic citizenship.

Political Conclusion

In contrast with the federalists who recommend a democratic pattern for the EU, Grimm warns against any further erosion of national competences by European law. The democratic deficit would not be effectively filled by a "statist shortcut" to the problem, but rather deepened. New political institutions, such as a European Parliament with the usual powers, a government formed out of the Commission, a Second Chamber replacing the Council, and a European Court of Justice with expanded competences, in themselves offer no solutions. If they are not filled with life, they will instead accelerate the tendencies toward autonomization of bureaucratized politics already apparent within the national frameworks. The real prerequisites for a European-wide integration of citizen will-formation have been absent up to now. Constitutional euroskepticism thus amounts to the empirically based argument that as long as there is not a European people that is sufficiently "homogeneous" to form a democratic will, there should be no constitution.

The Discussion

My reflections are directed against (1) the incomplete account of the alternatives and (2) the not entirely unambiguous normative justification of the functional requirements for democratic will-formation.

(1) Grimm presents us with the unwelcome consequences that would result from the transition of the European Community to a democratically constituted, federal state should the new institutions not take root. So long as a European-networked civil society, a European-wide political public sphere, and a common political culture are lacking, the supranational decision processes would become in-

creasingly independent of the still nationally organized processes of opinion- and will-formation. This prognosis of the dangers involved strikes me as plausible. But what is the alternative?

Grimm's preferred option seems to imply that the constitutional status quo can at least freeze the extant democratic deficit. Completely independently of constitutional innovations, however, this deficit expands day by day because the economic and social dynamics, even within the existing institutional framework, perpetuate the erosion of national powers through European law. As Grimm himself acknowledges, "The democratic principle is valid for the member states whose own decision capabilities are however diminishing: decisional capability is accruing to the European Community where the democracy principle is developing only weakly." But if the gap is steadily widening between the European authorities' expanding scope and the inadequate legitimation of the proliferating European regulations, then decisively adhering to an exclusively nation-state oriented mode of legitimation does not necessarily mean opting for the lesser evil. The federalists at least accept the foreseeable—and perhaps avoidable—risk of the autonomization of supranational organizations as a challenge. The euroskeptics have, from the start, acquiesced in the supposedly irresistible erosion of democratic substance so that they do not have to leave what appears to be the reliable shelter of the nation-state.

In fact, the shelter is becoming increasingly less comfortable. The debates on national economic competitiveness and the international division of labor in which we are engaged make us aware of quite another gap—a gap between the nation-state's increasingly limited maneuverability and the imperatives of modes of production interwoven worldwide. Modern revenue-states profit from their respective economies only as long as there are "national economies" that can still be influenced by political means. With the denationalization of the economy, especially of the financial markets and of industrial production itself, and above all with the globalization and rapid expansion of labor markets, national governments today are increasingly compelled to accept permanently high unemployment and the marginalization of a growing minority for the sake of international competitiveness. If the welfare state is to be preserved at least in its essentials and if the creation of a separate underclass is to be avoided, then institutions capable of acting supranationally must be formed. Only regionally comprehensive regimes like the European Community can still affect the global system along the lines of a coordinated world domestic policy.

In Grimm's account, the EU appears as an institution to be *put up with*, and with whose abstractions we must live. The reasons we should *want* it politically are not presented. I submit that the greater danger is posed by the autonomization of globalized networks and markets which simultaneously contribute to the fragmentation of public consciousness. If these systemic pressures are not met by politically capable institutions, there will be a resurgence of the crippling fatalism of the Old Empires in the midst of highly mobile modern economies. The decisive elements of this future scenario would be the postindustrial misery of the "surplus" population produced by the surplus society—the Third World within the First—and an accompanying moral erosion of political community. *This* future-present would in retrospect see itself as the future of a past illusion—the democratic illusion according to which societies could still determine their own destinies through political will and consciousness.

(2) I have not yet said anything about the ancillary problem of supranational bodies' becoming increasingly independent, a problem that Grimm rightly emphasizes. Naturally any assessment of the chances for a European-wide democracy depends in the first place upon empirically grounded arguments. But we first have to determine the functional requirements; and for that, the normative perspective in which these requirements are justified is crucial.

Grimm rejects a European constitution "because there is as yet no European people." This would seem at first sight to be founded upon the same premise that informed the tenor of the German Constitutional Court's Maastricht judgment—namely, the view that the state's democratic legitimation requires a certain homogeneity of the citizenry. However, Grimm immediately distances himself from Carl Schmitt's conception of *völkisch* or ethnic-cultural homogeneity: "The presuppositions for democracy are developed here not of the people, but from the society that wants to constitute itself as a political unit. But this presumes a collective identity, if it wants to settle its conflicts without violence, accept majority rule, and practice solidarity." This conception leaves open the question of how the called-for collective identity is to be understood. I see the nub of republicanism in the fact that the forms and procedures of the constitutional state, together with the democratic mode of legitimation, simultaneously forge a new level of social integration. Democratic citizenship establishes an abstract, legally mediated solidarity between strangers. This form of social integration, which first emerges with the nation-state, is realized in the form of a politically socializing *communicative context*. Indeed it depends upon the satisfaction of certain important functional requirements that cannot be fulfilled simply by administrative means. To these requirements belong conditions in which an ethical-political self-understanding of citizens can also develop and be reproduced communicatively—but not a collective identity that is *independent of the democratic process itself* and, as such, exists prior to that process. What unites a nation of citizens, as opposed to a *Volksnation,* is not some primordial substrate but rather an intersubjectively shared context of possible mutual understanding.

It is therefore crucial in this context whether one uses the term "people" in the juristically neutral sense of "state-constituting people," or whether one associates the term with notions of identity of some other kind. In Grimm's view the identity of a nation of citizens "need not" be "rooted in ethnic origin, but may also have other bases." I think on the contrary that it *must* have another basis if the democratic process is finally to guarantee the social integration of a differentiated—and today increasingly differentiating—society. This burden must not be shifted from the levels of political will-formation to presumed prepolitical substrates, for the constitutional state undertakes to foster social integration if necessary in the legally abstract form of political participation and to secure the substantive status of citizenship in democratic ways. The examples of culturally and ideologically pluralistic societies only serve to emphasize this normative point. The multicultural self-understanding of the nations of citizens formed in classical countries of immigration like the US is more instructive in this respect than that derived from the culturally assimilationist French model. If in the same democratic political community various cultural, religious, and ethnic forms of life are to exist among and with each other on equal terms, then the majority culture must become sufficiently detached from its traditional, historically explicable fusion with the *political* culture shared by all citizens.

To be sure, a politically constituted context of solidarity between citizens who, despite remaining strangers to one another, are supposed to stand up for each other is a communicative context *involving demanding preconditions*. On this point there is no disagreement. The core is formed by a political public sphere which enables citizens to take positions at the same time on the same topics of the same relevance. This public sphere must not be deformed through either external or internal coercion. It must be embedded in the context of a freedom-valuing political culture and be supported by a liberal associational structure of a civil society. Socially relevant experience from still-intact private spheres must flow into such a civil society so that they may be processed there for public treatment. Political parties that have not become integrated into the state apparatus must remain rooted in this complex so that they can mediate between the spheres of informal public communication, on the one hand, and the institutionalized deliberation and decision-making processes, on the other. Accordingly, from a normative perspective there can be no European federal state worthy of the title of a European democracy unless a European-wide, integrated public sphere develops in the ambit of a common political culture: a civil society encompassing interest associations, nongovernmental organizations, citizens' movements, etc., and naturally a party system appropriate to a European arena. In short, this entails public communication that transcends the boundaries of the thus far limited national public spheres.

Certainly, the ambitious functional requirement of democratic will-formation can scarcely be sufficiently fulfilled within the present nation-state framework; this is all the more true for Europe. What concerns me, however, is the perspective from which these functional prerequisites are normatively justified; for this normative standpoint in a certain sense prejudices the empirical evaluation of the present difficulties. These must, for the time being, seem insuperable if a prepolitical collective identity is regarded as necessary, as independent cultural substrate which is *merely articulated* in the fulfillment of the said functional requirements. But a communicative understanding of democracy, one that Grimm also seems to favor, can no longer rest upon such a concretist understanding of "the people." This notion falsely projects homogeneity where in fact there is only heterogeneity.

The ethical-political self-understanding of citizens in a democratic community must not be taken as a historical-cultural a priori that makes democratic will-formation possible, but rather as the fluid content of a circulatory process that is generated through the legal institutionalization of citizens' communication. This is precisely how national identities were formed in modern Europe. Therefore it is to be expected that the political institutions that would be created by a European constitution would have a catalytic effect. Europe has been integrating economically, socially, and administratively for some time and in addition can base itself on a common cultural background and the shared historical experience of having happily overcome nationalism. Given the political will, there is no a priori reason it cannot create the politically necessary communicative context once the constitutional basis for such a context has been laid down. Even the requirement of a common language—English as a second first language—ought not be an insurmountable obstacle given the existing level of formal schooling. European identity can in any case mean nothing other than unity within national diversity. And perhaps German federalism, as it developed after Prussia was shattered and the confessional division overcome, might not be the worst model.

IV

Human Rights: Global and Internal

7

Kant's Idea of Perpetual Peace: At Two Hundred Years' Historical Remove

For Kant, the "perpetual peace" invoked by the Abbé St. Pierre is an ideal that should lend the idea of a cosmopolitan order attractiveness and intuitive force. With this Kant introduces a third dimension into his legal theory: cosmopolitan law (*das Recht der Weltbürger*), an innovation with far-reaching implications, takes its place alongside state law and international law. The republican order of a democratic state founded on human rights calls for something more than the weak regulation of belligerent international relations by international law. Rather, the legal principles implemented within single states should lead ultimately to a global legal order that unites all peoples and abolishes war: "All forms of the state are based on the idea of a constitution which is compatible with the natural rights of man, so that those who obey the law should also act as a unified body of legislators. And if we accordingly think of the commonwealth in terms of concepts of pure reason, it may be called a Platonic *ideal* (*respublica noumenon*), which is not an empty figment of the imagination, but the eternal norm of all civil constitutions whatsoever, and a means of ending all wars."[1] The conclusion—"ending all wars"—is surprising. It points to the fact that the norms of international law that regulate war and peace are only provisionally valid, that is, they are valid only until the process of legal pacification for which Kant prepares the ground with his work "Perpetual Peace" has brought about a cosmopolitan order and thereby abolished war.

Of course, Kant developed this idea within the conceptual framework of social contract theory (*Vernunftrecht*) and against the background of the specific historical experiences of his time. Both now separate us from Kant. With the undeserved hindsight of later generations, we can now see that his proposals are beset with conceptual difficulties and that they are no longer consonant with our historical experiences. Hence in the following I will first sketch the premises that form Kant's starting point. They affect all three steps of his argument: the definition of the goal, perpetual peace; the description of the actual project, the appropriate legal form of a federation of nations; and, finally, the solution in the philosophy of history to the problem posed by this project, the gradual realization of the idea of a cosmopolitan order (I). Following this, I will examine how Kant's idea stands up in light of the historical experience of the last two hundred years (II) and how it must be reformulated in light of the contemporary global situation (III). The present alternative to regression to the state of nature which has been proposed by legal scholars, political scientists, and philosophers, namely the idea of a cosmopolitan democracy,[2] has provoked strong objections. But these objections to the universalism of cosmopolitan law and a politics of human rights lose their force once we appropriately differentiate between law and morality in the concept of human rights (IV). This differentiation also provides the key to a metacriticism of Carl Schmitt's influential arguments against the humanistic foundation of legal pacifism (V).

I

Kant defines the *goal* of the sought-for "lawful condition" among peoples negatively, as the abolition of war: "there is to be no war;" the "heinous waging of war" must come to an end.[3] Kant justifies the desirability of such a peace in reference to the evils of the kind of warfare being waged by the princes of Europe at that time with the aid of their mercenary armies. Kant does not accord primary importance among these evils to the victims of war, but instead to the "horrors of violence" and the "devastation," and above all, to the plundering and impoverishment of the country resulting from the considerable burdens of debt that arise from war, and he mentions as possible consequences of war subjugation, the loss of liberty, and foreign domination. In addition, there is the corruption of morals that occurs when subjects are instigated by the government to commit such criminal acts as spying and spreading false information or to commit acts of treachery, for example, as snipers or assassins. Here we encounter the panorama of limited war, which became institutionalized as a legitimate means of solving conflicts via international law in the system of the balance of powers after the Peace of Westphalia of 1648. The outcome of such wars defines the state of peace. And just as a specific peace treaty ends the evil of a particular war, so the peace alliance is now supposed to "put an end to war forever" and abolish the evils of war as such. This is what is meant by "perpetual peace." But the peace in question is as limited as the war from which it arises.

Kant had in mind local wars between individual states or alliances; he had no inkling of world wars. He was thinking of wars between regimes and states, not yet of anything like ethnic and civil wars; of technically limited wars that still allowed for a distinction between combatants and the civilian population, not yet of anything like guerrilla warfare and terror bombing; of wars with politically defined aims, not yet of ideologically motivated wars of annihilation and expulsion.[4] Given the premise of local wars and limited warfare, the normative scope of international law extends only to rules for the conduct of war and for the regulation of peace. The right "to go to war," the so-called *ius ad bellum*, which has priority over right "in war" and "after war," is, strictly speaking, no right at all, for it merely expresses the arbitrary freedom that is accorded the subjects of international law in the state of nature, that is, in the lawless condition of their external relations.[5] The only norms of criminal law that can intervene in this lawless condition relate to the conduct of war itself, and even then they are only enforced by the courts of the states waging war. War crimes are crimes committed *in* war. Only since wars have become unlimited, and the concept of peace has undergone a corresponding extension, does the idea arise that war itself—in the form of a war of aggression—is a crime that deserves to be outlawed and punished. But Kant could not yet conceive of such a crime *of* war.

While perpetual peace is an important characteristic feature of a cosmopolitan order, it is still only a symptom of the latter. Kant must still solve the *problem* of how such a condition should be conceptualized from the point of view of law. He must specify what differentiates cosmopolitan law from classical international law—in other words, what is specific to *ius cosmopoliticum*.

Whereas international law, like all law in the state of nature, is only provisionally valid, cosmopolitan law would resemble state-sanctioned civil law in definitively bringing the state of nature to an end. Therefore, when describing the transition to the cosmopolitan order, Kant repeatedly draws on the analogy with the original social contract, that is, with that exit from the state of nature which establishes a particular state and makes it possible for citizens to live in legally secured freedom. Just as the social contract brought the state of nature between self-reliant individuals to an end, so too the state of nature between belligerent states should come to an end. In an essay published two years prior to "Perpetual Peace," Kant draws strict parallels between these two processes. Here, too, he mentions the destruction of welfare and the loss of freedom as the greatest evils and then continues: "And there is no possible way of counteracting this except through the constitution of a legal order among peoples [*Völkerrecht*], based upon enforceable public laws to which each state must submit (by analogy with the civil or political legal order among individual human beings). For a permanent universal peace by means of a so-called European balance of power is a pure illusion."[6] Kant speaks here of a "universal state [*Völkerstaat*] to whose power all the individual states would voluntarily submit." But just two years later Kant carefully distinguishes between "a federation of nations" (*Völkerbund*) and "a state of all peoples" (*Völkerstaat*).

The order henceforth described as "cosmopolitan" is supposed to differ from an internal legal order by virtue of the fact that states, unlike individual citizens, do not submit themselves to the public coercive laws of a superordinate power but retain their independence. The envisaged federation of free states which renounce war once and for all in their external relations is supposed to leave intact the sovereignty of its members. The permanently associated states preserve their supreme constitutional authority and are not subsumed into a world republic that would be endowed with all of the distinguishing features of a state. In place of the "positive idea of a world republic" is put the "negative substitute of a . . . federation likely to prevent war."[7] This federation is supposed to proceed from sovereign agreements under international law, which are now no longer understood on the model of the social contract. For these treaties do not establish any actionable legal rights of the parties against one another but only unite them into a permanent alliance, an "enduring and voluntary association." Thus this act of association into a federation of nations goes beyond the weak binding power of international law only in respect of its "permanence." Kant compares the federation of nations to a "permanent congress of states."[8]

The contradictory character of this construction is readily apparent. For in another passage Kant asserts that "By a *congress* is here understood only a voluntary coalition of different states which can be *dissolved* at any time, not a union (like that of the American states) which is based on a constitution. . . ."[9] Just how the permanence of this union, on which a "civilized" resolution of international conflict depends, can be guaranteed without the legally binding character of an institution analogous to a state constitution Kant never explains. On the one hand, he wants to preserve the sovereignty of its members by means of the proviso that they may dissolve their compact; this is what suggests the comparison with congresses and voluntary associations. On the other hand, the federation that founds a permanent peace is supposed to differ from merely transitory alliances in that its members feel *obligated* to subordinate their own *raison d'état* to the jointly declared goal of "not resolving their disputes by war, but by a process analogous to a court of law." Without this element of obligation, the peaceful congress of nations cannot become "permanent," nor can its voluntary association become "enduring;" instead, it remains hostage to an unstable constellation of interests and will inevitably fall apart, much as the League of Nations would years later. Kant cannot have *legal* obligation in mind here, since he does not conceive of the federation of nations as an organization with common institutions that could acquire the characteristics of a state and thereby obtain coercive authority. Hence he must rely exclusively on each government's own *moral* self-obligation. But such trust is scarcely reconcilable with Kant's own soberly realistic descriptions of the politics of his time.

Kant is very much aware of this problem but nevertheless glosses over it with a mere appeal to reason: "If (a) state says: 'There shall be no war between myself and other states, although I do not recognize any supreme legislative power which could secure my rights and whose rights I should in turn secure,' it is impossible to understand what justification I can have for placing any confidence in my rights, unless I can rely on some substitute for the union of civil society, i.e. on a free federation. If the concept of international right is to have any meaning at all, reason must necessarily couple it with a federation of this kind."[10] However, this affirmation leaves open the decisive question, namely, how the permanent self-obligation of states that retain their sovereignty can be ensured. Note that this does not yet concern the empirical issue of how the idea can be approximated, but rather how the idea itself is to be conceptualized. If the union of peoples is to be a legal, rather than a moral, arrangement, then it may not lack any of those characteristics of a "good political constitution" that Kant enumerates a couple of pages later—qualities of the constitution of a state that does not need to rely on "the good moral education" of its members, but ideally has the strength to foster such an education in turn.

Viewed historically, Kant's reticence concerning the project of a *constitutionally organized* community of nations was certainly realistic. The constitutional state which had only recently emerged from the American and French revolutions was still the exception rather than the rule. The balance of powers operated on the assumption that only sovereign states could be subjects of international law. Under these conditions, external sovereignty designates the capacity of a state to maintain its independence and hence the integrity of its borders in the international arena, if necessary by military force. Internal sovereignty refers to its capacity, based on the monopoly of the means of violence, to maintain law and order in its own territory by means of administrative power and positive law. Reason of state is defined in accordance with the principles of a power politics, which include engagement in prudent, limited wars, where domestic policy is subordinated to foreign policy. The clear separation between foreign and domestic policy rests on a narrow and politically sharply defined concept of power which is measured in the final analysis by the control over the reserve force of the military and the police.

As long as this classical-modern world of nation-states defines the horizon of thought, any conception of a cosmopolitan constitution that does not respect the sovereignty of member states necessarily seems unrealistic. This also explains why the possibility of a unification of peoples under the hegemony of a powerful state, which Kant evokes with the image of a "universal monarchy,"[11] does not represent a viable alternative: on the foregoing premises, such a ruling power would inevitably bring about "the most fearful despotism."[12] Because Kant does not transcend the horizon of his time, it is of course equally difficult for him to believe in any moral motivation for creating and maintaining a federation between free states dedicated to power politics. Kant sketches as a solution to this problem a philosophy of history with a cosmopolitan purpose which is supposed to lend plausibility, through a hidden "purpose of nature," to the improbable "agreement between politics and morality."

II

Kant identifies three basic quasi-natural tendencies that complement reason and are supposed to explain why a federation of nations could be in the enlightened self-interest of each state: (1) the peaceful character of republics, (2) the power of international trade to forge an association, and (3) the function of the political public sphere. Reviewing these arguments in a historical light is instructive in two respects. On the one hand their manifest content has been falsified by developments in the nineteenth and twentieth centuries. But on the other hand they direct our attention to historical developments that exhibit a dialectical tendency. Whereas these developments reveal that the premises on which Kant based his theory, shaped as they were by conditions as they appeared at the close of the eighteenth century, are no longer valid, they nevertheless also support the claim that a conception of cosmopolitan law appropriately reformulated for contemporary conditions might well meet with a supportive constellation of forces, depending on how we ourselves interpret the changed circumstances of the late twentieth century.

(1) Kant's first argument claims that international relations lose their belligerent character to the extent that the republican form of government prevails within states, because it is in the interest of the populations of constitutional states to compel their governments to pursue peaceful policies: "If . . . the consent of the citizens is required to decide whether or not war is to be declared, it is very natural that they will have great hesitation in embarking on so dangerous an enterprise. For this would mean calling down on themselves all the miseries of war. . . ."[13] This optimistic assumption has been refuted by the mobilizing power of an idea whose ambivalence Kant could not have recognized in 1795, that is, the idea of the nation. Nationalism was certainly a vehicle for the desired transformation of subordinated subjects into active citizens who identify with their state. However, it did not make the national state any more peace-loving than its predecessor, the dynastic absolutist state.[14] For from the perspective of nationalist movements the classical self-assertion of the sovereign state takes on the connotations of national independence. As a consequence the republican convictions of citizens were supposed to prove themselves in their willingness to fight and die for *Volk* and fatherland. Kant justifiably regarded the mercenary armies of his day as instruments for "the use of human beings as mere machines . . . in the hands of someone else" and called for the establishment of the citizen militia; but he could not foresee that the mass mobilization of recruits inflamed by nationalist passions would usher in an age of devastating, ideologically unlimited wars of liberation.

At the same time, the idea that a democratic order tends to foster nonbelligerent conduct toward other states is not completely false. Historical and statistical research shows that, although states with democratic constitutions do not necessarily conduct fewer wars than authoritarian regimes (of whatever kind), they are less likely to resort to force in their relations with one another. This finding can be given an interesting interpretation.[15] To the extent that the universalist value-orientations of a population accustomed to free institutions also shape foreign policy, a republican polity does not behave more peaceably all told, but the wars it conducts have a different character. The foreign policy of the state changes in tandem with the motivation of its citizenry. The deployment of military force is no longer exclusively determined by an essentially particularistic *raison d'état* but *also* by the desire to foster the international spread of nonauthoritarian states and governments. But if value preferences transcend the preservation of national interests to include the implementation of democracy and human rights, then the conditions under which the international balance of powers operates undergo a change.

(2) The subsequent history which we now look back on has dealt in a similarly dialectical way with the second argument. Kant was mistaken about the immediate situation, but indirectly he also turns out to have been correct. For Kant detected in the growing interdependence of societies generated by the exchange of information, persons, and commodities, but especially by the expansion of trade, a tendency favorable to the peaceful unification of peoples.[16] Trade relations expanded in the early modern period into the dense network of a world market, which according to Kant grounds an interest in securing peaceful relations through "mutual self-interest": "For the *spirit of commerce* sooner or later takes hold of every people, and it cannot exist side by side with war. And of all the powers (or means) at the disposal of the power of the state, *financial power* can probably be relied on most. Thus states find themselves compelled to promote the noble cause of peace."[17] However, Kant had not yet learned—as Hegel soon would from his reading of the English economists[18]— that capitalist development would lead to a conflict between social classes that threatens in two ways the peace and the presumptive peacefulness of politically liberal societies in particular. Kant did not foresee that the social tensions that initially intensify in the course of accelerating capitalist industrialization would both encumber domestic politics with class struggles and direct foreign policy into the channels of violent imperialism. Throughout the nineteenth and the first half of the twentieth centuries, European governments repeatedly exploited the mobilizing power of nationalism to deflect social conflicts outward and to neutralize them with foreign policy

successes. It was only after the catastrophes of the Second World War led to the depletion of the energies of integral nationalism that the class antagonisms were successfully pacified by means of the welfare state. This so altered the internal situation of the industrialized nations that, at least in the OECD sphere, the growing interdependencies between national economies led to the kind of "economization of international politics"[19] that Kant rightly hoped would have a pacifying effect. Today, globally dispersed media, networks, and systems in general necessitate increasingly dense symbolic and social interrelations, which lead to the constant reciprocal influence of local and far distant events.[20] These processes of globalization have rendered complex societies, with their delicate technological infrastructures, ever more vulnerable. Although military confrontations between the nuclear superpowers are becoming increasingly unlikely because of the huge risks involved, local conflicts with relatively numerous and horrible casualties are becoming ever more frequent. At the same time, globalization raises questions about the fundamental presuppositions of classical international law—the sovereignty of states and the sharp division between domestic and foreign policy.

Nongovernmental actors such as multinational corporations and internationally influential private banks undermine the formal sovereignty of nation-states. Today each of the thirty largest corporations operating on a global scale has an annual turnover greater than the gross domestic product of ninety countries represented in the UN. But even the governments of the economically most powerful countries are keenly aware of the gulf that is opening up between the limits of the range of action of nation states and the imperatives, not of world trade, but of global networks of productive relations. Sovereign states could profit from their economies only as long as they functioned as "national economies" over which they could exercise influence by political means. But with the denationalization of the economy, in particular with the increasing global interconnection of financial markets and industrial production itself, national politics loses its control over the general conditions of production[21] and with it any leverage for maintaining its standard of living.

At the same time, there is a blurring of the boundaries between domestic and foreign policy that are constitutive of state sovereignty.

The classical image of power politics is being altered not only by the additional normative standpoints of the politics of democratization and of human rights, but also by a peculiar diffusion of power itself. With the growing pressure for cooperation, more or less indirect forms of influence are gaining increasing importance—influence on the structuring of perceived situations, on the forging of contacts or the interruption of flows of communication, and on the definition of agendas and problems. Influence on the parameters within which other actors make their decisions is often more important than the direct implementation of one's own goals, the exercise of executive power, or the threat of violence.[22] "Soft power" displaces "hard power" and robs the subjects to whom Kant's association of free states was tailored of the very basis of their independence.

(3) Something similar holds, in turn, for the third argument Kant employs to dispel the suspicion that the projected federation of nations is a "mere chimera." In a republican polity, constitutional principles become the standards by which policies must admit of being publicly assessed. Such regimes cannot afford to "base their policies publicly on opportunistic machinations alone,"[23] even if they are only compelled to pay lip service to constitutional principles. To this extent the political public sphere has a surveillance function: it can prevent the implementation of "shady" policies that are inconsistent with publicly defensible maxims by exposing them to public criticism. On Kant's view, the public sphere can acquire an additional programmatic function to the extent that philosophers, in their capacity as "public teachers of the law," can "freely and publicly discuss the maxims of waging war and instituting peace" and can convince the public of citizens of the validity of their basic principles. Kant surely had the example of Frederick II and Voltaire in mind when he wrote this moving sentence: "It is not to be expected that kings will philosophize or that philosophers will become kings; nor is it to be desired, however, since the possession of power inevitably corrupts the free judgment of reason. Kings and sovereign peoples (i.e. those who govern themselves by egalitarian laws) should not, however, force the class of philosophers to disappear or to remain silent, but should allow them to speak publicly. This is essential to both in order that light may be thrown on their affairs and . . . is beyond suspicion."[24]

As the atheism controversy involving Fichte would reveal just a few years later, Kant had every reason to fear censorship. We may also forgive his trust in the persuasive power of philosophy and in the integrity of philosophers; historicist skepticism about reason is a product of the nineteenth century, and it was only in our century that intellectuals committed the ultimate betrayal. What is more important is that Kant still counted on the transparency of a surveyable public sphere shaped by literary means and open to arguments and which is sustained by a public composed of a relatively small stratum of educated citizens. He could not foresee the structural transformation of this bourgeois public sphere into a semantically degenerated public sphere dominated by the electronic mass media and pervaded by images and virtual realities. He could scarcely imagine that this milieu of "conversational" enlightenment could be adapted both to nonverbal indoctrination and to deception *by means of* language.

This veil of ignorance probably explains his bold, far-sighted anticipation, whose prescience is only today becoming apparent, of a *global* public sphere. For such a global public sphere is only beginning to emerge as a result of global communication: "The peoples of the earth (!) have thus entered in varying degrees into a universal community, and it has developed to the point where a violation of rights in *one* part of the world is felt *everywhere*. The idea of a cosmopolitan right is therefore not fantastical or overstrained; it is a necessary complement to the unwritten code of political and international right, transforming it into a universal right of humanity. Only under this condition [namely, that of a functioning global public sphere—J. H.] can we flatter ourselves that we are continually advancing toward a perpetual peace."[25]

The first events that actually captured the attention of the world public sphere and polarized opinions on a global scale were presumably the Vietnam War and the Gulf War. It was only very recently that the UN organized in quick succession a series of conferences on global issues of ecology (in Rio de Janeiro), on problems of population growth (in Cairo), on poverty (in Copenhagen), and on global warming (in Berlin). These "global summits" can be interpreted as so many attempts to bring at least some political pressure to bear on governments simply by thematizing problems important for human survival for the global public, that is, by an appeal to world opinion. To be sure one should not overlook the fact that this temporary, issue-specific public attention is still channeled through the established structures of national public spheres. Supporting structures are needed to institute permanent communication between geographically distant participants who simultaneously exchange contributions on the same themes with the same relevance. In this sense, there is not yet a global public sphere, nor even the urgently needed European public sphere. However, the central role played by a new type of organization—namely, nongovernmental organizations such as Greenpeace or Amnesty International—not only in these conferences but more generally in the creation and mobilization of transnational public spheres is at least an indication of the growing impact on the press and media of actors who confront states from within the network of an international civil society.[26]

The important role that Kant rightly accords publicity and the public sphere directs our attention to the relationship between the legal constitution and the political culture of a polity.[27] For a liberal political culture provides the soil in which the institutions of freedom put down their roots; at the same time, it is the medium through which progress in the political education of a populace is realized.[28] To be sure, Kant speaks of the growth of culture that leads to "greater agreement over principles"[29]; he also takes it that the public use of communicative freedoms translates into processes of enlightenment that affect the attitudes and modes of thought of the populace via political socialization. Kant speaks in this context of "the sympathetic interest which the enlightened man inevitably feels for anything good which he fully comprehends."[30] However, these remarks do not assume any systematic import on his theory, for the dichotomous conceptual frame of transcendental philosophy separates the internal from the external, morality from legality. In particular, Kant ignores the continuum that a liberal political culture establishes between the prudent pursuit of one's interests, moral insight, and custom; he ignores the connection between tradition on the one hand and critique on the other. The practices of such a culture mediate between morality, law, and politics and provide at the same time a suitable context for a public sphere that fosters political learning processes.[31] Hence Kant did not really need to fall back on a metaphysical purpose of nature in order to explain how a "pathologically enforced social union can be transformed into a moral whole."[32]

As these critical reflections indicate, Kant's idea of a cosmopolitan order must be reformulated if it is not to lose touch with a global situation that has changed fundamentally. The requisite revision of Kant's basic conceptual framework is made easier by the fact that the cosmopolitan idea itself has not remained fixed: ever since President Wilson's initiative and the founding of the League of Nations, it has been repeatedly taken up and implemented at political level. Since the end of the Second World War, the idea of perpetual peace has taken on a more tangible form in the institutions, declarations, and policies of the UN (as well as those of other international organizations). The challenge posed by the unprecedented catastrophes of the twentieth century has also given new impetus to Kant's idea. Against this somber background, the World Spirit, as Hegel would have put it, has lurched forward.

The First World War confronted the European societies with the terror and horrors of a territorially and technologically unlimited war, the Second World War with the mass crimes of an ideologically unlimited war. Behind the veil of the total war instigated by Hitler, the breakdown of civilization was so complete that it unleashed a worldwide upheaval and facilitated the transition from international law to cosmopolitan law. First, the outlawing of war already proclaimed by the Briand-Kellogg Pact of 1928 was translated into punishable criminal offenses by the Nuremberg and Tokyo military tribunals. These offenses are no longer limited to crimes committed during war, but incriminate war itself as a crime. Henceforth the "crime *of* war" can be prosecuted. Second, criminal law was extended to include "crimes against humanity," crimes carried out under the instructions of state organs and with the assistance of countless members of organizations, functionaries, civil servants, businessmen, and private individuals. With these two innovations, the states as subjects of international law for the first time lost the general presumption of innocence of an assumed state of nature.

III

A fundamental conceptual revision of Kant's proposal must focus on three aspects: (1) the external sovereignty of states and the altered character of relations among them; (2) the internal sovereignty of states and the normative limitations of classical power politics; and (3) the stratification of world society and the globalization of dangers that necessitate a reconceptualization of what is meant by "peace."

(1) Kant's concept of a permanent federation of nations that nonetheless respects the sovereignty of states is, as we have seen, inconsistent. Cosmopolitan law must be institutionalized in such a way that it is binding on the individual governments. The community of peoples must be able to ensure that its members act at least in conformity with the law through the threat of sanctions. Only in this way will the unstable system of states that assert their sovereignty through mutual threats be transformed into a federation with common institutions which assume state functions, that is, which legally regulate the relations between its members and monitor their compliance with these rules. The external character of international relations between states that form environments for each other is thereby transformed into a domestic relationship between the members of a common organization based on a legal code or a constitution. This is the significance of the UN Charter which (with the prohibition of violence in Article 2.4) outlaws offensive wars and (in Chapter VII) authorizes the Security Council to use appropriate means, and if necessary to initiate military actions, whenever "any threat to the peace, breach of the peace, or act of aggression" exists. At the same time, the UN is expressly forbidden to interfere in the internal affairs of a state (Article 2.7). Each state retains the right of military self-defense. In December 1991, the General Assembly once again reaffirmed this principle (Resolution 46/182): "The sovereignty, territorial integrity, and national unity of a state must be fully respected in accordance with the Charter of the UN."[33]

With these ambiguous regulations, which both restrict and guarantee the sovereignty of individual states, the Charter shows itself to be a response to a transitional situation. The UN does not yet have its own military forces; it does not even have forces it could deploy under its own command, let alone have a monopoly over the means of violence. For the implementation of its resolutions it depends on the voluntary cooperation of its members who have the competence to act. The lack of a power base was supposed to be compensated for by the creation of the Security Council, which binds the major world powers to the world organization as permanent members with veto rights. As is well known, this arrangement has led to decades of stalemate between the superpowers. And when the Security Council does take the initiative, it uses its discretion in a highly selective manner, completely disregarding the principle of equal treatment.[34] This problem has gained renewed currency as a result of the Gulf War.[35] Even the International Court in the Hague possesses only a symbolic if not completely negligible significance, as it only convenes when a suit is brought and moreover its judgments are not even binding (as was shown once again in the case of Nicaragua versus the United States).

Nowadays international security, at least in the relations between the nuclear powers, is guaranteed not by the normative framework of the UN but by arms reduction agreements and above all by "security partnerships." These bilateral treaties establish coordination mechanisms and inspections between the competing power blocks, so that a nonnormative, purely purposively grounded reliability of expectations is established through transparency in planning and the calculability of motives.

(2) Because Kant regarded the bounds of national sovereignty as inviolable, he conceived of the cosmopolitan community as a federation of states, not of world citizens. This was inconsistent in that Kant derived every legal order, and not just that within the state, from the original right that attaches to every person "qua human being." Every individual has a right to equal liberties under universal laws ("since everyone decides for everyone and each decides for himself"[36]). This founding of law in general on human rights privileges individuals as the bearers of rights and lends all modern legal orders an essentially individualistic character.[37] But if Kant holds that this guarantee of freedom—"what human beings ought to do by the laws of freedom"—is the essential purpose of perpetual peace and is so

moreover "in all three areas of public law—civil, international and cosmopolitan law,"[38] then he must not allow the autonomy of citizens to be preempted even by the sovereignty of their states.

The point of cosmopolitan law is, rather, that it bypasses the collective subjects of international law and directly establishes the legal status of the individual subjects by granting them unmediated membership in the association of free and equal world citizens. Carl Schmitt grasped this point and recognized that this conception implies that "each individual is simultaneously a world citizen (in the full juridical sense of the word) and a citizen of a state."[39] Since the supreme constitutional authority (*Kompetenz-Kompetenz*) now resides in the "world federal state" and individuals acquire immediate legal standing in this international community, the individual state is transformed into "a mere agency (*Kompetenz*) for individual human beings who assume double roles in their international and national functions."[40] The most important implication of a form of law that bypasses the sovereignty of states is the personal liability of individuals for crimes committed in the course of government and military service.

Current developments have also outstripped Kant in this regard. Based on the August 1941 North Atlantic Charter, the UN Charter of June 1945 imposes on its member states a general obligation to respect and promote human rights. The General Assembly specified these rights in an exemplary fashion in December 1948 in its "General Declaration of Human Rights" and has developed them further in the interim in numerous resolutions.[41] The UN does not leave the protection of human rights solely up to the nation-states; it has its own mechanisms for establishing that human rights violations have occurred. The Human Rights Commission has monitoring agencies and reporting procedures for basic social, economic, and cultural rights that are subject to the "proviso of the possible;" in addition, for cases of civil and political rights it has set up formal complaint procedures. Though it is not universally recognized by all signatory states, the individual right of appeal, which gives individual citizens means of legal recourse against their own governments, is in theory of greater significance than states' right of appeal. But until now there has existed no supranational criminal court that could bring confirmed cases of human rights violations to trial and pass judgment on them. At the recent Vienna conference on human rights it was not possible to win agreement even on the proposal to appoint a UN High Commissioner for Human Rights. Ad hoc war crime tribunals on the model of the Nuremberg and Tokyo international military tribunals have thus far remained the exception.[42] To be sure, the UN General Assembly has recognized the guiding principles on which the judgments of these tribunals were based as "principles of international law." To this extent it is false to claim that the trials of leading Nazi military figures, diplomats, ministers, doctors, bankers, and industrial leaders were "once-off" occurrences without the power to establish legal precedents.[43]

The weak link in the global protection of human rights remains the absence of an executive power that could enforce the General Declarations of Human Rights, if necessary by curtailing the sovereign power of nation-states. Since human rights would have to be implemented in many cases despite the opposition of national governments, international law's prohibition of intervention is in need of revision. Where a functioning state power is not entirely absent, as in the case of Somalia, the world organization undertakes an intervention only with the agreement of the governments concerned (as in Liberia and in Bosnia/Croatia).[44] However, during the Gulf War the UN took the first steps in a new direction—if not in its legal justification, then at least de facto—with Resolution 688 of April 1991. In that instance it appealed to the right of intervention which Chapter VII of its Charter grants it in cases of "threats to international security;" in this sense, from a juridical point of view they did not intervene in "the internal affairs" of a sovereign state even in this case. But that this is precisely what they in effect did was not lost on the allies, when they instituted no-fly zones in Iraqi air space and deployed ground troops in northern Iraq to secure "safe havens" for Kurdish refugees (which Turkey has in the interim abused) to protect members of a national minority against their own state.[45] The British Foreign Minister spoke on this occasion of an "expansion of the limits of international action."[46]

(3) The basic conceptual revisions necessitated by changes in the nature of international relations and the normative curtailment of the room for maneuver of sovereign states have implications for the

conception of a federation of peoples and a cosmopolitan order. These are reflected in part in the demanding norms that already exist; but there is still a large discrepancy between the letter and the observance of these norms. The contemporary world situation can be understood at best as a transitional stage between international and cosmopolitan law. But many indications seem to point instead to a regression to nationalism. This judgment depends in the first place on how one assesses the dynamic of "accommodating" trends. We have traced the dialectical unfolding of the developments that Kant examined under the headings of the peacefulness of republics, the unifying power of global markets, and the normative pressure of liberal public spheres. Today these tendencies are confronted with an unforeseen constellation of circumstances.

Kant envisaged that the association of free states would expand in such a way that more and more states would crystallize around a core of an avant garde of peaceful republics: "For if by good fortune one powerful and enlightened nation can form a republic . . . , this will provide a focal point for a federal association among other states . . . and the whole will gradually spread further and further by a series of alliances of this kind."[47] But, as a matter of fact, the present world organization unites virtually *all* states under its roof, regardless of whether or not they already have republican constitutions and respect human rights. World political unity finds expression in the UN General Assembly in which all governments have equal rights of representation. At the same time, the world organization abstracts not only from the differences in legitimacy among its members within the community of *states,* but also from differences in their status within a stratified world *society.* I speak of a "world society" because communication systems and markets have created a global network; at the same time, one must speak of a "stratified" world society because the mechanism of the world market couples increasing productivity with growing impoverishment and, more generally, processes of economic development with processes of underdevelopment. Globalization splits the world in two and at the same time forces it to act cooperatively as a community of shared risks.

From the perspective of political science, the world since 1917 has disintegrated into three worlds. To be sure, the symbols of the First, Second, and Third Worlds have taken on a new meaning since

1989.[48] The *Third World* today consists of territories where the state infrastructure and monopoly of the means of violence are so weakly developed (Somalia) or have disintegrated to such an extent (the former Yugoslavia), where the social tensions are so extreme and the threshold of tolerance of political culture so low, that indirect violence of a Mafia-like or fundamentalist variety disrupts internal order. These societies are threatened by processes of national, ethnic, or religious disintegration. In fact, the vast majority of the wars that have raged in recent decades, often unnoticed by the global public, were civil wars. By contrast, the *Second World* is shaped by the legacy of power politics inherited from Old Europe by the nation-states that emerged from decolonization. Internally these states often seek to compensate for instabilities through authoritarian constitutions and in their foreign relations obstinately insist on sovereignty and non-intervention (as, for example, in the Gulf region). They rely on military force and are guided exclusively by the logic of the balance of power. Only the states of the *First World* can afford to harmonize their national interests to a certain extent with the norms that define the halfhearted cosmopolitan aspirations of the UN.

R. Cooper lists as indicators that a state belongs to the First World the increasing irrelevance of territorial disputes and the tolerance of internal pluralism; the mutual cross-national exercise of influence on matters that have traditionally counted as domestic concerns and, more generally, the increasing fusion of domestic and foreign policy; the sensitivity to the influence of liberal public spheres; the renunciation of military force as a means of solving conflicts and the juridification of international relations; and, finally, the preference for partnerships that base security on the transparency and reliability of expectations. The First World thus defines so to speak the meridian of a present by which the political simultaneity of economic and cultural nonsimultaneity is measured. Kant, who as a child of the eighteenth century still thought unhistorically, ignored these facts and thereby overlooked the real abstraction that must be accomplished by the community of nations and that the world organization must take into account in its policies.

The politics of the UN can take account of this "real abstraction" only if it works to overcome existing social tensions and economic imbalances. In turn, this aim can succeed only if, in spite of the stratification of world society, a consensus emerges in at least three areas: a shared historical consciousness of the nonsimultaneity of societies which are nevertheless simultaneously dependent on a peaceful coexistence; a normative agreement concerning human rights whose interpretation at the moment is a matter of dispute between the West, on the one hand, and the Asians and Africans, on the other[49]; and finally a shared conception of the desirable state of peace. A purely negative conception of peace was sufficient for Kant's purposes. Today this is unsatisfactory not only because of the breakdown of the limits on the conduct of war, but above all because wars have social causes.

According to a proposal offered by Dieter and Eva Senghass,[50] the complexity of the causes of war calls for a conception of peace as a *process* which unfolds in a nonviolent manner and which aims not merely to prevent violence but to satisfy the real preconditions for a peaceful coexistence of groups and peoples. The implementation of regulations should neither harm the existence and self-respect of the members, nor so impair vital interests and justice concerns that the parties to the conflict end up resorting to violence when the procedural possibilities have been exhausted. Policies that take their orientation from such a concept of peace will employ all means short of military force, including humanitarian intervention, to influence the internal affairs of formally sovereign states with the goal of promoting self-sustaining economies and tolerable social conditions, democratic participation, the rule of law, and cultural tolerance. Such strategies of nonviolent intervention designed to promote processes of democratization[51] rely on the fact that global interconnections have rendered *all* states dependent on their environments and have made them sensitive to the "soft" power of indirect influence, up to and including explicitly imposed economic sanctions.

Of course, with the increasing complexity of goals and the increasing costliness of strategies, the difficulties of implementation also increase, which tends to dissuade the leading powers from taking the initiative and bearing the costs. I would like to mention just four variables that are important in this regard: the composition and the voting-regulations of the Security Council whose members have to act in concert; the political culture of states whose governments can be induced to adopt short-term "selfless" policies only if they are subject to the normative pressures emanating from mobilized public spheres; the formation of regional regimes, which would for the first time provide the world organization with an effective infrastructure; and, finally, the gentle pressure toward globally coordinated action exerted by the awareness of global dangers. The dangers are manifest: ecological imbalances, asymmetries in standards of living and economic power, large-scale technologies, the arms trade (in particular, the spread of atomic, biological, and chemical weapons), terrorism, drug-related criminality, and so forth. Those who do not completely despair of the learning capacity of the international system have to rest their hopes on the fact that the globalization of these dangers has in fact long since united the world into an involuntary community of shared risks.

IV

The timely reformulation of the Kantian idea of a cosmopolitan pacification of the state of nature between states has on the one hand inspired efforts to reform the UN and, more generally, to expand supranational agencies in the different regions of the world. Such efforts aim to improve the institutional framework for a politics of human rights, which has made headway since the Presidency of Jimmy Carter but has also suffered debilitating setbacks (1). On the other hand, the politics of human rights has met with strong opposition from those who view the attempt to implement human rights at the institutional level as a self-destructive moralization of politics. However, this criticism is often based on a confused conception of human rights that does not differentiate sufficiently between the dimensions of politics, law, and morality (2).

(1) The "rhetoric of universalism" against which this criticism is directed finds its boldest expression in proposals to extend the UN into a "cosmopolitan democracy." These reform proposals focus on three points: the establishment of a world parliament, the construction of a global judicial system, and the long overdue reorganization of the Security Council.[52]

The UN still exhibits features of a "permanent congress of states." If it is to shed the character of a mere assembly of government delegations, the General Assembly must be transformed into a kind of upper house and divide its competences with a second chamber.[53] In this parliament, peoples would be represented as the totality of world citizens not by their governments but by directly elected representatives. Countries that refuse to permit deputies to be elected by democratic procedures (giving special consideration to their national minorities) could be represented in the interim by nongovernmental organizations appointed by the World Parliament itself as the representatives of oppressed populations.

The World Court in the Hague currently lacks the authorization to initiate prosecutions; it cannot make binding judgments and must restrict itself to arbitration functions. Moreover, its jurisdiction is restricted to relations between states; it does not extend to conflicts between individual persons or between individual citizens and their governments. In all of these respects, the powers of the Court would have to be expanded in accordance with proposals already worked out by Hans Kelsen a half century ago.[54] International criminal courts, which until now have only been convened on an ad hoc basis for specific war crime trials, would have to be institutionalized on a permanent basis.

The Security Council was intended to counterbalance the egalitarian General Assembly; it is supposed to reflect the de facto relations of power in the world. But some five decades later, this reasonable principle needs to be adapted to the altered global situation, and the requisite adaptations should not be limited to extending the representation to include other influential nation-states (for example, making Germany and Japan permanent members). Instead, it has been proposed that alongside global powers (such as the United States), regional regimes (such as the European Union) should be granted privileged voting rights. In addition, the requirement of unanimity between the permanent members must be abolished in favor of an appropriate form of qualified majority rule. In sum, the Security Council could be transformed into an executive branch capable of implementing policies on the model of the Council of Ministers of the European Union. Moreover, states will be willing to adapt their traditional foreign policy to the imperatives of a world domestic politics only if the world organization can deploy military forces under its own command and exercise police functions.

The foregoing reflections are conventional in taking their orientation from the organizational components of national constitutions. The implementation of a properly clarified conception of cosmopolitan law evidently calls for somewhat more institutional imagination. In any event, the moral universalism that informed Kant's proposals remains the authoritative normative intuition. However, a criticism has been made of this moral-practical self-understanding of modernity[55] which has been especially influential in Germany, beginning with Hegel's criticisms of Kant's moral philosophy, and has left deep traces down to the present. Carl Schmitt gave this argument its most incisive formulation and offered a justification that is in part insightful, in part confused.

Schmitt distills the slogan "Whoever speaks of 'humanity' is a liar" into the striking formula "Humanity, Bestiality." On this view, "the deception of humanism" has its roots in the hypocrisy of a legal pacifism that wants to conduct "just wars" under the banner of peace and cosmopolitan law: "When a state fights its political enemy in the name of humanity, it is not a war for the sake of humanity, but rather a war wherein a particular state seeks to usurp a universal concept in its struggle against its enemy, in the same way that one can misuse peace, justice, progress, and civilization in order to claim these as one's own and to deny the same to the enemy. The concept of humanity is an especially useful ideological instrument . . . ."[56]

Schmitt later extends this argument, which in 1932 was still directed against the United States and the other victors of Versailles, to the actions of the League of Nations and the UN. The politics of a world organization that takes its inspiration from Kant's idea of perpetual peace and is directed to the creation of a cosmopolitan order hearkens to the same logic, according to Schmitt: its pan-interventionism would inevitably lead to a pan-criminalization,[57] and hence to the perversion of the goal it is supposed to serve.

(2) Before I examine the specific context of these reflections, I would like to deal with the argument at a general level and uncover its problematic core. The two crucial statements are, first, that the politics of human rights leads to wars which under the guise of

police actions take on a moral character; and second, that this moralization brands opponents as enemies, and the resulting criminalization for the first time gives inhumanity a completely free hand: "We are familiar with the secret law behind this vocabulary and know that today the most terrible wars are conducted in the name of peace and that the worst inhumanity is committed in the name of humanity."[58] Schmitt justifies both statements in the light of two further premises: (a) that the politics of human rights implements norms that are part of a universalistic morality; and (b) that since moral judgments are governed by the code of "good" and "evil," the moral criticism of an opponent in war (or a political opponent) destroys the legally institutionalized restrictions on military conflicts (or on political disputes). Whereas the first premise is false, the second premise suggests a false assumption in the context of a politics of human rights.

(a) Human rights in the modern sense can be traced back to the Virginia Bill of Rights and the American Declaration of Independence of 1776 and to the *Declaration des droits de l'homme et du citoyen* of 1789. These declarations were inspired by the political philosophy of modern natural law, especially that of Locke and Rousseau. It is no accident that human rights first take on a concrete form in the context of these first constitutions, specifically as basic rights that are guaranteed within the frame of a national legal order. However, they seem to have a double character: as constitutional norms they enjoy positive validity, but as rights possessed by each person qua human being they are also accorded a suprapositive validity.

In the philosophical discussion of human rights this ambiguity has provoked much irritation.[59] On one conception, human rights are supposed to have a status somewhere between moral and positive law; on the other conception, they can assume either the form of moral or of juridical rights, though their content remains identical—that is, they constitute "a law (*Recht*) valid (*gültig*) prior to any state, though not for that reason already in force (*geltend*)." Human rights are "neither actually granted or denied, but are either respected or disrespected."[60] These formulas reflect a certain philosophical embarrassment and suggest that the constitutional legislator merely dresses up moral norms, however they are justified, in the form of positive law. In my view, this appeal to the classical distinction between natural and positive law sets the wrong parameters for the debate. The concept of human rights does not have its origins in morality, but rather bears the imprint of the modern concept of individual liberties, hence of a specifically juridical concept. Human rights are juridical *by their very nature*. What lends them the appearance of moral rights is not their content, and most especially not their structure, but rather their mode of validity, which points beyond the legal orders of nation-states.

The texts of historical constitutions appeal to "innate" rights and often have the solemn form of "declarations;" both features are supposed to dissuade us from what we would now call a positivist misunderstanding and express the fact that human rights are "not at the disposal" of the legislator.[61] But this rhetorical proviso cannot preserve human rights from the fate of all positive law; they, too, can be changed or be suspended, for example, following a change of regimes. Of course, as a component of a democratic legal order like the other legal norms, they enjoy "validity" in the dual sense that they are not only valid de facto, and hence are enforced by the sanctioning power of the state, but can also claim normative legitimacy, that is, they should be capable of being rationally justified. But apart from this typical feature, basic rights do indeed have a remarkable status regarding their justification.

As constitutional norms, human rights enjoy a certain privilege, which is manifested in part by the fact that they are constitutive for the legal order as a whole and to this extent determine a framework within which normal legislation must be conducted. But basic rights enjoy a privileged status even within the ensemble of constitutional norms. On the one hand, liberal and social basic rights have the form of general norms addressed to citizens in their capacity as human beings (not merely as members of a state). Though human rights are for the time being only realized within the framework of a nation legal order, within this sphere of validity they ground rights for all persons and not merely for citizens. The further normal legislation exhausts the implications of human rights, the more the legal status of resident aliens comes to resemble that of citizens.[62] It is this universal range of application, which refers to human beings as such, that basic rights share with moral norms. As is shown by the recent controversy (in Germany) over the voting rights of resident aliens, this also holds in certain respects for political rights. This points to a second and even more important aspect. Basic rights are equipped with a universal validity claim because they can be justified *exclusively* from the moral point of view. Certainly, other legal norms are *also* justified with the help of moral arguments, but in general further ethical-political and pragmatic considerations play a role in their justification, considerations that are inseparable from the concrete form of life of a historical legal community or from the concrete goals of particular policies. Basic rights, by contrast, regulate matters of such generality that moral arguments are *sufficient for their justification*. These arguments show why the implementation of such rules is in the equal interest of all persons qua persons, and thus why they are equally good for *everybody*.

On the other hand, this form of justification by no means robs the basic rights of their juridical character—it does not turn them into moral norms. Legal norms—in the modern sense of positive law—preserve their legal form, regardless of the kinds of reasons on the basis of which their claim to legitimacy can be justified. For they owe this character to their structure, not to their content. Basic rights are actionable individual rights whose meaning at least in part is to free legal persons in a carefully circumscribed manner from the binding force of moral commands by creating domains of legal conduct in which actors can act in accordance with their own preferences. Whereas moral rights only derive from duties that bind the free will of autonomous persons, legal entitlements to act in accordance with one's preferences enjoy priority over legal duties, which in turn arise from legal restrictions on these individual liberties.[63]

This conceptual privileging of rights over duties follows from the structure of modern coercive law first elaborated by Hobbes. Hobbes initiated a shift in perspective away from premodern law, which was still elaborated from a religious or metaphysical perspective.[64] In contrast to deontological morality which grounds duties, law serves to protect individual freedom of choice in accordance with the principle that everything is permitted which is not explicitly forbidden by general laws that set limits to freedom. To be sure, the generality of such laws must satisfy the moral point of view if the individual rights derived from them are to be legitimate—liberties must be equally distributed among citizens. But the concept of subjective right that circumscribes a domain of freedom of choice has structural consequences for modern legal orders in general. Hence Kant conceives of law as "the sum of the conditions under which the choice of one can be united with the choice of another in accordance with a universal law of freedom."[65] According to Kant, all special human rights are grounded in the "single original" right to equal individual liberties: "*Freedom* (independence from being constrained by another's choice), insofar as it can coexist with the freedom of everyone else in accordance with a universal law, is the only original right belonging to every man by virtue of his humanity."[66]

Consistent with this foundation, human rights take their place in the Doctrine of Right and only there. Like other subjective rights, they—and they preeminently—have a moral content. But without prejudice to this content, human rights belong structurally to a positive and coercive legal order which founds actionable individual legal claims. To this extent, it is part of the meaning of human rights that they claim the status of basic rights which are implemented within the context of *some* existing legal order, be it national, international, or global. The erroneous conflation of human rights with moral rights is suggested by the fact that, in spite of their *claim* to universal validity, human rights have thus far managed to achieve an unambiguous positive form only within the national legal orders of democratic states. Moreover, they remain only a weak force in international law and still await institutionalization within the framework of a cosmopolitan order that is only now beginning to take shape.

(b) But if the first premise—that human rights are in essence moral rights—is false, then the first of Schmitt's two statements is also undercut, that is, his statement that the global implementation of human rights obeys a moral logic and hence would lead to interventions that would be merely thinly disguised police actions. At the same time, the second statement—that an interventionist politics of human rights would inevitably degenerate into a "struggle against evil"—comes under severe pressure. At any rate, this statement suggests the false assumption that a classical international law tailored to limited wars would suffice to channel military conflicts in a "civilized" direction. Even if this assumption would withstand empirical objections, the police actions of a politically competent and democratically legitimated world organization would better merit the title of a "civil" regulation of international conflicts than would wars, however limited. For the establishment of a cosmopolitan order means that violations of human rights are no longer judged and combated *immediately* from the moral point of view, but rather are prosecuted, *like* criminal actions within the framework of a state-organized legal order, in accordance with institutionalized legal procedures. Precisely the juridification of the state of nature among states prevents a moral de-differentiation of law and guarantees the accused full legal protection, and hence protection against unmediated moral discrimination, even in the currently relevant cases of war crimes and crimes against humanity.[67]

V

I would like to develop this argument further through a metacritical examination of Carl Schmitt's objections. But first I must say something about the context of these objections, because the way Schmitt links the different levels of argument is not especially transparent. The criticism of a form of cosmopolitan law that bypasses the sovereignty of individual states concerned Schmitt primarily in connection with the "discriminatory conception of war"—as a war of aggression. This seems to lend his argument a sharply-defined legal focus. He consistently attacks the penalization of wars of aggression inscribed in the UN Charter and the ascription of legal liability to individual persons for a type of war crime that was unknown to that classical international law that held sway until the First World War. But Schmitt weighs down this legal approach, which is harmless in itself, with political considerations and metaphysical arguments. Hence we must first uncover the underlying theory (1), in order to get at the critique of morality that forms the core of the argument (2).

(1) Taken at face value, the juridical argument aims to civilize war through international law (a); and it is connected with a political argument whose sole concern seems to be to preserve the established international order (b).

(a) Schmitt does not reject the distinction between offensive and defensive wars for the pragmatic reason that it is difficult to operationalize. The juridical reason is rather that only a morally neutral concept of war, which also excludes personal responsibility for a penalized war, is consistent with the sovereignty of states as subjects of international law; for the *ius ad bellum*—that is, the right to go to war for any reason whatsoever—is constitutive of the sovereignty of states. At this stage in the argument, Schmitt is not as yet concerned with the supposedly disastrous consequences of moral universalism (as is made clear by the relevant text[68]), but rather with restrictions on how wars are conducted. Only the practice of noncondemnation of war can succeed in limiting military actions in war and provide protection against the evils of a total war, which Schmitt had already analyzed with admirable clarity before the Second World War.[69]

In this way Schmitt presents his call for a return to the status quo ante of limited wars merely as a more realistic alternative to a cosmopolitan pacification of the state of nature between states; in comparison with the effort to "civilize" war in terms of classical international law, abolishing war altogether is a much more far-reaching and, so it seems, utopian goal. But there are good empirical reasons for doubting the "realism" of Schmitt's proposal as well. The bare appeal to international law, which developed out of the wars of religion as one of the great achievements of Western rationalism, does not of itself show how the classical-modern world of the balance of powers can be reestablished as a practical matter. For international law in its classical form has manifestly failed in the face of total wars. Behind the territorial, technical, and ideological expansion of war there lurk momentous forces. These forces are still more likely to be tamed through the sanctions and interventions of an organized community of nations than through the legally ineffectual appeal to sovereign governments to conduct themselves in a reasonable manner; a return to the classical system of international law would effectively restore complete freedom of action to the collective actors who would have to reform their uncivilized conduct. This weakness in the argument is a first indication that the juridical line of argument is merely a façade behind which Schmitt conceals concerns of a different sort.

After the Second World War, Schmitt could save the consistency of his legal argument only by consigning the mass crimes of the Nazi period to a sui generis category in order thereby to preserve at least the appearance of moral neutrality for war itself. In 1945 in a brief prepared for the Nuremberg defendant Friedrich Flick, Schmitt consistently distinguished between war crimes and "atrocities" that transcend human comprehension "as characteristic expressions of a peculiarly inhuman mentality": "The command of a superior cannot justify or excuse such outrages."[70] That Schmitt made this distinction for purely tactical reasons in his role as a lawyer emerges with brutal clarity in the texts of his diary of a few years later. It is clear from this "Glossarium" that Schmitt not only wanted to see offensive war decriminalized but also the barbarous extermination of the Jews. He asks, "Was it a 'crime against humanity'? Is there such a thing as a crime against love?" and he doubts whether such "crimes" can be considered juridical matters at all, because the "objects of protection and attack" of such a crime cannot be circumscribed with sufficient precision: "Genocide, the murder of peoples—a touching concept; I have experienced an example of it myself: the extermination of the German-Prussian civil service in 1945." This rather prickly understanding of genocide led Schmitt to the more far-reaching conclusion: "'Crimes against humanity' is only the most general of all general clauses for destroying an enemy." In another passage, Schmitt asserts: "There are crimes against humanity and crimes for humanity. Crimes against humanity are committed by the Germans. Crimes for humanity are perpetrated on the Germans."[71]

Here another argument clearly emerges. The implementation of cosmopolitan law, with the consequent discriminatory conception of war, is not only considered as a false reaction to the evolution toward total war, but rather as its cause. Total war is seen as the contemporary manifestation of the "just war" that necessarily issues from an interventionist politics of human rights: "What is decisive is that the total character of war goes hand-in-hand with its claim to be just."[72]

Moral universalism now assumes the role of the explanandum and the argument shifts from the juridical to the moral level. Schmitt seemed to have recommended the return to classical international law in the first instance as a means of avoiding total war. But it is not even clear whether he regarded the total extension of war, hence the inhuman conduct of war, as the real evil, or whether his main fear was the devaluation of war as such. In any case, in a corollary to *The Concept of the Political* written in 1938, Schmitt describes the totalizing extension of the conduct of war to nonmilitary areas in such a way that total war takes on the merit of enhancing "national health": "The step beyond the purely military represents not only a quantitative expansion but a qualitative leap. For this reason it (i.e., total war) does not betoken an alleviation, but rather an intensification of hostility. The mere possibility of such an increase in intensity means that the concepts of friend and foe become political once again and are freed from the sphere of private and psychological rhetoric, even where their political character was completely attenuated."[73]

(b) Since there is no reason that an inveterate foe of pacifism should be overly concerned with the taming of totalized war, Schmitt's real concern may lie elsewhere, namely, in the preservation of an international order in which wars can still be waged and conflicts resolved in this way. The practice of refusing to condemn war maintains the regulatory mechanism of unconstrained national self-assertion. From this point of view, the evil to be avoided is not total war but the disintegration of a sphere of the political that rests on the classical division between domestic and foreign policy. Schmitt rationalizes this in terms of his own peculiar theory of the political. According to this theory, a legally pacified domestic policy must be supplemented by a belligerent foreign policy licensed by international law because the state, which enjoys a monopoly over the means of violence, can only uphold law and order in the face of the virulent force of subversive domestic enemies so long as it preserves and regenerates its political substance in the struggle against external enemies. This substance supposedly can only be renewed in the willingness of a nation to kill and be killed, since "the political" itself is essentially related to "the real possibility of physical killing."[74]

The political is manifested in the ability and the will of a people to recognize the enemy and to assert itself in the face of "the negation of its own existence" by "the otherness of the foreign."

These scurrilous reflections on "the essence of the political" need interest us here only for the role they play in Schmitt's argument. A political existentialism that imbues the concept of the political with vitalistic connotations forms the background for the assumption that the creativity of political power will be transformed into a destructive force once it is barred from the predatory international arena of "conquering violence." The global implementation of human rights and democracy, which is designed to foster world peace, would have the unintended effect of allowing war to go beyond the "formally just" bounds within which it was held by international law. Without the safety valve of a domain in which it is given free rein, war will become autonomous and overwhelm all spheres of civil life in modern society, and thereby destroy the complexity of functionally differentiated societies. This warning against the catastrophic consequences of an abolition of war through legal pacification can only be explained by a metaphysics that appealed to the then fashionable but by now rather hackneyed aesthetic of "the storm of steel."

(2) One can certainly distill one specific argument out of this belligerent *Lebensphilosophie*. According to Schmitt, behind the ideologically grounded "war against war," which transforms the limited military struggle between "organized national units" into an unlimited paramilitary civil war, lies the universalism of that humanist morality developed by Kant.

It is clear that Schmitt's reaction to UN peacekeeping and peacemaking interventions would have been no different than Hans Magnus Enzensberger's: "The rhetoric of universalism is specific to the West. Its postulates are supposed to hold in the same way for all people without exception. Universalism knows no distinction of near and far; it is unconditional and abstract. . . . But since all of our possibilities of action are finite, the gap between claim and reality yawns ever wider. Soon the threshold of objective hypocrisy is overstepped; universalism then reveals itself as a moral trap."[75] Thus it is allegedly the false abstractions of moral humanism that plunge us into self-delusion and mislead us into overburdening ourselves in a hypocritical manner. The presumed anthropological limits over which such a morality elevates itself are determined by Enzensberger, following Arnold Gehlen, in terms of spatial proximity and social distance: a being which is hewn from such crooked timber can function morally only in its immediate environment.[76]

When Schmitt speaks of hypocrisy he has instead Hegel's criticism of Kant in mind. He furnishes his contemptuous formula "Humanity, Bestiality" with an ambiguous commentary, which at first glance might just as well have come from Horkheimer: "We say: the main city cemetery and tactfully keep quiet about the slaughter house. But slaughtering is taken for granted; and it would be inhumane, even bestial, to utter the word 'slaughter' aloud."[77] This aphorism is ambiguous: it seems at first sight to be directed against the false, because mystifying, abstraction of Platonic general concepts by which we all too often suppress the reverse side of a civilization of victors, namely, the suffering of its marginalized victims. But this reading, after the fashion of a critique of ideology, would require precisely the kind of egalitarian respect and universal compassion invoked by the moral universalism Schmitt so vehemently opposes. What his antihumanism seeks to affirm (along with Mussolini's and Lenin's Hegel[78]) is not the sacrificial lamb, but rather slaughter—Hegel's slaughter-bank of peoples, the "honor of war"—for he goes on: "Humanity as such cannot wage war . . . . The concept of humanity excludes the concept of the enemy."[79] This is Schmitt's argument: moral humanism dangerously abstracts from the natural order of the political, the supposedly unavoidable distinction between friend and foe. Because it subsumes "political" relations under the categories of "good" and "evil," it turns the enemy into "an inhuman monster that must not only be repulsed but must be totally annihilated."[80] And because the discriminatory concept of war can be traced back to the universalism of human rights, it is ultimately the infection of international law by morality that explains the inhumanity of modern wars and civil wars perpetrated "in the name of humanity."

The reception of this critique of morality has had baleful effects, quite apart from the context in which Schmitt employs it. For it fuses a correct insight with a fatal mistake which draws sustenance from the friend-foe conception of the political. The kernel of truth is that an *unmediated* moralization of law and politics does in fact break through those protective zones that we want to have secured for legal persons for good, indeed moral, reasons. But it is a mistake to assume that this moralization can only be prevented by keeping international politics free from law and the law free from or purged of morality. Both assumptions are false given the premises of the rule of law and democracy: the idea of the constitutional state demands that the coercive force of the state be channeled both externally and internally through legitimate law; and the democratic legitimation of law is intended to guarantee that law remains in harmony with recognized moral principles. Cosmopolitan law is a logical consequence of the idea of the constitutive rule of law. It establishes for the first time a symmetry between the juridification of social and political relations both within and beyond the state's borders.

Schmitt's most revealing inconsistency is his insistence upon an asymmetry between a pacified legal order in the domestic sphere and a belligerent posture in foreign relations. Since he also conceives of internally imposed civil peace merely as a latent conflict between governmental authority and its repressed enemies, he grants the wielders of state power the right to declare representatives of the opposition to be internal enemies—a practice which has left its mark on the Federal Republic.[81] In contrast with the constitutional state, where independent courts and the whole body of citizens (in extreme cases, activated through civil disobedience) decide sensitive questions regarding unconstitutional measures, Schmitt leaves it to the discretion of the current rulers to criminalize political opponents as opponents in a civil war. Because constitutional controls are loosened in these marginal areas of internal affairs, precisely that state of affairs results which Schmitt fears will follow from the pacification of relations between states: the penetration of moral categories into a legally protected zone of political action and the tarnishing of opponents as agents of evil. But then it is inconsistent to demand that international relations should remain immune from regulations analogous to those of the constitutional state.

As a matter of fact, an *unmediated* moralization of politics would be just as harmful in the international arena as in the conflict between governments and their internal enemies—something that ironically Schmitt permits, because he locates the harm in the wrong place. But in both cases the harm results solely from the fact that a legally protected domain of political or state action is falsely coded in two ways: first it is moralized, that is, judged according to criteria of "good" and "evil," and then it is criminalized, hence condemned in accordance with criteria of "legal" and "illegal," without—and this is the decisive point that Schmitt suppresses—the legal preconditions of an impartial judicial authority and a neutral system of criminal punishment in place. The human rights politics of a world organization becomes inverted into a human rights fundamentalism only when it provides a moral legitimation under the cover of a sham legal legitimation for an intervention which is in reality nothing more than a struggle of one party against the other. In such cases, the world organization (or an alliance acting in its name) engages in deception, because it passes off a military conflict between two warring parties as a neutral police measure justified by enforceable law and by the judgments of a criminal court. "Morally justified appeals are in danger of taking on fundamentalist features when their goal is not to implement legal procedures for [enacting as well as] applying and implementing human rights, but instead are applied directly to the interpretive scheme by means of which accountability for violations of human rights is determined, and when they are the sole basis for the demanded sanctions"[82] (my interpolation).

Schmitt defends the further position that the juridification of power politics beyond the boundaries of a state, and hence the international implementation of human rights in an arena previously dominated by military force, *always and necessarily* leads to such human rights fundamentalism. This assertion is ill founded in that it is based on the false premise that human rights are moral in nature and hence that their implementation would imply a kind of moralization. The problematic aspect of the juridification of international affairs already mentioned does not result from the fact that actions previously understood as political are henceforth subsumed under legal categories. For, in contrast with morality, the legal code does not require that actions be subjected to an immediate moral evaluation in accordance with criteria of "good" and "evil." Klaus Günther clarifies the key point: "That a political interpretation (in

Carl Schmitt's sense) of violations of human rights is inadmissible does not mean that an unmediated moral interpretation can take its place."[83] Human rights should not be confused with moral rights.

But neither does the distinction between law and morality which Günther upholds imply that positive law has no moral content. Through the democratic procedure of political legislation, moral arguments (among other sorts) also flow into the justification of enacted norms and thereby into law itself. As Kant recognized, law differs from morality in the formal properties of legality. Certain aspects of conduct open to moral assessment (for example, convictions and motives) are per se exempted from legal regulation. But, above all, the legal code binds the judgments and sanctions of the prosecuting agencies to narrowly interpreted, intersubjectively testable conditions of constitutional procedures, which are designed to protect those accused. Whereas the moral person stands so to speak naked before the inner court of his or her conscience, the legal person remains wrapped in the protective mantle of—morally well-grounded—individual liberties. Therefore the correct response to the danger of an unmediated moralization of power politics is "not the demoralization of politics, but rather the democratic transformation of morality into a system of positive laws with legal procedures for their application and implementation."[85] Human rights fundamentalism is avoided not by renouncing the politics of human rights, but only through a cosmopolitan transformation of the state of nature among states into a legal order.

8
Struggles for Recognition in the Democratic Constitutional State

Modern constitutions owe their existence to a conception found in modern natural law according to which citizens come together voluntarily to form a legal community of free and equal consociates. The constitution puts into effect precisely those rights that individuals must grant one another if they want to order their life together legitimately by means of positive law. This conception presupposes the notion of individual rights (*subjektive Rechte*) and individual legal persons as the bearers of rights. Although modern law establishes a basis for state-sanctioned relations of intersubjective recognition, the rights derived from these relations protect the vulnerable integrity of legal subjects who are in every case individuals. In the final analysis it is a question of protecting these individual legal persons, even if the integrity of the individual—in law no less than in morality—depends on relations of mutual recognition remaining intact. Can a theory of rights that is so individualistically constructed deal adequately with struggles for recognition, in which what seems to be at stake is the articulation and assertion of collective identities?

A constitution can be thought of as a historical project that each generation of citizens continues to pursue. In the democratic constitutional state the exercise of political power is coded in a dual manner: the institutionalized handling of problems and the procedurally regulated mediation of interests must be understandable simultaneously as actualizing a system of rights.[1] But in the political arena those who encounter one another are collective actors contending about collective goals and the distribution of collective goods. Only in the courtroom and in legal discourse are rights asserted and defended as actionable individual rights, for which one can bring suit. Existing law also has to be interpreted in new ways in different contexts in view of changing needs and interests. This struggle over the interpretation and satisfaction of historically unredeemed claims is a struggle for legitimate rights in which once again collective actors are involved, combating a lack of respect for their dignity. In this "struggle for recognition" participants voice collective experiences of violated integrity, as Axel Honneth has shown.[2] Can these phenomena be reconciled with a theory of rights that is individualistically designed?

The political achievements of liberalism and social democracy that are the product of the bourgeois emancipation movements and the European labor movement suggest an affirmative answer to this question. Both attempted to overcome the disenfranchisement of underprivileged groups and with it the division of society into social classes; but where liberal social reform came into play, the struggle against the oppression of collectivities who were deprived of equal social opportunities took the form of a struggle for the social-welfarist universalization of civil rights. Since the bankruptcy of state socialism, this perspective has indeed been the only one remaining: the status of a dependent wage earner is to be supplemented with rights to social and political participation, and the mass of the population is thereby to be given the opportunity to live in realistic expectation of security, social justice, and affluence. A more equitable distribution of collective goods is to compensate for the unequal conditions of life in capitalist societies. This aim is thoroughly compatible with the theory of rights, because the primary goods (in Rawls's sense) are either distributed among individuals (like money, free time, and services) or used by individuals (like the infrastructures of transportation, health care, and education) and can thus take the form of individual claims to benefits.

At first glance, however, claims to the recognition of collective identities and to equal rights for cultural forms of life are a different matter. Feminists, minorities in multicultural societies, peoples struggling for national independence, and formerly colonized regions suing for the equality of their cultures on the international stage are all currently fighting for such claims. Does not the recognition of cultural forms of life and traditions that have been marginalized, whether in the context of a majority culture or in a Eurocentric global society, require guarantees of status and survival—in other words, some kind of collective rights that shatter the outmoded self-understanding of the democratic constitutional state, which is tailored to individual rights and in that sense is "liberal"?

Charles Taylor provides a complex answer to this question, an answer that advances the discussion significantly.[3] As the commentaries on his essay published in the same volume indicate, his original ideas also inspire criticism. Taylor remains ambiguous on the decisive point. He distinguishes two readings of the democratic constitutional state, for which Michael Walzer provides the terms *Liberalism 1* and *Liberalism 2*. These designations suggest that the second reading, which Taylor favors, merely corrects an inappropriate understanding of liberal principles. On closer examination, however, Taylor's reading attacks the principles themselves and calls into question the individualistic core of the modern conception of freedom.

I   Taylor's "Politics of Recognition"

Amy Gutmann makes the incontrovertible point that

full public recognition as equal citizens may require two forms of respect: (1) respect for the unique identities of each individual, regardless of gender, race, or ethnicity, and (2) respect for those activities, practices, and ways of viewing the world that are particularly valued by, or associated with, members of disadvantaged groups, including women, Asian-Americans, African-Americans, Native Americans, and a multitude of other groups in the United States.[4]

The same thing holds, of course, for *Gastarbeiter* [foreign workers] and other foreigners in Germany, for Croats in Serbia, Russians in the Ukraine, and Kurds in Turkey; for the disabled, homosexuals, and so on. The demand for respect is aimed not so much at equalizing living conditions as it is at protecting the integrity of the traditions and forms of life in which members of groups that have been discriminated against can recognize themselves. Normally, of course, the failure of cultural recognition is connected with gross social discrimination, and the two reinforce each other. The question that concerns us here is whether the demand for respect for one's cultural traditions follows from the principle of equal respect for each individual, or whether, at least in some cases, these two demands will necessarily come into conflict with one another.

Taylor proceeds on the assumption that the protection of collective identities comes into competition with the right to equal individual liberties (*subjektive Freiheiten*)—Kant's one original human right—so that in the case of conflict a decision must be made about which takes precedence. The argument runs as follows: Because the second claim distinguished by Gutmann requires consideration of precisely those particularities from which the first claim seems to abstract, the principle of equal rights has to be put into effect in two kinds of politics that run counter to one another—a politics of consideration of cultural differences on the one hand and a politics of universalization of individual rights on the other. The one is supposed to compensate for the price the other exacts with its equalizing universalism. Taylor spells out this opposition—an opposition that is falsely construed, as I will try to show—using the concepts of the good and the just, drawn from moral theory. Liberals like Rawls and Dworkin call for an ethically neutral legal order that is supposed to assure everyone equal opportunity to pursue his or her own conception of the good. In contrast, communitarians like Taylor and Walzer dispute the ethical neutrality of the law and thus can expect the constitutional state, if need be, actively to advance specific conceptions of the good life.

Taylor gives the example of the French-speaking minority that forms the majority in the Canadian province of Quebec. The francophone group claims the right for Quebec to form a "distinct society" within the nation as a whole. It wants to safeguard the integrity of its form of life against the Anglo-Saxon majority culture, among other things by means of regulations that forbid immigrants and the French-speaking population to send their children to English-language schools, that establish French as the language in which firms with more than fifty employees will operate, and that in general prescribe French as the language of business. According to

Taylor, a theory of rights of the first type would necessarily be closed to collective goals of this kind:

A society with collective goals like Quebec's violates this model. . . . On this model, there is a dangerous overlooking of an essential boundary in speaking of fundamental rights to things like commercial signage in the language of one's choice. One has to distinguish the fundamental liberties, those that should never be infringed and therefore ought to be unassailably entrenched, on one hand, from privileges and immunities that are important, but that can be revoked or restricted for reasons of public policy—although one would need a strong reason to do this—on the other.[5]

Taylor proposes an alternative model that under certain conditions would permit basic rights to be restricted by guarantees of status aimed at promoting the survival of endangered cultural forms of life and thus would permit policies that "actively seek to *create* members of the community, for instance, in their assuring that future generations continue to identify as French-speakers. There is no way that these policies could be seen as just providing a facility to already existing people."[6]

Taylor makes the case for his thesis of incompatibility by first presenting the theory of rights through a selective reading of Liberalism 1. He does not clearly define either the Canadian example or the legal reference of his problematic. Before I take up these two problems, I would like to show that when properly understood the theory of rights is by no means blind to cultural differences.

Taylor understands Liberalism 1 as a theory according to which all legal consociates are guaranteed equal individual freedoms of choice and action in the form of basic rights. In cases of conflict the courts decide who has which rights; thus the principle of equal respect for each person holds only in the form of a legally protected autonomy that every person can use to realize his or her personal life project. This interpretation of the system of rights is paternalistic in that it ignores half of the concept of autonomy. It does not take into consideration that those to whom the law is addressed can acquire autonomy (in the Kantian sense) only to the extent that they can understand themselves as the authors of the laws to which they are subject as private legal persons. Liberalism 1 fails to recognize that private and public autonomy are co-original. It is not that public autonomy supplements and remains external to private autonomy but rather that there is an internal, that is, conceptually necessary connection between the two. For in the final analysis, private legal persons cannot even attain the enjoyment of equal individual liberties unless they themselves, by jointly exercising their autonomy as citizens, arrive at a clear understanding about what interests and criteria are justified and in what respects equal things will be treated equally and unequal things unequally in any particular case.

But once we take this *internal* connection between democracy and the constitutional state seriously, it becomes clear that the system of rights is blind neither to unequal social conditions nor to cultural differences. The color blindness of the selective reading vanishes once we recognize that we ascribe to the bearers of individual rights an identity that is conceived intersubjectively. Persons, including legal persons, become individualized only through a process of socialization.[7] A correctly understood theory of rights requires a politics of recognition that protects the integrity of the individual in the life contexts in which his or her identity is formed. This does not require an alternative model that corrects the individualistic design of the system of rights through other normative perspectives. All that is required is the consistent actualization of the system of rights. There would be little likelihood of this, of course, without social movements and political struggles.

I would like to show this with reference to the history of feminism, which has had to make repeated attempts to realize its legal and political goals in the face of strong resistance. Like the development of law in Western societies in general, the feminist politics of equality during the past hundred years follows a pattern that can be described as a dialectic of *de jure* and *de facto* equality. Equality under the law grants freedoms of choice and action that can be realized differently and thus do not promote actual equality in life circumstances or positions of power. The factual prerequisites for the equal opportunity to make use of equally distributed legal competence must certainly be fulfilled if the normative meaning of legal equality is not to turn into its opposite. But the intended equalization of actual life circumstances and positions of power should not lead to *normalizing* interventions that perceptibly restrict the capacities of the presumed beneficiaries to shape their lives autonomously. As long as policies are focused on safeguarding private autonomy, while the internal connection between the individual rights of private persons and the public autonomy of the citizens who participate in making the laws is obscured from view, the politics of rights will oscillate helplessly between the poles of a liberal paradigm in the Lockean sense and an equally shortsighted social-welfare paradigm. This is true of equal treatment for men and women as well.[8]

Initially, the goal of the *liberal policies* was to detach the acquisition of status from gender and to guarantee women equal opportunity to compete for jobs, social standing, education, political power, and so on, regardless of the outcomes. But the formal equality that was partially achieved thereby only made the *de facto* unequal treatment of women all the more obvious. *Social-welfare policies,* especially in the areas of social, labor, and family law, responded to this with special regulations regarding pregnancy, motherhood, and the social burdens of divorce. Since then, of course, not only unfulfilled liberal demands but also the ambivalent consequences of successfully implemented social-welfare programs have become the object of feminist criticism—for example, the increased employment risks that women suffer as a result of these compensations, the over-representation of women in the lower wage brackets, the problematic notion of "child welfare," the increasing "feminization" of poverty in general, and so on. From the legal point of view there is a structural basis for this reflexively produced discrimination, namely, the over-generalized classifications of disadvantageous situations and disadvantaged groups. These "false" classifications lead to "normalizing" interventions into the way people lead their lives, with the result that the intended compensations turn into new forms of discrimination and instead of being guaranteed liberties people are deprived of freedom. In the domains of law that feminism is particularly concerned with, social-welfare paternalism is precisely that, because legislation and adjudication are oriented to traditional patterns of interpretation and thus serve only to strengthen existing gender stereotypes.

The classification of sex roles and gender-dependent differences touches fundamental levels of a society's cultural self-understanding.

Radical feminism is only now making us aware of the fallible nature of this self-understanding, which is fundamentally debatable and in need of revision. Radical feminism rightly insists that such *classifications,* which imbue with political significance the differences in experiences and life circumstances of specific groups of men and women with respect to the equal opportunity to exercise individual liberties, must be clarified in the political public sphere, specifically in public debates about the appropriate interpretation of needs.[9] Hence this struggle for equality for women is a particularly good illustration of the need for a change in the paradigmatic understanding of rights. The debate about whether the autonomy of legal persons is better ensured through the individual freedom of private persons to compete or through objectively guaranteed claims to benefits for clients of welfare-state bureaucracies is being replaced by a proceduralist conception of rights according to which the democratic process has to safeguard both private and public autonomy at the same time. The individual rights that are supposed to guarantee women the autonomy to shape their private lives cannot even be appropriately formulated unless those affected articulate and justify in public discussion what is relevant to equal or unequal treatment in typical cases. Safeguarding the private autonomy of citizens with equal rights must go hand in hand with activating their autonomy as citizens of the nation.

A "liberal" version of the system of rights that fails to take this connection into account will necessarily misconstrue the universalism of basic rights as an abstract leveling of distinctions, a leveling of both cultural and social differences. These differences must be interpreted in increasingly context-sensitive ways if the system of rights is to be actualized democratically. The process of universalizing civil rights continues to fuel the differentiation of the legal system, which cannot ensure the integrity of legal subjects without strict equal treatment, directed by the citizens themselves, of the life contexts that safeguard their identities. If the selective reading of the theory of rights is corrected to include a democratic understanding of the actualization of basic rights, there is no need to contrast a truncated Liberalism 1 with a model that introduces a notion of collective rights that is alien to the system.

II Struggles for Recognition: The Phenomena and Levels of Analysis

Feminism, multiculturalism, nationalism, and the struggle against the Eurocentric heritage of colonialism are related phenomena that should not be confused with one another. They are related in that women, ethnic and cultural minorities, and nations and cultures defend themselves against oppression, marginalization, and disrespect and thereby struggle for the recognition of collective identities, whether in the context of a majority culture or within the community of peoples. We are concerned here with emancipation movements whose collective political goals are defined primarily in cultural terms, even though social and economic inequalities as well as political dependencies are always also involved.

(a) Feminism is not, of course, a minority cause, but it is directed against a dominant culture that interprets the relationship of the sexes in an asymmetrical manner that excludes equal rights. Gender-specific differences in life circumstances and experiences do not receive adequate consideration, either legally or informally. Women's cultural understanding of themselves does not receive due recognition, any more than does their contribution to the common culture; given the prevailing definitions, women's needs cannot even be adequately articulated. Thus their political struggle for recognition begins as a struggle over the interpretation of gender-specific achievements and interests. Insofar as it is successful, it changes the relationship between the sexes along with the collective identity of women, thereby directly affecting men's understanding of themselves as well. The scale of values of the society as a whole is up for discussion; the consequences of this problematization extend into core private areas and affect the established boundaries between the private and public spheres as well.[10]

(b) The struggle of oppressed ethnic and cultural minorities for recognition of their collective identities is a different matter. Since these emancipation movements also aim at overcoming an illegitimate division of society, the majority culture's understanding of itself cannot remain untouched by them. But from the point of view of members of the majority culture, the revised interpretation of the achievements and interests of others does not necessarily alter their own role in the same way that the reinterpretation of the relations between the sexes alters the role of men.

Emancipation movements in multicultural societies are not a uniform phenomenon. They present different challenges depending on whether the situation is one of endogenous minorities becoming aware of their identity or new minorities arising through immigration, and on whether the nation faced with the challenge has always understood itself to be open to immigration on the basis of its history and political culture or whether the national self-understanding first needs to be adjusted to accommodate the integration of alien cultures. The challenge becomes all the greater the more profound are the religious, racial, or ethnic differences, or the historical-cultural disjunctions to be bridged. The challenge becomes all the more painful the more the tendencies to self-assertion take on a fundamentalist and separatist character, whether because experiences of impotence lead the minority struggling for recognition to take a regressive position or because the minority in question has to use mass mobilization to awaken consciousness in order to articulate a newly constructed identity.

(c) The position of ethnic and cultural minorities differs from that of peoples who see themselves nationalistically, as ethnically and linguistically homogeneous groups against the background of a common historical fate and who want to protect their identity not only as an ethnic community but as a people forming a nation with the capacity for political action. Nationalist movements have almost always modeled themselves on the republican nation-state that emerged from the French Revolution. Compared with the first generation of nation-states, Italy and Germany were "belated nations." The period of decolonialization after the Second World War represents yet another context. And the constellations that formed at the collapse of empires like the Ottoman Empire, the Austro-Hungarian Empire, or the Soviet Union were different still. The situation of national minorities like the Basques, the Kurds, or the Northern Irish, which emerged in the course of the formation of nation-states, is again different. A special case is the founding of the state of Israel, which emerged from both a national-religious movement and as a response to the horrors of Auschwitz, in the British Mandate of Palestine claimed by Arabs.

(d) Eurocentrism and the hegemony of Western culture are in the last analysis catchwords for a struggle for recognition on the international level. The Gulf War made us aware of this. Under the shadow of a colonial history that is still vivid in people's minds, the allied intervention was regarded by religiously motivated masses and secularized intellectuals alike as a failure to respect the identity and autonomy of the Arabic-Islamic world. The historical relationship between the Occident and the Orient, and especially the relationship of the First to the former Third World, continues to bear the marks of a denial of recognition.

This cursory classification of the phenomena nevertheless allows us to place the constitutional struggle between the Canadian government and Quebec on the borderline between (b) and (c). Below the threshold of a separatist movement to found their own state, the struggle of the French-speaking minority is clearly one for rights that would be accorded them as a matter of course if they were to declare themselves an independent nation—as Croatia, Slovenia, and Slovakia, the Baltic States, and Georgia have recently done. But they are aspiring to become a "state within a state," something for which a broad spectrum of forms of federalist constructions is available, ranging from a federal state to a loose confederation. In Canada the decentralization of sovereign state powers is bound up with the question of cultural autonomy for a minority that would like to become a relative majority within its own house. New minorities would arise in turn, of course, with a change in the complexion of the majority culture.

In addition to distinguishing the phenomena categorized above, we need to distinguish different levels of their analysis. Taylor's remarks touch on at least three discourses to which these phenomena have given rise.

(e) In the debate about political correctness these phenomena served as an occasion for American intellectuals to engage in a process of self-reflection about the status of modernity.[11] Neither of the two parties to the debate wants to pursue the project of modernity on its own terms, as a project that should not be abandoned.[12]

What the "radicals" see as an encouraging step into postmodernity and toward overcoming totalizing figures of thought is, for the "traditionalists," the sign of a crisis that can be dealt with only through a return to the classical traditions of the West. We can leave this debate aside, since it contributes little to an analysis of struggles for recognition in the democratic constitutional state and virtually nothing to their political resolution.[13]

(f) The more strictly *philosophical* discourses which take these phenomena as a point of departure for describing general problems are on a different level. The phenomena are well suited to illustrate the difficulties of intercultural understanding. They illuminate the relationship of morality to ethical life (*Sittlichkeit*) and the internal connection between meaning and validity, and they provide new fuel for the old question of whether it is even possible to transcend the context of our own language and culture or whether all standards of rationality remain bound up with specific worldviews and traditions. The overwhelming evidence of the fragmentation of multicultural societies and the Babylonian confusion of tongues in an overly complex global society seems to impel us toward holistic conceptions of language and contextualist conceptions of worldviews that make us skeptical about universalist claims, whether cognitive or normative. The complex and still unsettled debate about rationality also has implications, of course, for the concepts of the good and the just with which we operate when we examine the conditions of a "politics of recognition." But Taylor's proposal itself has a different reference, which lies at the level of law and politics.

(g) The question of the *rights* of offended and disrespected minorities takes on a legal sense when it is posed in these terms. Political decisions must make use of the regulatory form of positive law if they are to be at all effective in complex societies. In the medium of law, however, we are dealing with an artificial structure with certain normative presuppositions. Modern law is *formal* in that it rests on the premise that anything that is not explicitly forbidden is permitted. It is *individualistic* in that it makes the individual person the bearer of rights. It is *coercive* in that it is sanctioned by the state and applies only to legal or rule-conforming behavior—it permits the practice of religion but it cannot prescribe religious views. It is *positive* law in that it derives from the (modifiable) decisions of a political legislature; and finally, it is *procedurally enacted* law in that it is legitimated by a democratic process. Positive law requires purely legal behavior, but the law must be legitimate; although it does not prescribe the motives for obeying the law, it must be such that its addressees can always obey it out of respect for the law. A legal order is legitimate when it safeguards the autonomy of all *citizens* to an equal degree. The citizens are autonomous only if the addressees of the law can also see themselves as its authors. And its authors are free only as participants in legislative processes that are regulated in such a way and take place in forms of communication such that everyone can presume that the regulations enacted in that way deserve general and rationally motivated assent. In normative terms, there is no such thing as a constitutional state without democracy. Since, on the other hand, the democratic process itself has to be legally institutionalized, the principle of popular sovereignty requires those fundamental rights without which there can be no legitimate law at all: first and foremost, the right to equal individual freedom of choice and action, which in turn presupposes comprehensive legal protection of individuals.

As soon as we treat a problem as a legal problem, we bring into play a conception of modern law that forces us—on conceptual grounds alone—to operate with the architectonics of the constitutional state and its wealth of presuppositions. This has implications for the way we deal with the problem of securing equal legal rights and equal recognition for groups that are culturally defined, that is, collectivities that are distinguished from other collectivities on the basis of tradition, forms of life, ethnic origins, and so on—and whose members want to be distinguished from all other collectivities in order to maintain and develop their identity.

III The Permeation of the Constitutional State by Ethics

From the point of view of legal theory, the primary question that multiculturalism raises is the question of the ethical neutrality of law and politics. By "ethical" I mean all questions that relate to conceptions of the good life, or a life that is not misspent. Ethical questions cannot be evaluated from the "moral point of view" of whether something is "equally good for everyone;" rather, impartial judgment of such questions is based on strong evaluations and determined by the self-understanding and perspectival life-projects of particular groups, that is, by what is from their point of view "good for us," all things considered. The first-person reference, and hence the relationship to the identity of a group (or an individual), is grammatically inscribed in ethical questions. I will use the example of the Canadian constitutional debate to look at the liberal demand for ethical neutrality of the law in relation to the ethical-political self-understanding of a nation of citizens.

The neutrality of the law—and of the democratic process of enacting laws—is sometimes understood to mean that political questions of an ethical nature must be kept off the agenda and out of the discussion by "gag rules" because they are not susceptible to impartial legal regulation. On this view, in the sense of Liberalism 1, the state is not to be permitted to pursue any collective goals beyond guaranteeing the personal freedom and the welfare and security of its citizens. The alternative model (in the sense of Liberalism 2), in contrast, expects the state to guarantee these fundamental rights in general but also beyond that to intervene on behalf of the survival and advancement of a "particular nation, culture, religion, or of a (limited) set of nations, cultures and religions," in Michael Walzer's formulation. Walzer regards this model too as fundamental; it leaves room, however, for citizens to choose to give priority to individual rights under certain circumstances. Walzer shares Taylor's premise that conflicts between these two fundamental normative orientations are quite possible and that in such cases only Liberalism 2 permits collective goals and identities to be given precedence. Now, the theory of rights does assert the absolute precedence of rights over collective goods, so that arguments about goals, as Dworkin shows, can only "trump" claims based on individual rights if these goals can in turn be justified in the light of other rights that take precedence.[14] But that alone is not sufficient to support the communitarian view, which Taylor and Walzer share, that the system of rights is blind to claims to the protection of cultural forms of life and collective identities and is thus "leveling" and in need of revision.

Earlier I used the example of the feminist politics of equality to make a general point, namely, that the democratic elaboration of a system of rights incorporates not only general political goals but also the collective goals that are articulated in struggles for recognition. For in distinction to moral norms which regulate possible interactions between speaking and acting subjects in general, legal norms refer to the network of interactions in a specific society. Legal norms are derived from the decisions of a local lawmaking body and apply within a particular geographical area of the state to a socially delimited collectivity of members of that state. Within this well-defined sphere of validity, legal norms put the political decisions with which a society organized as a state acts upon itself into the form of collectively binding programs. To be sure, consideration of collective goals is not permitted to dissolve the structure of the law. It may not destroy the form of the law as such and thereby negate the difference between law and politics. But it is inherent in the concrete nature of the matters to be regulated that in the medium of law—as opposed to morality—the process of setting normative rules for modes of behavior is open to influence by the society's political goals. For this reason every legal system is *also* the expression of a particular form of life and not merely a reflection of the universal content of basic rights. Of course, legislative decisions must be understood as actualizing the system of rights, and policies must be understood as an elaboration of that system; but the more concrete the matter at hand, the more the self-understanding of a collectivity and its form of life (as well as the balance between competing group interests and an informed choice between alternative ends and means) are expressed in the acceptability of the way the matter is legally regulated. We see this in the broad spectrum of reasons that enter into the rational process by which the legislature's opinion and will are formed: not only moral considerations, pragmatic considerations, and the results of fair negotiations, but ethical reasons as well enter into deliberations and justifications of legislative decisions.

To the extent to which the shaping of citizens' political opinion and will is oriented to the idea of actualizing rights, it certainly cannot, as the communitarians suggest, be equated with a process by which citizens reach agreement about their ethical-political self-understanding.[15] But the process of actualizing rights is indeed embedded in contexts that require such discourses as an important component of politics—discussions about a shared conception of the good and a desired form of life that is acknowledged to be authentic. In such discussions the participants clarify the way they want to understand themselves as citizens of a specific republic, as inhabitants of a specific region, as heirs to a specific culture, which traditions they want to perpetuate and which they want to discontinue, how they want to deal with their history, with one another, with nature, and so on. And of course the choice of an official language or a decision about the curriculum of public schools affects the nation's ethical self-understanding. Because ethical-political decisions are an unavoidable part of politics, and because their legal regulation expresses the collective identity of a nation of citizens, they can spark cultural battles in which disrespected minorities struggle against an insensitive majority culture. What sets off the battles is not the ethical neutrality of the legal order but rather the fact that every legal community and every democratic process for actualizing basic rights is inevitably permeated by ethics. We see evidence of this, for instance, in the institutional guarantees enjoyed by Christian churches in countries like Germany—despite freedom of religion—or in the recently challenged constitutional guarantee of status accorded the conventional family but not to other marriage-like arrangements.

In this context, it is of interest that both empirically and normatively such ethical-political decisions depend on the contingent composition of the citizenry of the nation-state. The social makeup of the population of a state is the result of historical circumstances extrinsic to the system of rights and the principles of the constitutional state. It determines the totality of persons who live together in a territory and are bound by the constitution, that is, by the decision of the founding fathers to order their life together legitimately by means of positive law; as descendants, citizens have implicitly (or as naturalized citizens even explicitly) agreed to continue to pursue a preexisting constitutional project. Through their socialization processes, however, the persons of which a state is composed at any given time also embody the cultural forms of life in which they have developed their identity—even if they have in the meantime become disengaged from the traditions of their origins. Persons—or better, their personality structures—form the nodal points, as it were, in an ascriptive network of cultures and traditions, of intersubjectively shared contexts of life and experience. And this network also forms the horizon within which the citizens of the nation, willingly or not, conduct the ethical-political discourses in which they attempt to reach agreement on their self-understanding. If the population of citizens as a whole shifts, this horizon will change as well; new discourses will be held about the same questions, and new decisions will be reached. National minorities are at least intuitively aware of this, and it is an important motive for demanding their own state, or, as in the unsuccessful Meech Lake draft constitution, for demanding to be recognized as a "distinct society." If the francophone minority in Canada were to constitute itself as a legal community, it would form other majorities on important ethical-political questions through the same democratic processes and would arrive at regulatory decisions different from the ones Canadians as a whole have hitherto reached.

As the history of the formation of nation-states shows,[16] the creation of new national boundaries gives rise to new national minorities. The problem does not disappear, except at the price of "ethnic cleansing"—a price that cannot be politically or morally justified. The double-edged nature of the "right" to national self-determination is demonstrated clearly in the case of the Kurds, who are spread across three different countries, or Bosnia-Herzogovina, where ethnic groups are battling one another mercilessly. On the one hand, a collectivity that thinks of itself as a community with its own identity attains a new level of recognition by taking the step of becoming a nation in its own right. It cannot reach this level as a prepolitical linguistic and ethnic community, or even as an incorporated or fragmented "cultural nation." The need to be recognized as a nation-state is intensified in times of crisis, when the populace clings to the ascriptive signs of a regressively revitalized collective identity, as for instance after the dissolution of the Soviet empire. This kind of support offers dubious compensation for well-founded fears about the future and lack of social stability. On the other hand,

national independence is often to be had only at the price of civil
wars, new kinds of repression, or ensuing problems that perpetuate
the initial conflicts with the signs reversed.

The situation is different in Canada, where reasonable efforts are
being made to find a federalist solution that will leave the nation as
a whole intact but will try to safeguard the cultural autonomy of a
part of it by decentralizing state powers.[17] If these efforts succeed,
the portion of the citizenry that participates in the democratic process in specific areas of policy will change, but the principles of that
process will not. For the theory of rights in no way forbids the
citizens of a democratic constitutional state to assert a conception of
the good in their general legal order, a conception they either
already share or have come to agree on through political discussion.
It does, however, forbid them to privilege one form of life at the
expense of others within the nation. In federal versions of the nation-state this is true at both the federal and the state levels. If I am
not mistaken, in Canada the debate is not about this principle of
equal rights but about the nature and extent of the state powers that
are to be transferred to the Province of Quebec.

IV Equal Rights to Coexistence vs. the Preservation of Species

Federalization is a possible solution only when members of different
ethnic groups and cultural lifeworlds live in more or less separate
geographical areas. In multicultural societies like the United States
this is not the case. Nor will it be the case in countries like Germany,
where the ethnic composition of the population is changing under
the pressure of global waves of migration. Even if Quebec were to
become culturally autonomous, it would find itself in the same situation, having merely traded an English majority culture for a French
one. Let us assume for the sake of argument that a well-functioning
public sphere with open communication structures that permit and
promote discussions oriented to self-understanding exists in such
multicultural societies against the background of a liberal culture
and on the basis of voluntary associations. Then the democratic
process of actualizing equal individual rights can also extend to
guaranteeing different ethnic groups and their cultural forms of life

equal rights to coexistence. This does not require special justification or an alternative principle. For from a normative point of view, the integrity of the individual legal person cannot be guaranteed without protecting the intersubjectively shared experiences and life contexts in which the person has been socialized and has formed his or her identity. The identity of the individual is interwoven with collective identities and can be stabilized only in a cultural network that cannot be appropriated as private property any more than the mother tongue itself can be. Hence the individual remains the bearer of "rights to cultural membership," in Will Kymlicka's phrase.[18] But as the dialectic of legal and factual equality plays itself out, it gives rise to extensive guarantees of status, rights to self-administration, infrastructural benefits, subsidies, and so on. In arguing for such guarantees, endangered indigenous cultures can advance special moral reasons arising from the history of a country that has been appropriated by the majority culture. Similar arguments in favor of "reverse discrimination" can be advanced for the long-suppressed and disavowed cultures of former slaves.

These and similar obligations arise from legal claims and not from a general assessment of the value of the culture in question. Taylor's politics of recognition would be standing on shaky ground if it depended on the "presumption of equal value" of cultures and their specific contributions to world civilization. The right to equal respect, which everyone can demand in the life contexts in which his or her identity is formed as well as elsewhere, has nothing to do with the presumed excellence of his or her culture of origin, that is, with generally valued accomplishments. Susan Wolf also emphasizes this:

At least one of the serious harms that a failure of recognition perpetuates has little to do with the question of whether the person or the culture who goes unrecognized has anything important to say to all human beings. The need to correct those harms, therefore, does not depend on the presumption or the confirmation of the presumption that a particular culture is distinctively valuable to people outside the culture.[19]

Thus coexistence with equal rights for different ethnic groups and their cultural forms of life need not be safeguarded through the sort of collective rights that would overtax a theory of rights tailored to individual persons. Even if such group rights could be granted in a constitutional democracy, they would be not only unnecessary but questionable from a normative point of view. For in the last analysis, the protection of forms of life and traditions in which identities are formed is supposed to foster the recognition of their members; it does not represent a kind of preservation of species by administrative means. The ecological perspective on species conservation cannot be transferred to cultures. Cultural heritages and the forms of life articulated within them normally reproduce themselves by convincing those whose personality structures they shape, that is, by motivating them to appropriate and continue the traditions productively. The constitutional state can make this hermeneutic achievement of the cultural reproduction of worlds possible, but it cannot guarantee it. For to *guarantee* survival would necessarily rob the members of the freedom to say yes or no, which nowadays is crucial if they are to remain able to appropriate and preserve their cultural heritage. When a culture has become reflexive, the only traditions and forms of life that can sustain themselves are those that *bind* their members, while at the same time allowing members to subject the traditions to critical examination and leaving later generations the *option* of learning from other traditions or converting and setting out for other shores. This is true even of relatively closed sects like the Pennsylvania Amish.[20] Even if we considered it a meaningful goal to protect cultures as though they were endangered species, the hermeneutic conditions necessary for them to reproduce themselves successfully would be incompatible with the goal of "maintain[ing] and cherish[ing] distinctness, not just now but forever" (Taylor).

On this point it helps to recall the many subcultures and lifeworlds that flourished in early modern Europe with its occupational stratification, or the forms of life of rural laborers and the deracinated, proletarianized urban masses of the first phase of industrialization that succeeded them. Those forms of life were caught up and crushed in the process of modernization, but by no means did all of them find their "Meister Anton" and have committed members to defend them against the alternatives presented by the new era. Forms of life that were culturally vibrant and attractive enough to stimulate the will to self-assertion, like the urban culture of the nineteenth century, were able to preserve some of their features only through self-transformation. Even a majority culture that does not consider itself threatened preserves its vitality only through an unrestrained revisionism, by sketching out alternatives to the status quo or by integrating alien impulses—even to the point of breaking with its own traditions. This is especially true of immigrant cultures, which initially define themselves stubbornly in ethnic terms and revive traditional elements under the assimilationist pressure of the new environment but then quickly develop a mode of life equally distant from both assimilation and tradition.[21]

In multicultural societies, the coexistence of forms of life with equal rights means ensuring every citizen the opportunity to grow up within the world of a cultural heritage and to have his or her children grow up in it without suffering discrimination. It means the opportunity to confront this (and every other) culture and to perpetuate it in its conventional form or to transform it, as well as the opportunity to turn away from its commands with indifference or break with it self-critically and then live spurred on by having made a conscious break with tradition, or even with a divided identity. The accelerated pace of change in modern societies explodes all stationary forms of life. Cultures survive only if they draw the strength to transform themselves from criticism and secession. Legal guarantees can be based only on the fact that within his or her own cultural milieu, each person retains the possibility of regenerating this strength. And this in turn develops not only by setting oneself apart but at least as much through exchanges with strangers and things alien.

In the modern era rigid forms of life succumb to entropy. Fundamentalist movements can be understood as an ironic attempt to give one's own lifeworld ultrastability by restorative means. The irony lies in the way traditionalism misunderstands itself. In fact, it emerges from the vortex of social modernization even as it apes a substance that has already disintegrated. As a reaction to the overwhelming push for modernization, fundamentalism is itself a thoroughly modern movement of renewal. Nationalism too can turn into fundamentalism, but it should not be confused with it. The nationalism of the French Revolution allied itself with the universalistic principles of the democratic constitutional state; at that time nationalism and republicanism were kindred spirits. On the other hand, fundamentalism afflicts not only societies that are collapsing but even the established democracies of the West. All world religions have produced their own forms of fundamentalism, although by no means do all sectarian movements display those traits.

As the Rushdie case reminded us, a fundamentalism that leads to a practice of intolerance is incompatible with constitutional democracy. Such a practice is based on religious or historico-philosophical interpretations of the world that claim exclusiveness for a privileged way of life. Such conceptions lack an awareness of the fallibility of their claims, as well as a respect for the "burdens of reason" (Rawls). Of course, religious convictions and global interpretations of the world are not obliged to subscribe to the kind of fallibilism that currently accompanies hypothetical knowledge in the experimental sciences. But fundamentalist worldviews are dogmatic in a different sense: they leave no room for reflection on their relationship with the other worldviews with which they share the same universe of discourse and against whose competing validity claims they can advance their positions only on the basis of reasons. They leave no room for "reasonable disagreement."[22]

In contrast with fundamentalist worldviews, the subjectivized "gods and demons" of the modern world are distinguished by a reflexive attitude that does more than allow for a modus vivendi— something that can be legally enforced given religious freedom. In a spirit of tolerance à la Lessing, the nonfundamentalist worldviews that Rawls characterizes as "not unreasonable comprehensive doctrines"[23] allow for a civilized debate between convictions, in which one party can recognize the other parties as co-combatants in the search for authentic truths without sacrificing its own claims to validity. In multicultural societies the national constitution can tolerate only forms of life articulated within the medium of such nonfundamentalist traditions, because coexistence with equal rights for these forms of life requires the mutual recognition of the different cultural memberships: all persons must also be recognized as members of ethical communities integrated around different conceptions of the good. Hence the ethical integration of groups and subcultures with their own collective identities must be uncoupled from the abstract political integration that includes all citizens equally.

The political integration of citizens ensures loyalty to the common political culture. The latter is rooted in an interpretation of constitutional principles from the perspective of the nation's historical experience. To this extent that interpretation cannot be ethically neutral. Perhaps one would do better to speak of a common *horizon* of interpretation within which current issues give rise to public debates about the citizens' political self-understanding. The "historians' debate" in 1986—1987 in Germany is a good example of this.[24] But the debates are always about the best interpretation of the same constitutional rights and principles. These form the fixed point of reference for any constitutional patriotism that situates the system of rights within the historical context of a legal community. They must be enduringly linked with the motivations and convictions of the citizens, for without such a motivational anchoring they could not become the driving force behind the dynamically conceived project of producing an association of free and equal individuals. Hence the shared political culture in which citizens recognize themselves as members of their polity is also permeated by ethics.

At the same time, the ethical substance of a constitutional patriotism cannot detract from the legal system's neutrality vis-à-vis communities that are ethically integrated at a subpolitical level. Rather, it has to sharpen sensitivity to the diversity and integrity of the different forms of life coexisting within a multicultural society. It is crucial to maintain the distinction between the two levels of integration. If they are collapsed into one level, the majority culture will usurp state prerogatives at the expense of the equal rights of other cultural forms of life and violate their claim to mutual recognition. The neutrality of the law vis-à-vis internal ethical differentiations stems from the fact that in complex societies the citizenry as a whole can no longer be held together by a substantive consensus on values but only by a consensus on the procedures for the legitimate enactment of laws and the legitimate exercise of power. Citizens who are politically integrated in this way share the rationally based conviction that unrestrained freedom of communication in the political public sphere, a democratic process for settling conflicts, and the constitutional channeling of political power together provide a basis for checking illegitimate power and ensuring that administrative power is used in the equal interest of all. The universalism of legal principles manifests itself in a procedural consensus, which must be embedded through a kind of constitutional patriotism in the context of a historically specific political culture.

V Immigration, Citizenship, and National Identity

Legal experts have the advantage of discussing normative questions in connection with cases to be decided. Their thinking is oriented to application. Philosophers avoid this decisionist pressure; as contemporaries of classical ideas that extend over more than two thousand years, they are not embarrassed to consider themselves participants in a conversation that will go on forever. Hence it is all the more fascinating when someone like Charles Taylor attempts to grasp his own times in ideas and to show the relevance of philosophical insights to the pressing political questions of the day. His essay is an example of this, as unusual as it is brilliant—although, or rather because, he does not follow the fashionable path of an "applied ethics."

After the upheavals in Central and Eastern Europe there has been another theme on the agenda of the day in Germany and in the European Community as a whole: immigration. After a comprehensive presentation of this problem, a Dutch colleague arrives at the following unadorned prognosis:

Western European countries . . . will do their utmost to prevent immigration from Third World countries. To this end they will grant work permits to persons who have skills of immediate relevance to the society in fairly exceptional cases only (soccer players, software specialists from the US, scholars from India, etc.). They will combine a very restrictive entry policy with policies aimed at dealing more quickly and effectively with requests for asylum, and with a practice of deporting without delay those whose request has been denied. . . . The conclusion is, that they will individually and jointly use *all means* at their disposal to stem the tide.[25]

This description fits precisely the compromise on political asylum that the government and the opposition in Germany made the basis for a constitutional change in 1993. There is no doubt that the great majority of the population welcomes this policy. Xenophobia is widespread these days in the European Community as well. It is more marked in some countries than in others, but the attitudes of the Germans do not differ substantially from those of the French and the English.[26] Taylor's example encourages us to see how a philosophical point of view can help answer the question of whether this policy of sealing ourselves off from immigration is justified. I will begin by discussing the question in the abstract and then reviewing the German debate on political asylum of 1992–1993 and its historical background. I will then outline the alternatives that would have to be discussed in a public debate—one that has not yet been openly conducted—about the ethical-political self-understanding of the enlarged Federal Republic of Germany.

Although modern law differs from posttraditional morality by its specific formal characteristics, the system of rights and the principles of the constitutional state are in harmony with this morality by virtue of their universalistic content. At the same time, as we have seen, legal systems are "ethically permeated" in that they reflect the political will and the form of life of a specific legal community. The United States, whose political culture is stamped by a constitutional tradition that is two hundred years old, is a clear example of this. But the juridified ethos of a nation-state cannot come into conflict with civil rights so long as the political legislature is oriented to constitutional principles and thus to the idea of actualizing basic rights. The ethical substance of a political integration that unites all the citizens of the nation must remain "neutral" with respect to the differences between the ethical-cultural communities within the nation, each of which is integrated around its own conception of the good. The uncoupling of these two levels of integration notwithstanding, a nation of citizens can sustain the institutions of freedom only by developing a certain measure of loyalty to their own state, a loyalty that cannot be legally enforced.

It is this ethical-political self-understanding on the part of the nation that is affected by immigration; for the influx of immigrants alters the composition of the population in ethical-cultural respects as well. Thus the question arises whether the desire for immigration runs up against limits in the right of a political community to maintain its political-cultural form of life intact. Assuming that the autonomously developed state order is indeed shaped by ethics, does the right to self-determination not include the right of a nation to affirm its identity vis-à-vis immigrants who could give a different cast to this historically developed political-cultural form of life?

From the perspective of the recipient society, the problem of immigration raises the question of legitimate conditions of entry. Ignoring the intermediate stages, we can focus on the act of naturalization, with which a state controls the expansion of the political community defined by the rights of citizenship. Under what conditions can the state deny citizenship to those who advance a claim to naturalization? Aside from the usual provisos (as against criminals), the most relevant question in our context is in what respect can a democratic constitutional state demand that immigrants assimilate in order to maintain the integrity of its citizens' way of life. Philosophically, we can distinguish two levels of assimilation:

1. assent to the principles of the constitution within the scope of interpretation determined at a particular time by the ethical-political self-understanding of the citizens and the political culture of the country; in other words, assimilation to the way in which the autonomy of the citizens is institutionalized in the recipient society and the way the "public use of reason" is practiced there; and

2. the further level of a willingness to become acculturated, that is, not only to conform externally but to become habituated to the way of life, the practices, and customs of the local culture across their full range. This means an assimilation that penetrates to the level of ethical-cultural integration and thereby has a deeper impact on the collective identity of the immigrants' culture of origin than the political socialization required under (1) above.

The results of the immigration policy practiced in the United States support a liberal interpretation that exemplifies (1), the weaker expectation of assimilation limited to political socialization.[27]

An example of (2) is provided by the Prussian policy on immigration from Poland under Bismarck, which despite variations was oriented primarily to Germanization.[28]

A democratic constitutional state that is serious about uncoupling these two levels of integration can require of immigrants only the political socialization described in (1) above (and practically speaking can expect to see it only in the second generation). This enables it to preserve the identity of the political community, which nothing, including immigration, is permitted to encroach upon, since that identity is founded on the constitutional principles anchored in the political culture and not on the basic ethical orientations of the cultural form of life predominant in that country. Accordingly, all that needs to be expected of immigrants is the willingness to enter into the political culture of their new homeland, without having to give up the cultural form of life of their origins by doing so. The right to democratic self-determination does indeed include the right of citizens to insist on the inclusive character of their own political culture; it safeguards the society from the danger of segmentation—from the exclusion of alien subcultures and from a separatist disintegration into unrelated subcultures. As I indicated above, political integration does not extend to fundamentalist immigrant cultures. But neither does it justify compulsory assimilation for the sake of the self-affirmation of the cultural form of life dominant in the country.[29]

This constitutional alternative has the implication that the legitimately asserted identity of the political community will by no means be preserved from alterations *indefinitely* in the wake of waves of immigration. Because immigrants cannot be compelled to surrender their own traditions, as other forms of life become established the horizon within which citizens henceforth interpret their common constitutional principles may also expand. Then the mechanism comes into play whereby a change in the cultural composition of the active citizenry changes the context to which the ethical-political self-understanding of the nation as a whole refers: "People live in communities with bonds and bounds, but these may be of different kinds. In a liberal society, the bonds and bounds should be compatible with liberal principles. Open immigration would change the character of the community, but it would not leave the community without any character."[30]

Let me now turn from the question of which conditions a democratic constitutional state may impose on the reception of immigrants to another question: Who has the right to immigrate?

There are sufficient moral grounds for an individual legal claim to political asylum (in the sense of Article 16 of the German Basic Law, which must be interpreted with reference to the protection of human dignity guaranteed in Article 1 and in connection with the guarantee of legal recourse established in Article 19). I do not need to go into them here. What is important is the definition of a refugee. In accordance with Article 13 of the Geneva Convention on the Status of Refugees, someone is considered to be entitled to asylum if he is fleeing from a country "where his life or freedom would be threatened on account of his race, religion, nationality, membership of a particular social group or political opinion." In light of recent experience, this definition needs to be extended to include the protection of women from mass rapes. The right to temporary asylum for refugees from civil war regions is also unproblematic. But since the discovery of America, and especially since the explosive increase in worldwide immigration in the eighteenth century, the great bulk of those wanting to immigrate has consisted of individuals immigrating in order to work as well as refugees from poverty who want to escape a miserable existence in their homeland. And so it is today. It is against this immigration from the impoverished regions of the East and South that a European chauvinism of affluence is now arming itself.

From the moral point of view we cannot regard this problem solely from the perspective of the inhabitants of affluent and peaceful societies; we must also take the perspective of those who come to foreign continents seeking their well-being, that is, an existence worthy of human beings, rather than protection from political persecution. The question of whether a *legal* claim to immigration exists over and above a *moral* claim is particularly relevant in the current situation, where the number of people wanting to immigrate manifestly exceeds the willingness to receive them.

One can cite good grounds for a moral claim. People do not normally leave their homelands except under dire circumstances; as a rule the mere fact that they have fled is sufficient evidence of their need for help. A moral obligation to provide assistance arises in particular from the growing interdependencies of a global society that has become so enmeshed through the capitalist world market and electronic mass communications that the UN has assumed something like an overall political responsibility for safeguarding life on the planet, as the recent example of Somalia indicates. Further, special duties are devolved upon the First World as a result of the history of colonization and the uprooting of regional cultures by the incursion of capitalist modernization. We should also note that in the period between 1800 and 1960 Europeans were disproportionately represented in intercontinental migratory movements, making up 80 percent of those involved, and they profited from this—that is, they improved their living conditions in comparison with other migrants and with those of their compatriots who did not emigrate. At the same time, the exodus of the nineteenth and early twentieth centuries improved the economic situations in the countries from which they fled, just as decisively as did, conversely, the immigration to Europe during the reconstruction period following the Second World War.[31] Either way, Europe was the beneficiary of these streams of migration.

These and other related reasons that could be given do not, to be sure, justify guaranteeing actionable individual legal rights to immigration but they do justify a moral obligation to have a liberal immigration policy that opens one's own society to immigrants and regulates the flow of immigration in relation to existing capacities. In the defensive slogan "the boat is full" one hears a lack of willingness to take the perspective of the other side—of the "boat people" in their rickety crafts, for example, trying to escape the terror in Indochina. European societies, shrinking demographically and dependent on immigration if only for economic reasons, have certainly not reached the limits of their capacity to absorb immigrants. The moral basis for a liberal immigration policy also gives rise to an obligation not to limit immigration quotas to the recipient country's economic needs, that is, not to "welcome (only) technical expertise," but instead to establish quotas in accordance with criteria that are acceptable from the perspective of all parties involved.

VI The Politics of Asylum in a United Germany

If one takes these principles as a point of departure, the compromise on political asylum negotiated between the German government and the opposition Social Democrats, which was put into effect in early 1993, cannot be justified in normative terms. Without going into detail, I will list the four central flaws of the agreement and criticize the premises on which they are based.

(a) The regulations provided for by the agreement are limited to political asylum, that is, to measures directed against "abuses" of the right to asylum. They ignore the fact that Germany needs an immigration policy that provides immigrants with other legal options as well. The problem of immigration is falsely defined in a way that has numerous implications. Anyone who dissolves the connection between the question of political asylum and the question of immigration to escape poverty is implicitly declaring that he or she wants to evade Europe's moral obligation to refugees from the impoverished regions of the world and instead tacitly tolerates a flow of illegal immigration that can always be exploited as "abuse of asylum" for domestic political purposes.

(b) Parliament's addition of Article 16a to the Basic Law, as a result of the interparty agreement of January 15, 1993, weakens the substance of the individual legal right to political asylum because it allows refugees coming into the country from a so-called "safe Third Country" to be deported without legal recourse. This shifts the burden of immigration to Eastern Europe, to our neighbors Poland, the Czech Republic, Slovakia, Hungary, and Austria—in other words, to countries that are currently ill prepared to handle this problem in a legally unobjectionable way. In addition, curtailing the guarantee of legal protection for refugees from countries defined as "free of persecution" from Germany's point of view is problematic.[32]

(c) Rather than making it easier for foreigners already residing in Germany, especially the *Gastarbeiter* [literally, guest workers] whom we recruited, to acquire citizenship, the asylum compromise left the naturalization laws unchanged. The dual citizenship that those foreigners understandably prefer is denied them; even children born to them in Germany do not automatically receive the rights of citizenship. Foreigners who are willing to renounce their previous citizenship can be naturalized only after they have been living in Germany for at least fifteen years. In contrast, the so-called *Volksdeutschen* or ethnic Germans—primarily Poles and Russians who can prove German ancestry—have a constitutional right to naturalization. In 1992, in addition to approximately 500,000 asylum seekers (of which 130,000 were from the civil war regions of the former Yugoslavia), 220,000 ethnic-German immigrants were accepted into Germany on this basis.

(d) The German policy on political asylum rests on the repeatedly reaffirmed premise that Germany is not a land of immigration. This contradicts not only what we all see in the streets and subways of our metropolises—today twenty-six percent of the population of Frankfurt consists of foreigners—but also the historical facts. To be sure, since the early nineteenth century almost eight million Germans have emigrated to the United States alone. But at the same time, major waves of immigration have occurred over the last hundred years. By the First World War, 1.2 million immigrant workers had entered the country, and 12 million "displaced persons" were left behind at the end of the Second World War—primarily forced labor deported from Poland and the Soviet Union. In 1955, following the path laid out by the Nazi policy of forced foreign labor, and despite relatively high unemployment in Germany, came the organized recruitment of a cheap, unmarried male workforce from southern and southeastern Europe. This continued until recruitment ceased in 1973. Today the families and offspring of those *Gastarbeiter* who did not return to their own countries live in the paradoxical situation of immigrants with no clear prospects for immigration—Germans with foreign passports.[33] They form the bulk of the 8.2 percent of the 1990 German population composed of foreigners living in Germany. Without them, the economic boom now comparable only to that of Japan would not have been possible, and it is even harder to understand the resistance to the full integration of these foreigners when one considers that by 1990 West Germany had integrated 15 million refugees, immigrants, and foreigners who were either German or of German descent—thus also *Neubürger,* new citizens: "If a foreign population of about 4.8 million is added, nearly one-third of the West German population has resulted from immigration movements since World War II."[34]

If the notion that "we are not a land of immigration" continues to be put forth in the political public sphere in the face of this evidence, this indicates that it is a manifestation of a deep-seated mentality—and that a painful change is necessary in the way we conceive of ourselves as a nation. It is no accident that our naturalization decisions are based on the principle of ancestry and not, as in other Western nations, on the principle of territoriality. The shortcomings described above in the way Germany is dealing with the problem of immigration must be understood against the historical background of the Germans' understanding of themselves as a nation of *Volksgenossen* or ethnic comrades centered around language and culture. Anyone who is born in France is considered to be French and holds the rights of a French citizen. In Germany, until the end of the Second World War fine distinctions were still being made between *Deutschen,* or citizens of German descent, *Reichsdeutschen,* or German citizens of non-German descent, and *Volksdeutschen,* or individuals of German descent living in other countries.

In France national consciousness could develop within the framework of a territorial state, while in Germany it was originally linked with the romantically inspired educated middle-class notion of a *Kulturnation,* a nation defined by its culture. This idea represented an imaginary unity that had to seek support in a shared language, tradition, and ancestry in order to transcend the reality of the existing small states in Germany. Still more important was the fact that the French national consciousness could develop in step with the establishment of democratic civil liberties and in the struggle against the sovereignty of the French king, whereas German nationalism arose out of the struggle against Napoleon, thus against an external enemy, independently of the battle for democratic civil liberties and long before the *kleindeutsche* nation-state was imposed from above. Having emerged from a "war of liberation" of this kind, national consciousness in Germany could be linked with the pathos of the uniqueness of its culture and ancestry—a particularism that has indelibly stamped the Germans' self-understanding.

The Federal Republic of Germany turned away from this *Sonder-bewußtsein* or sense of exceptionalness after 1945, after the shock of the collapse of civilization in the Nazi mass exterminations, a shock it only gradually came to terms with. Loss of sovereignty and a marginal position in a polarized world reinforced this. Reunification and the dissolution of the Soviet Union have changed this constellation in a fundamental way. Hence the reactions to the right-wing radicalism that has flared up again—and in this context the deceptive debate on asylum as well—raise the question of whether the enlarged Federal Republic will continue on its path toward a more civilized politics or whether the old *Sonderbewußtsein* is being regenerated in a different form. This question is complicated by the fact that the process of national unification was pushed through and administratively manipulated from above and has set a false course for the country in this respect as well. Discussion and clarification of the ethical-political self-understanding of the citizens of two German states with widely divergent historical fates is urgently needed but has not yet taken place. The "accession" of new Länder, or federal states—a constitutionally dubious legal option—prevented a constitutional debate, and positions in the debate about the seat of the German capital are skewed. In the meantime the citizens of the former East Germany, humiliated in many ways and deprived of their spokespersons and a political public sphere of their own, have other problems to contend with; in place of clearly articulated contributions to the debate there arise smoldering resentments.

All repression produces symptoms. One challenge after another—from the Gulf War, Maastricht, the civil war in Yugoslavia, the asylum issue and right-wing radicalism, to the deployment of German military forces outside the NATO area—arouses a sense of helplessness in the political public sphere and in an immobilized government. The changed constellation of power and a changed domestic situation certainly demand new responses. The question is, with what kind of consciousness will Germany make the adaptations required if it continues its pattern of reacting with ad hoc decisions and subliminal mood shifts?

Historians who dash off books with titles like "Back to History" and "Fear of Power" offer us a backward-looking "farewell to the old Federal Republic" that purports to expose the recently celebrated success story of postwar German democracy as a *Sonderweg* or special path of its own. The former West Germany is said to have embodied the forced abnormality of a defeated and divided nation, and now, having recovered its national greatness and sovereignty, it must be led out of its utopianism, with its obliviousness to power, and back to the path of self-conscious preeminence in Central Europe, the path of power politics marked out by Bismarck. This celebration of the caesura of 1989 hides the repeatedly frustrated desire for normalization of those who did not want to accept the caesura of 1945.[35] They reject an alternative that does not necessarily lead to different options at every turn in the short run but instead opens up another perspective. In this alternative view, the orientation of the old Federal Republic to the West represents not a shrewd but a transitory foreign policy decision, and above all not solely a *political* decision, but rather a profound *intellectual* break with those specifically German traditions that stamped the Wilhelminian Empire and contributed to the downfall of the Weimar Republic. That break set the stage for a shift in mentality that affected broad segments of the public after the youth revolt of 1968 under the favorable conditions of an affluent society, a shift that made it possible for democracy and the constitutional state to take political and cultural root in German soil for the first time. Today what is at stake is adapting Germany's political role to new realities, without letting the process of civilizing politics that was underway until 1989 be broken off under the pressure of the economic and social problems of unification, and without sacrificing the normative achievements of a national self-understanding that is no longer based on ethnicity but founded on citizenship.

V

What is Meant by "Deliberative Politics"?

9

Three Normative Models of Democracy

In what follows I refer to the idealized distinction between the "liberal" and the "republican" understanding of politics—terms which mark the fronts in the current debate in the United States initiated by the so-called communitarians. Drawing on the work of Frank Michelman, I will begin by describing the two polemically contrasted models of democracy with specific reference to the concept of the citizen, the concept of law, and the nature of processes of political will-formation. In the second part, beginning with a critique of the "ethical overload" of the republican model, I introduce a third, procedural model of democracy for which I propose to reserve the term "deliberative politics."

I

The crucial difference between liberalism and republicanism consists in how the role of the democratic process is understood. According to the "liberal" view, this process accomplishes the task of programming the state in the interest of society, where the state is conceived as an apparatus of public administration, and society is conceived as a system of market-structured interactions of private persons and their labor. Here politics (in the sense of the citizens' political will-formation) has the function of bundling together and bringing to bear private social interests against a state apparatus that specializes in the administrative employment of political power for collective goals.

On the republican view, politics is not exhausted by this mediating function but is constitutive for the socialization process as a whole. Politics is conceived as the reflexive form of substantial ethical life. It constitutes the medium in which the members of quasi-natural solidary communities become aware of their dependence on one another and, acting with full deliberation as citizens, further shape and develop existing relations of reciprocal recognition into an association of free and equal consociates under law. With this, the liberal architectonic of government and society undergoes an important change. In addition to the hierarchical regulatory apparatus of sovereign state authority and the decentralized regulatory mechanism of the market—that is, besides administrative power and self-interest—*solidarity* appears as a third source of social integration.

This horizontal political will-formation aimed at mutual understanding or communicatively achieved consensus is even supposed to enjoy priority, both in a genetic and a normative sense. An autonomous basis in civil society independent of public administration and market-mediated private commerce is assumed as a precondition for the practice of civic self-determination. This basis prevents political communication from being swallowed up by the government apparatus or assimilated to market structures. Thus, on the republican conception, the political public sphere and its base, civil society, acquire a strategic significance. Together they are supposed to secure the integrative power and autonomy of the communicative practice of the citizens.[1] The uncoupling of political communication from the economy has as its counterpart a coupling of administrative power with the communicative power generated by political opinion- and will-formation.

These two competing conceptions of politics have different consequences.

(a) In the first place, their concepts of the citizen differ. According to the liberal view, the citizen's status is determined primarily by the individual rights he or she has vis-à-vis the state and other citizens. As bearers of individual rights citizens enjoy the protection of the government as long as they pursue their private interests within the boundaries drawn by legal statutes—and this includes protection against state interventions that violate the legal prohibition on government interference. Individual rights are negative rights that guarantee a domain of freedom of choice within which legal persons are freed from external compulsion. Political rights have the same structure: they afford citizens the opportunity to assert their private interests in such a way that, by means of elections, the composition of parliamentary bodies, and the formation of a government, these interests are finally aggregated into a political will that can affect the administration. In this way the citizens in their political role can determine whether governmental authority is exercised in the interest of the citizens as members of society.[2]

According to the republican view, the status of citizens is not determined by the model of negative liberties to which these citizens can lay claim as private persons. Rather, political rights—preeminently rights of political participation and communication—are positive liberties. They do not guarantee freedom from external compulsion, but guarantee instead the possibility of participating in a common practice, through which the citizens can first make themselves into what they want to be—politically responsible subjects of a community of free and equal citizens.[3] To this extent, the political process does not serve just to keep government activity under the surveillance of citizens who have already acquired a prior social autonomy through the exercise of their private rights and prepolitical liberties. Nor does it act only as a hinge between state and society, for democratic governmental authority is by no means an original authority. Rather, this authority proceeds from the communicative power generated by the citizens' practice of self-legislation, and it is legitimated by the fact that it protects this practice by institutionalizing public freedom.[4] The state's *raison d'être* does not lie primarily in the protection of equal individual rights but in the guarantee of an inclusive process of opinion- and will-formation in which free and equal citizens reach an understanding on which goals and norms lie in the equal interest of all. In this way the republican citizen is credited with more than an exclusive concern with his or her private interests.

(b) The polemic against the classical concept of the legal person as bearer of individual rights reveals a controversy about the concept of law itself. Whereas on the liberal conception the point of a legal order is to make it possible to determine which individuals in each case are entitled to which rights, on the republican conception these "subjective" rights owe their existence to an "objective" legal order that both enables and guarantees the integrity of an autonomous life in common based on equality and mutual respect. On the one view, the legal order is conceived in terms of individual rights; on the other, their objective legal content is given priority.

To be sure, this conceptual dichotomy does not touch on the *intersubjective* content of rights that demand reciprocal respect for rights and duties in symmetrical relations of recognition. But the republican concept at least points in the direction of a concept of law that accords equal weight to both the integrity of the individual and the integrity of the community in which persons as both individuals and members can first accord one another reciprocal recognition. It ties the legitimacy of the laws to the democratic procedure by which they are generated and thereby preserves an internal connection between the citizens' practice of self-legislation and the impersonal sway of the law:

For republicans, rights ultimately are nothing but determinations of prevailing political will, while for liberals, some rights are always grounded in a "higher law" of transpolitical reason or revelation. . . . In a republican view, a community's objective, common good substantially consists in the success of its political endeavor to define, establish, effectuate, and sustain the set of rights (less tendentiously, laws) best suited to the conditions and *mores* of that community. Whereas in a contrasting liberal view, the higher-law rights provide the transactional structures and the curbs on power required so that pluralistic pursuit of diverse and conflicting interests may proceed as satisfactorily as possible.[5]

The right to vote, interpreted as a positive right, becomes the paradigm of rights as such, not only because it is constitutive for political self-determination, but because it shows how inclusion in a community of equals is connected with the individual right to make autonomous contributions and take personal positions on issues:

[T]he claim is that we all take an interest in each others' enfranchisement because (i) our choice lies between hanging together and hanging separately; (ii) hanging together depends on reciprocal assurances to all of having one's vital interests heeded by others; and (iii) in the deeply pluralized conditions of contemporary American society, such assurances are not attainable through virtual representation, but only by maintaining at least the semblance of a politics in which everyone is conceded a voice.[6]

This structure, read off from the political rights of participation and communication, is extended to *all* rights via the legislative process constituted by political rights. Even the authorization guaranteed by private law to pursue private, freely chosen goals simultaneously imposes an obligation to respect the limits of strategic action which are agreed to be in the equal interest of all.

(c) The different ways of conceptualizing the role of citizen and the law express a deeper disagreement about the nature of the political process. On the liberal view, politics is essentially a struggle for positions that grant access to administrative power. The political process of opinion- and will-formation in the public sphere and in parliament is shaped by the competition of strategically acting collectives trying to maintain or acquire positions of power. Success is measured by the citizens' approval of persons and programs, as quantified by votes. In their choices at the polls, voters express their preferences. Their votes have the same structure as the choices of participants in a market, in that their decisions license access to positions of power that political parties fight over with a success-oriented attitude similar to that of players in the market. The input of votes and the output of power conform to the same pattern of strategic action.

According to the republican view, the political opinion- and will-formation in the public sphere and in parliament does not obey the structures of market processes but rather the obstinate structures of a public communication oriented to mutual understanding. For politics as the citizens' practice of self-determination, the paradigm is not the market but dialogue. From this perspective there is a structural difference between communicative power, which proceeds from political communication in the form of discursively generated majority decisions, and the administrative power possessed by the governmental apparatus. Even the parties that struggle over access to positions of governmental power must bend themselves to the deliberative style and the stubborn character of political discourse:

Deliberation . . . refers to a certain attitude toward social cooperation, namely, that of openness to persuasion by reasons referring to the claims of others as well as one's own. The deliberative medium is a good faith exchange of views—including participants' reports of their own understanding of their respective vital interests— . . . in which a vote, if any vote is taken, represents a pooling of judgments.[7]

Hence the conflict of opinions conducted in the political arena has legitimating force not just in the sense of an authorization to occupy positions of power; on the contrary, the ongoing political discourse also has binding force for the way in which political authority is exercised. Administrative power can only be exercised on the basis of policies and within the limits laid down by laws generated by the democratic process.

II

So much for the comparison between the two models of democracy that currently dominate the discussion between the so-called communitarians and liberals, above all in the US. The republican model has advantages and disadvantages. In my view it has the advantage that it preserves the radical democratic meaning of a society that organizes itself through the communicatively united citizens and does not trace collective goals back to "deals" made between competing private interests. Its disadvantage, as I see it, is that it is too idealistic in that it makes the democratic process dependent on the virtues of citizens devoted to the public weal. For politics is not concerned in the first place with questions of ethical self-understanding. The mistake of the republican view consists in an ethical foreshortening of political discourse.

To be sure, ethical discourses aimed at achieving a collective self-understanding—discourses in which participants attempt to clarify how they understand themselves as members of a particular nation, as members of a community or a state, as inhabitants of a region, etc., which traditions they wish to cultivate, how they should treat each other, minorities, and marginal groups, in what sort of society they want to live—constitute an important part of politics. But under conditions of cultural and social pluralism, behind politically relevant goals there often lie interests and value-orientations that are by no means constitutive of the identity of the political community as a whole, that is, for the totality of an intersubjectively shared form of life. These interests and value-orientations, which conflict with one another within the same polity without any prospect of consensual resolution, need to be counterbalanced in a way that cannot be effected by ethical discourse, even though the results of this nondiscursive counterbalancing are subject to the proviso that they must not violate the basic values of a culture. The balancing of interests takes the form of reaching a compromise between parties who rely on their power and ability to sanction. Negotiations of this sort certainly presuppose a readiness to cooperate, that is, a willingness to abide by the rules and to arrive at results that are acceptable to all parties, though for different reasons. But compromise-formation is not conducted in the form of a rational discourse that neutralizes power and excludes strategic action. However, the fairness of compromises is measured by presuppositions and procedures which for their part are in need of rational, indeed normative, justification from the standpoint of justice. In contrast with ethical questions, questions of justice are not by their very nature tied to a particular collectivity. Politically enacted law, if it is to be legitimate, must be at least in harmony with moral principles that claim a general validity that extends beyond the limits of any concrete legal community.

The concept of deliberative politics acquires empirical relevance only when we take into account the multiplicity of forms of communication in which a common will is produced, that is, not just ethical self-clarification but also the balancing of interests and compromise, the purposive choice of means, moral justification, and legal consistency-testing. In this process the two types of politics which Michelman distinguishes in an ideal-typical fashion can interweave and complement one another in a rational manner. "Dialogical" and "instrumental" politics can *interpenetrate* in the medium of deliberation if the corresponding forms of communication are sufficiently institutionalized. Everything depends on the conditions of communication and the procedures that lend the institutionalized opinion- and will-formation their legitimating force. The third model of democracy, which I would like to propose, relies precisely on those conditions of communication under which the political process can be presumed to produce rational results because it operates deliberatively at all levels.

Making the proceduralist conception of deliberative politics the cornerstone of the theory of democracy results in differences both from the republican conception of the state as an ethical community and from the liberal conception of the state as the guardian of a market society. In comparing the three models, I take my orientation from that dimension of politics which has been our primary concern, namely, the democratic opinion- and will-formation that issue in popular elections and parliamentary decrees.

According to the liberal view, the democratic process takes place exclusively in the form of compromises between competing interests. Fairness is supposed to be guaranteed by rules of compromise-formation that regulate the general and equal right to vote, the representative composition of parliamentary bodies, their order of business, and so on. Such rules are ultimately justified in terms of liberal basic rights. According to the republican view, by contrast, democratic will-formation is supposed to take the form of an ethical discourse of self-understanding; here deliberation can rely for its content on a culturally established background consensus of the citizens, which is rejuvenated through the ritualistic reenactment of a republican founding act. Discourse theory takes elements from both sides and integrates them into the concept of an ideal procedure for deliberation and decision making. Weaving together negotiations and discourses of self-understanding and of justice, this democratic procedure grounds the presumption that under such conditions reasonable or fair results are obtained. According to this proceduralist view, practical reason withdraws from universal human rights or from the concrete ethical life of a specific community into the rules of discourse and forms of argumentation that derive their normative content from the validity-basis of action oriented to reaching understanding, and ultimately from the structure of linguistic communication.[8]

These descriptions of the structures of democratic process set the stage for different normative conceptualizations of state and society. The sole presupposition is a public administration of the kind that emerged in the early modern period together with the European state system and in functional interconnection with a capitalist economic system. According to the republican view, the citizens' political opinion- and will-formation forms the medium through which society constitutes itself as a political whole. Society is centered in the state; for in the citizens' practice of political self-determination the polity becomes conscious of itself as a totality and acts on itself via the collective will of the citizens. Democracy is synonymous with the political self-organization of society. This leads to a polemical understanding of politics as directed against the state apparatus. In Hannah Arendt's political writings one can see the thrust of republican arguments: in opposition to the civic privatism of a depoliticized population and in opposition to the acquisition of legitimation through entrenched parties, the political public sphere should be revitalized to the point where a regenerated citizenry can, in the forms of a decentralized self-governance, (once again) appropriate the governmental authority that has been usurped by a self-regulating bureaucracy.

According to the liberal view, this separation of the state apparatus from society cannot be eliminated but only bridged by the democratic process. However, the weak normative connotations of a regulated balancing of power and interests stands in need of constitutional channeling. The democratic will-formation of self-interested citizens, construed in minimalist terms, constitutes just one element within a constitution that disciplines governmental authority through normative constraints (such as basic rights, separation of powers, and legal regulation of the administration) and forces it, through competition between political parties, on the one hand, and between government and opposition, on the other, to take adequate account of competing interests and value orientations. This state-centered understanding of politics does not have to rely on the unrealistic assumption of a citizenry capable of acting collectively. Its focus is not so much the input of a rational political will-formation but the output of successful administrative accomplishments. The thrust of liberal arguments is directed against the disruptive potential of an administrative power that interferes with the independent social interactions of private persons. The liberal model hinges not on the democratic self-determination of deliberating citizens but on the legal institutionalization of an economic society that is supposed to guarantee an essentially nonpolitical common good through the satisfaction of the private aspirations of productive citizens.

Discourse theory invests the democratic process with normative connotations stronger than those of the liberal model but weaker than those of the republican model. Once again, it takes elements from both sides and fits them together in a new way. In agreement with republicanism, it gives center stage to the process of political opinion- and will-formation, but without understanding the constitution as something secondary; on the contrary, it conceives the basic principles of the constitutional state as a consistent answer to the question of how the demanding communicative presuppositions of a democratic opinion- and will-formation can be institutionalized. Discourse theory does not make the success of deliberative politics depend on a collectively acting citizenry but on the institutionalization of corresponding procedures. It no longer operates with the concept of a social whole centered in the state and conceived as a goal-oriented subject writ large. But neither does it localize the whole in a system of constitutional norms mechanically regulating the interplay of powers and interests in accordance with the market model. Discourse theory altogether jettisons the assumptions of the philosophy of consciousness, which invite us either to ascribe the citizens' practice of self-determination to one encompassing macro-subject or to apply the anonymous rule of law to competing individuals. The former approach represents the citizenry as a collective actor which reflects the whole and acts for its sake; on the latter, individual actors function as dependent variables in systemic processes that unfold blindly because no consciously executed collective decisions are possible over and above individual acts of choice (except in a purely metaphorical sense).

Discourse theory works instead with the *higher-level intersubjectivity* of communication processes that unfold in the institutionalized deliberations in parliamentary bodies, on the one hand, and in the informal networks of the public sphere, on the other. Both within and outside parliamentary bodies geared to decision making, these subjectless modes of communication form arenas in which a more or less rational opinion- and will-formation concerning issues and problems affecting society as a whole can take place. Informal opinion-formation result in institutionalized election decisions and legislative decrees through which communicatively generated power is transformed into administratively utilizable power. As on the liberal model, the boundary between state and society is respected; but here civil society, which provides the social underpinning of autonomous publics, is as distinct from the economic system as it is from the public administration. This understanding of democracy leads to the normative demand for a new balance between the three resources of money, administrative power, and solidarity from which modern societies meet their need for integration and regulation. The normative implications are obvious: the integrative force of solidarity, which can no longer be drawn solely from sources of communicative action, should develop through widely expanded autonomous public spheres as well as through legally institutionalized procedures of democratic deliberation and decision making and gain sufficient strength to hold its own against the other two social forces—money and administrative power.

III

This view has implications for how one should understand legitimation and popular sovereignty. On the liberal view, democratic will-formation has the exclusive function of *legitimating* the exercise of political power. The outcomes of elections license the assumption of governmental power, though the government must justify the use of power to the public and parliament. On the republican view, democratic will-formation has the significantly stronger function of *constituting* society as a political community and keeping the memory of this founding act alive with each new election. The government is not only empowered by the electorate's choice between teams of leaders to exercise a largely open mandate, but is also bound in a programmatic fashion to carry out certain policies. More a committee than an organ of the state, it is part of a self-governing political community rather than the head of a separate governmental apparatus. Discourse theory, by contrast, brings a third idea into play: the

procedures and communicative presuppositions of democratic opin-
ion- and will-formation function as the most important sluices for
the discursive rationalization of the decisions of a government and
an administration bound by law and statute. On this view, *rationalization* signifies more than mere legitimation but less than the constitution of political power. The power available to the administration
changes its general character once it is bound to a process of democratic opinion- and will-formation that does not merely retrospec-
tively monitor the exercise of political power but also programs it in
a certain way. Notwithstanding this discursive rationalization, only
the political system itself can "act." It is a subsystem specialized for
collectively binding decisions, whereas the communicative structures
of the public sphere comprise a far-flung network of sensors that
respond to the pressure of society-wide problems and stimulate
influential opinions. The public opinion which is worked up via
democratic procedures into communicative power cannot itself
"rule" but can only channel the use of administrative power in
specific directions.

The concept of *popular sovereignty* stems from the republican appropriation and revaluation of the early modern notion of sovereignty originally associated with absolutist regimes. The state, which
monopolizes the means of legitimate violence, is viewed as a concentration of power which can overwhelm all other temporal powers.
Rousseau transposed this idea, which goes back to Bodin, to the will
of the united people, fused it with the classical idea of the self-rule
of free and equal citizens, and sublimated it into the modern concept of autonomy. Despite this normative sublimation, the concept
of sovereignty remained bound to the notion of an embodiment in
the (at first actually physically assembled) people. According to the
republican view, the at least potentially assembled people are the
bearers of a sovereignty that cannot in principle be delegated: in
their capacity as sovereign, the people cannot let themselves be
represented by others. Constitutional power is founded on the citizens' practice of self-determination, not on that of their representatives. Against this, liberalism offers the more realistic view that,
in the constitutional state, the authority emanating from the people
is exercised only "by means of elections and voting and by specific
legislative, executive, and judicial organs."[9]

These two views exhaust the alternatives only on the dubious assumption that state and society must be conceived in terms of a whole and its parts, where the whole is constituted either by a sovereign citizenry or by a constitution. By contrast to the discourse theory of democracy corresponds the image of a *decentered* society, though with the political public sphere it sets apart an arena for the detection, identification, and interpretation of problems affecting society as a whole. If we abandon the conceptual framework of the philosophy of the subject, sovereignty need neither be concentrated in the people in a concretistic manner nor banished into the anonymous agencies established by the constitution. The "self" of the self-organizing legal community disappears in the subjectless forms of communication that regulate the flow of discursive opinion- and will-formation whose fallible results enjoy the presumption of rationality. This is not to repudiate the intuition associated with the idea of popular sovereignty but rather to interpret it in intersubjective terms. Popular sovereignty, even though it has become anonymous, retreats into democratic procedures and the legal implementation of their demanding communicative presuppositions only to be able to make itself felt as communicatively generated power. Strictly speaking, this communicative power springs from the interactions between legally institutionalized will-formation and culturally mobilized publics. The latter for their part find a basis in the associations of a civil society distinct from the state and the economy alike.

The normative self-understanding of deliberative politics does indeed call for a discursive mode of socialization for the *legal community;* but this mode does not extend to the whole of the society in which the constitutionally established political system is *embedded.* Even on its own proceduralist self-understanding, deliberative politics remains a component of a complex society, which as a whole resists the normative approach of legal theory. In this regard, the discourse-theoretic reading of democracy connects with an objectifying sociological approach that regards the political system neither as the peak nor the center, nor even as the structuring model of society, but as just *one* action system among others. Because it provides a kind of surety for the solution of the social problems that threaten integration, politics must indeed be able to communicate, via the medium of law, with all of the other legitimately ordered spheres of action, however these may be structured and steered. But the political system remains dependent on other functional mechanisms, such as the revenue-production of the economic system, in more than just a trivial sense; on the contrary, deliberative politics, whether realized in the formal procedures of institutionalized opinion- and will-formation or only in the informal networks of the political public sphere, stands in an internal relation to the contexts of a rationalized lifeworld that meets it halfway. Deliberatively filtered political communications are especially dependent on the resources of the lifeworld—on a free and open political culture and an enlightened political socialization, and above all on the initiatives of opinion-shaping associations. These resources emerge and regenerate themselves spontaneously for the most part—at any rate, they can only with difficulty be subjected to political control.

10

On the Internal Relation between the Rule of Law and Democracy

In academia we often mention law and politics in the same breath, yet at the same time we are accustomed to consider law, the rule of law, and democracy as subjects of different disciplines: jurisprudence deals with law, political science with democracy, and each deals with the constitutional state in its own way—jurisprudence in normative terms, political science from an empirical standpoint. The scholarly division of labor continues to operate even when legal scholars attend to law and the rule of law, on the one hand, and will-formation in the constitutional state, on the other; or when social scientists, in the role of sociologists of law, examine law and the constitutional state and, in the role of political scientists, examine the democratic process. The constitutional state and democracy appear to us as entirely separate objects. There are good reasons for this. Because political rule is always exercised in the form of law, legal systems exist where political force has not yet been domesticated by the constitutional state. And constitutional states exist where the power to govern has not yet been democratized. In short, there are legally ordered governments without constitutional institutions, and there are constitutional states without democratic constitutions. Of course, these empirical grounds for a division of labor in the academic treatment of the two subjects by no means imply that, from a normative standpoint, the constitutional state could exist without democracy.

In this paper I want to treat several aspects of this internal relation between the rule of law and democracy. This relation results from the concept of modern law itself (section 1) as well as from the fact that positive law can no longer draw its legitimacy from a higher law (section 2). Modern law is legitimated by the autonomy guaranteed equally to each citizen, and in such a way that private and public autonomy reciprocally presuppose each other (section 3). This conceptual interrelation also makes itself felt in the dialectic of legal and factual equality. It was this dialectic that first elicited the social-welfare paradigm of law as a response to the liberal understanding of law, and today this same dialectic necessitates a proceduralist self-understanding of constitutional democracy (section 4). In closing I will elucidate this proceduralist legal paradigm with the example of the feminist politics of equality (section 5).

1 Formal Properties of Modern Law

Since Locke, Rousseau, and Kant, a certain concept of law has gradually prevailed not only in philosophical thought but in the constitutional reality of Western societies. This concept is supposed to account simultaneously for both the positivity and the freedom-guaranteeing character of coercible law. The positivity of law—the fact that norms backed by the threat of state sanction stem from the changeable decisions of a political lawgiver—is bound up with the demand for legitimation. According to this demand, positively enacted law should guarantee the autonomy of all legal persons equally; and the democratic procedure of legislation should in turn satisfy this demand. In this way, an internal relation is established between the coercibility and changeability of positive law on the one hand, and a mode of lawmaking that engenders legitimacy on the other. Hence from a normative perspective there is a conceptual or internal relation—and not simply a historically, accidental relation—between law and democracy, between legal theory and democratic theory.

At first glance, the establishment of this internal relation has the look of a philosophical trick. Yet, as a matter of fact, the relation is deeply rooted in the presuppositions of our everyday practice of law.

For in the mode of validity that attaches to law, the facticity of the state's legal enforcement is intermeshed with the legitimating force of a legislative procedure that claims to be rational in that it guarantees freedom. This is shown in the peculiar ambivalence with which the law presents itself to its addressees and expects their obedience: that is, it leaves its addressees free to approach the law in either of two ways. They can either consider norms merely as factual constraints on their freedom and take a strategic approach to the calculable consequences of possible rule-violations, or they can comply with legal statutes in a performative attitude, indeed comply out of respect for results of a common will-formation that claim legitimacy. Kant already expressed this point with his concept of "legality," which highlighted the connection between these two moments without which legal obedience cannot be reasonably expected: legal norms must be fashioned so that they can be viewed simultaneously in two ways, as coercive and as laws of freedom. These two aspects belong to our understanding of modern law: we consider the validity of a legal norm as equivalent to the explanation that the state can simultaneously guarantee factual enforcement and legitimate enactment—thus it can guarantee, on the one hand, the legality of behavior in the sense of average compliance, which can if necessary be compelled by sanctions; and, on the other hand, the legitimacy of the rule itself, which must always make it possible to comply with the norm out of respect for the law.

Of course, this immediately raises the question of how the legitimacy of rules should be grounded when the rules in question can be changed at any time by the political legislator. Constitutional norms too are changeable; and even the basic norms that the constitution itself has declared nonamendable share with all positive law the fate that they can be abrogated, say, after a change of regime. As long as one was able to fall back on a religiously or metaphysically grounded natural law, the whirlpool of temporality enveloping positive law could be held in check by morality. Situated in a hierarchy of law, temporalized positive law was supposed to remain *subordinate* to an eternally valid moral law, from which it was to receive its lasting orientations. But even aside from the fact that in pluralistic societies such integrating worldviews and collectively binding comprehensive doctrines have in any case disintegrated, modern law, simply by virtue of its formal properties, resists the direct control of a posttraditional morality of conscience, which is, so to speak, all we have left.

2 The Complementary Relation between Positive Law and Autonomous Morality

Modern legal systems are constructed on the basis of individual rights. Such rights have the character of releasing legal persons from moral obligations in a carefully circumscribed manner. By introducing rights that concede to agents the latitude to act according to personal preferences, modern law as a whole implements the principle that whatever is not explicitly prohibited is permitted. Whereas in morality an inherent symmetry exists between rights and duties, legal duties are a consequence of entitlements, that is, they result only from statutory constraints on individual liberties. This basic conceptual privileging of rights over duties is explained by the modern concepts of the "legal person" and of the "legal community." The moral universe, which is *unlimited* in social space and historical time, includes *all natural persons* with their complex life histories; morality itself extends to the protection of the integrity of fully individuated persons (*Einzelner*). By contrast, the legal community, which is always localized in space and time, protects the integrity of its members precisely insofar as they acquire the artificial status of *rights bearers*. For this reason, the relation between law and morality is more one of complementarity than of subordination.

The same is true if one compares their relative scope. The matters that require legal regulation are at once both narrower and broader in scope than morally relevant concerns: narrower inasmuch as legal regulation has access only to external, that is, coercible, behavior, and broader inasmuch as law, as an organizational form of politics, pertains not only to the regulation of interpersonal conflicts but also to the pursuit of political goals and the implementation of policies. Hence legal regulations touch not only on moral questions in the narrow sense, but also on pragmatic and ethical questions, and on forming compromises among conflicting interests. Moreover, unlike the clearly delimited normative validity claimed by moral norms, the *legitimacy* claimed by legal norms is based on various sorts of reasons. The legislative practice of justification depends on a complex network of discourses and bargaining, and not just on moral discourse.

The idea from natural law of a hierarchy of laws at different levels of dignity is misleading. Law is better understood as a functional complement to morality. As positively valid, legitimately enacted, and actionable, law can relieve the morally judging and acting person of the considerable cognitive, motivational, and organizational demands of a morality based entirely on individual conscience. Law can compensate for the weaknesses of a highly demanding morality that—if we judge from its empirical results—provides only cognitively indeterminate and motivationally unreliable results. Naturally, this does not absolve legislators and judges from the concern that the law be in harmony with morality. But legal regulations are too concrete to be legitimated solely through their compatibility with moral principles. From what, then, can positive law borrow its legitimacy, if not from a superior moral law?

Like morality, law too is supposed to protect the autonomy of all persons equally. Law too must prove its legitimacy under this aspect of securing freedom. Interestingly enough, though, the positive character of law forces autonomy to split up in a peculiar way, which has no parallel in morality. Moral self-determination in Kant's sense is a unified concept insofar as it demands of each person, *in propria persona,* that she obey just those norms that she herself posits according to her own impartial judgment, or according to a judgment reached in common with all other persons. However, the binding quality of legal norms does not stem solely from processes of opinion- and will-formation, but arises also from the collectively binding decisions of authorities who make and apply law. This circumstance makes it conceptually necessary to distinguish the role of authors who make (and adjudicate) law from that of addressees who are subject to established law. The autonomy that in the moral domain is all of a piece, so to speak, appears in the legal domain only in the dual form of private and public autonomy.

However, these two moments must then be mediated in such a way that the one form of autonomy does not detract from the other. Each form of autonomy, the individual liberties of the subject of private law and the public autonomy of the citizen, makes the other form possible. This reciprocal relation is expressed by the idea that legal persons can be autonomous only insofar as they can understand themselves, in the exercise of their civic rights, as authors of just those rights which they are supposed to obey as addressees.

3   The Mediation of Popular Sovereignty and Human Rights

It is therefore not surprising that modern natural law theories have answered the legitimation question by referring, on the one hand, to the principle of *popular sovereignty* and, on the other, to the *rule of law* as guaranteed by human rights. The principle of popular sovereignty is expressed in rights of communication and participation that secure the public autonomy of citizens; the rule of law is expressed in those classical basic rights that guarantee the private autonomy of members of society. Thus the law is legitimated as an instrument for the equal protection of private and public autonomy. To be sure, political philosophy has never really been able to strike a balance between popular sovereignty and human rights, or between the "freedom of the ancients" and the "freedom of the moderns." The political autonomy of citizens is supposed to be embodied in the self-organization of a community that gives itself its laws through the sovereign will of the people. The private autonomy of citizens, on the other hand, is supposed to take the form of basic rights that guarantee the anonymous rule of law. Once the issue is set up in this way, either idea can be upheld only at the expense of the other. The intuitively plausible co-originality of both ideas falls by the wayside.

Republicanism, which goes back to Aristotle and the political humanism of the Renaissance, has always given the public autonomy of citizens priority over the prepolitical liberties of private persons. *Liberalism,* which goes back to John Locke, has invoked the danger of tyrannical majorities and postulated the priority of human rights. According to republicanism, human rights owed their legitimacy to the ethical self-understanding and sovereign self-determination achieved by a political community; in liberalism, such rights were supposed to provide, from the very start, legitimate barriers that prevented the sovereign will of the people from encroaching on inviolable spheres of individual freedom. In their concepts of the legal person's autonomy, Rousseau and Kant certainly aimed to conceive of sovereign will and practical reason as unified in such a way that popular sovereignty and human rights would reciprocally interpret one another. But even they failed to do justice to the co-originality of the two ideas; Rousseau suggests more of a republican reading, Kant more of a liberal one. They missed the intuition they wanted to articulate: that the idea of human rights, which is expressed in the right to equal individual liberties, must neither be merely imposed on the sovereign legislator as an external barrier, nor be instrumentalized as a functional requisite for legislative goals.

To express this intuition properly it helps to view the democratic procedure—which alone provides legitimating force to the lawmaking process in the context of social and ideological pluralism—from a discourse-theoretical standpoint. Here I assume a principle that I cannot discuss in detail, namely, that a regulation may claim legitimacy only if all those possibly affected by it could consent to it after participating in rational discourses. Now, if discourses—and bargaining processes as well, whose fairness is based on discursively grounded procedures—represent the place where a reasonable political will can develop, then the presumption of reasonability, which the democratic procedure is supposed to ground, ultimately rests on an elaborate communicative arrangement: the presumption depends on the conditions under which one can legally institutionalize the forms of communication necessary for legitimate lawmaking. In that case, the desired internal relation between human rights and popular sovereignty consists in this: human rights themselves are what satisfy the requirement that a civic practice of the public use of communicative freedom be legally institutionalized. Human rights, which make the exercise of popular sovereignty legally possible, cannot be imposed on this practice as an external constraint. Enabling conditions must not be confused with such constraints.

Naturally, this analysis is at first plausible only for those political civil rights, specifically the rights of communication and participation, that safeguard the exercise of political autonomy. It is less plausible for the classical human rights that guarantee the citizens' private autonomy. Here we think in the first instance of the fundamental right to the greatest possible degree of equal individual liberties, though also of basic rights that constitute membership status in a state and provide the individual with comprehensive legal protection. These rights, which are meant to guarantee everyone an equal opportunity to pursue his or her private conception of the good, have an intrinsic value, or at least they are not reducible to their instrumental value for democratic will-formation. We will do justice to the intuition that the classical liberties are co-original with political rights only if we state more precisely the thesis that human rights legally enable the citizens' practice of self-determination. I turn now to this more precise statement.

4 The Relation between Private and Public Autonomy

However well-grounded human rights are, they may not be paternalistically foisted, as it were, on a sovereign. Indeed, the idea of citizens' legal autonomy demands that the addressees of law be able to understand themselves at the same time as its authors. It would contradict this idea if the democratic legislator were to discover human rights as though they were (preexisting) moral facts that one merely needs to enact as positive law. At the same time, one must also not forget that when citizens occupy the role of co-legislators they are no longer free to choose the medium in which alone they can realize their autonomy. They participate in legislation only as legal subjects; it is no longer in their power to decide which language they will make use of. The democratic idea of self-legislation *must* acquire its validity in the medium of law itself.

However, when citizens judge in the light of the discourse principle whether the law they make is legitimate, they do so under communicative presuppositions that must themselves be legally institutionalized in the form of political civil rights, and for such institutionalization to occur, the legal code as such must be available. But in order to establish this legal code it is necessary to create the status of legal persons who as bearers of individual rights belong to a voluntary association of citizens and when necessary effectively claim their rights. There is no law without the private autonomy of legal persons in general. Consequently, without basic rights that secure the private autonomy of citizens there is also no medium for legally institutionalizing the conditions under which these citizens, as citizens of a state, can make use of their public autonomy. Thus private and public autonomy mutually presuppose each other in such a way that neither human rights nor popular sovereignty can claim primacy over its counterpart.

This mutual presupposition expresses the intuition that, on the one hand, citizens can make adequate use of their public autonomy only if, on the basis of their equally protected private autonomy, they are sufficiently independent; but that, on the other hand, they can arrive at a consensual regulation of their private autonomy only if they make adequate use of their political autonomy as enfranchised citizens.

The internal relation between the rule of law and democracy has been concealed long enough by the competition between the legal paradigms that have been dominant up to the present. The liberal legal paradigm reckons with an economic society that is institutionalized through private law—above all through property rights and contractual freedom—and left to the spontaneous workings of the market. Such a "private law society" is tailored to the autonomy of legal subjects who as market participants more or less rationally pursue their personal life-plans. This model of society is associated with the normative expectation that social justice can be realized by guaranteeing such a negative legal status, and thus solely by delimiting spheres of individual freedom. The well-founded critique of this supposition gave rise to the social welfare model. The objection is obvious: if the free "capacity to have and acquire" is supposed to guarantee social justice, then an equality in "legal capacity" must exist. As a matter of fact, however, the growing inequalities in economic power, assets, and living conditions have increasingly destroyed the factual preconditions for an equal opportunity to make effective use of equally distributed legal powers. If the normative content of legal equality is not to be inverted, then two correctives are necessary. On the one hand, existing norms of private law must be substantively specified, and on the other, basic social rights must be introduced, rights that ground claims to a more just distribution of socially produced wealth and to more effective protection against socially produced dangers.

In the meantime, of course, this *materialization* of law has in turn created the unintended side effects of welfare paternalism. Clearly, efforts to compensate for actual living conditions and power positions must not lead to "normalizing" interventions of a sort that once again restrict the presumptive beneficiaries' pursuit of an autonomous life-project. The further development of the dialectic of legal and factual equality has shown that both legal paradigms are equally committed to the productivist image of an economic society based on industrial capitalism. This society is supposed to function in such a way that the expectation of social justice can be satisfied by securing each individual's private pursut of his or her conception of the good life. The only dispute between the two paradigms concerns whether private autonomy can be guaranteed directly by negative liberties *(Freiheitsrechte)*, or whether on the contrary the conditions for private autonomy must be secured through the provision of welfare entitlements. In both cases, however, the internal relation between private and public autonomy drops out of the picture.

5   An Example: The Feminist Politics of Equality

In closing, I want to examine the feminist politics of equality to show that policies and legal strategies oscillate helplessly between the conventional paradigms as long as they remain limited to securing private autonomy and disregard how the individual rights of private persons are related to the public autonomy of citizens engaged in lawmaking. For, in the final analysis, private legal subjects cannot enjoy even equal individual liberties if they themselves do not jointly exercise their civic autonomy in order to specify clearly which interests and standards are justified, and to agree on the relevant respects that determine when like cases should be treated alike and different cases differently.

Initially, the goal of liberal policies was to uncouple the acquisition of status from gender identity and to guarantee to women equal opportunities in the competition for jobs, social recognition, education, political power, etc., regardless of the outcome. However, the formal equality that was partially achieved merely made more obvious the ways in which women were *in fact* treated unequally. Social welfare politics responded, especially in the areas of social, labor, and family law, by passing special regulations relating, for example, to pregnancy and child care, or to social hardship in the case of divorce. In the meantime feminist critique has targeted not only the unredeemed demands, but also the ambivalent consequences of successfully implemented welfare programs—for example, the higher risk of women losing their jobs as a result of compensatory regulations, the over-representation of women in lower wage brackets, the problematic issue of "what is in the child's best interests," and in general the progressive feminization of poverty. From a legal standpoint, one reason for this reflexively generated discrimination is found in the overgeneralized classifications used to label disadvantaged situations and disadvantaged groups of persons, because these "false" classifications lead to "normalizing" interventions into how people conduct their lives, interventions that transform what was intended as compensation for damages into new forms of discrimination. Thus instead of guaranteeing liberty, such overprotection stifles it. In areas of law that are of concern to feminism, welfare paternalism takes on a literal meaning to the extent that legislation and adjudication are oriented by traditional patterns of interpretation and thus serve to buttress existing stereotypes of sexual identity.

The classification of gender-specific roles and differences touches on fundamental levels of a society's cultural self-understanding. Radical feminism has only now made us aware of the fallible character of this self-understanding, an understanding that is essentially contested and in need of revision. It rightly insists that the appropriate interpretation of needs and criteria be a matter of public debate in the political public sphere. It is here that citizens must clarify the aspects that determine which differences between the experiences and living situations of (specific groups of) men and women are relevant for an equal opportunity to exercise individual liberties. Thus, this struggle for the equal status of women is a particularly good example of the need for a change of the legal paradigm.

The dispute between the two received paradigms—whether the autonomy of legal persons is better secured through individual liberties for private competition or through publicly guaranteed entitlements for clients of welfare bureaucracies—is superseded by a *proceduralist conception of law.* According to this conception, the democratic process must secure private and public autonomy at the same time: the individual rights that are meant to guarantee to women the autonomy to pursue their lives in the private sphere cannot even be adequately formulated unless the affected persons themselves first articulate and justify in public debate those aspects that are relevant to equal or unequal treatment in typical cases. The private autonomy of equally entitled citizens can be secured only insofar as citizens actively exercise their civic autonomy.

Notes

Editor's Introduction

1. It should be noted that "rule of law" generally translates the German term "*Rechtsstaat*," which literally means "constitutional state;" hence the relevant intuition can also be expressed as the claim that the constitutional state is not possible without participatory democracy. This guiding intuition is dealt with explicitly in chapters 9 and 10, which offer a succinct exposition of Habermas's political theory and hence are a suitable starting point for readers who are not familiar with his recent work.

2. This duality of "facticity" and "validity" is the central theme of Habermas's major work in legal and political philosophy, *Between Facts and Norms: Contributions to a Discourse Theory of Law and Democracy*, trans. W. Rehg (Cambridge, MA, 1996).

3. Habermas does not claim to develop a theory of justice for all possible human societies and is keenly aware that Western constitutional democracies emerged in response to contingent historical developments. At the same time, he rejects contextualist attempts to base the legitimacy of the constitutional state on supposedly "Western" values, on the grounds that the principles of justice enshrined in democratic constitutions can claim universal validity for modern societies.

4. Rawls takes this contextualist turn in *Political Liberalism* (New York, 1993; expanded pbk. ed., 1996).

5. The theory of communicative action holds that social actors are self-interpreting subjects who acquire and reproduce their identities through communicative interaction; that action oriented to reaching understanding plays a more fundamental role than strategic action in the reproduction of socio-cultural forms of life; and that communicative actors implicitly or explicitly raise validity claims, including normative claims, that admit of reasoned justification in discourse. These ambitious claims are developed and defended at length by Habermas in *The Theory of Communicative Action*, 2 vols., trans. T. McCarthy (Boston, 1985/1987).

6. Cf. Habermas, *Between Facts and Norms*, p. 107; also chapter 9, below, "Three Normative Models of Democracy," esp. pp. 248ff.

7. In chapter 1 below, "A Genealogical Analysis of the Cognitive Content of Morality," Habermas defends the strong cognitivist position that moral norms admit in principle of universal rational justification against a range of opposing philosophical positions that have been taken on the question of whether moral disputes admit of rational resolution.

8. Habermas's response to skepticism concerning the rational basis of the validity of norms mirrors a duality that characterizes his general approach to questions of normative justification: an internal reconstruction of the unavoidable pragmatic presuppositions of argumentation is complemented by an objectifying analysis of the role of communicative interaction in the reproduction of socio-cultural forms of life and of agents' identities. See Habermas, "Individuation through Socialization: On George Herbert Mead's Theory of Subjectivity," in *Postmetaphysical Thinking*, trans. W. M. Hohengarten (Cambridge, MA, 1992), pp. 149–204.

9. The corresponding conception of validity is captured by a principle of universalization which states that only those moral norms are valid that are such that all those affected by their general observance could freely accept their anticipated consequences for the satisfaction of everyone's interests; see Habermas, *Moral Consciousness and Communicative Action*, trans. C. Lenhardt and S. Weber Nicholsen (Cambridge, MA, 1990), pp. 92–93.

10. Cf. *Between Facts and Norms*, p. 122: "These three categories of rights result simply from the application of the discourse principle to the medium of law as such, that is, to the conditions for the legal form of a horizontal association of free and equal persons." On the justification of the system of basic rights as a whole see *ibid.*, pp. 118–131.

11. Thus the nature of the constitution-founding practice means that autonomy in the legal-political domain splits into private and public autonomy in a way that has no equivalent in the moral domain. On this account, the distinction between private and public domains is an artifact of modern legal systems, not a prepolitical fact whose preservation is the main raison d'être of the liberal state.

12. Habermas, following Kant, distinguishes between pragmatic, prudential, and moral dimensions of practical reason. Ethical questions or questions of what is good for me or for us have a different logic than do pragmatic questions of the appropriate means to certain practical ends and moral questions of what I or we ought to do. See Habermas, "On the Pragmatic, the Ethical, and the Moral Employments of Practical Reason," in *Justification and Application*, trans. C. Cronin (Cambridge, MA, 1993), pp. 1–17.

13. While *any* group of people can in principle come together to form a constitutional regime—provided that an ongoing scheme of social cooperation between them is possible—this does not mean that any like-minded minority within an existing constitutional state has the right to form an independent state of its own. On the contrary, Habermas takes a rather restrictive view of the right of secession because secessions generally create new minorities who do not necessarily consent to the new regime. Only when a minority suffers systematic discrimination against which its members have no genuine legal recourse—in which case the existing regime is illegitimate because it systematically violates the rights of some of its subjects—can it claim a right to secede.

14. For example, Habermas's scheme is opposed to the increasing concentration of ownership of print and electronic media and the increasing subordination of such media to economic interests. Such developments tend to degrade public political discourse and undermine its legitimating function by restricting access to the media and making them susceptible to ideological exploitation.

15. For an extended discussion, see *Between Facts and Norms,* pp. 168ff.

16. See *Between Facts and Norms,* pp. 144–168, 341ff.

17. These three interrelated lines of criticism are dealt with respectively in the three main sections of chapter 2, "Reconciliation through the Public Use of Reason."

18. For Rawls's detailed responses and countercriticisms see his "Reply to Habermas," *The Journal of Philosophy* 92 (3), 1995: 132–180 (reprinted as an appendix to the paperback edition of *Political Liberalism*).

19. See chapter 3, below, "'Reasonable' vs. 'True' or the Morality of Worldviews," pp. 89ff. Habermas's description of this shared standpoint as the "moral point of view" is potentially misleading in light of the importance he attaches to the distinction between morality and legality in his political theory. This looseness in terminology reflects the fact that the perspective from which citizens justify *basic* constitutional principles approximates in its abstractness and universality to the moral point of view.

20. See Rawls, "Reply to Habermas," pp. 138, 179. Rawls correctly argues that no theory of justice can be purely procedural, in the sense of avoiding any appeal to substantive ideals, and that Habermas's discourse theory is no exception in this regard. The important difference, however, is how they ground their respective substantive principles. Whereas Rawls appeals to normative ideas implicit in the political culture of liberal democracies, thereby restricting the scope of his theory, Habermas argues that a fully universal principle of normative validity can be grounded in certain normative presuppositions of speech and action that communicative actors unavoidably make once they engage in practical argumentation. Thus the procedure of practical discourse itself, and not a comprehensive metaphysical conception of reason or the person, is the source of normative constraints.

21. See Rawls, "Reply to Habermas," pp. 139–141, 143–145.

22. For a discussion of some of the relevant issues see T. McCarthy, "Kantian Constructivism and Reconstructivism: Rawls and Habermas in Dialogue," *Ethics* 105 (1), 1994: 44–63.

23. See J. Rawls, "The Law of Peoples," in S. Shute and S. Hurley, eds., *On Human Rights: The Oxford Amnesty Lectures 1993* (New York, 1993). pp. 41–82.

24. See K. Polanyi's classic, *The Great Transformation* (Boston, 1944).

25. See especially chapter 4, below, "The European Nation-State: On the Past and Future of Sovereignty and Citizenship," and chapter 5, below, "On the Relation between the Nation, the Rule of Law, and Democracy."

26. See C. Schmitt, *The Concept of the Political*, trans. G. Schwab (Chicago, 1996), and *The Crisis of Parliamentary Democracy*, trans. E. Kennedy (Cambridge, MA, 1985).

27. See, Habermas, *Between Facts and Norms*, chapter 3, part 3, and "The European Nation State," pp. 117ff.

28. See, e.g., D. P. Forsythe, *The Internationalization of Human Rights* (Lexington, MA, 1991).

29. See I. Kant, "Perpetual Peace: a Philosophical Sketch," in H. Reiss, ed., *Kant: Political Writings*, trans. H. B. Nisbet (Cambridge, 1991), pp. 93–130; Kant, *Werkausgabe*, Vol. XI, ed. W. Weischedel (Frankfurt am Main, 1968), pp. 195–251.

30. See chapter 7, "Kant's Idea of Perpetual Peace," pp. 169ff.

31. Kant, "On the Common Saying: 'This May be True in Theory, but it does not Apply in Practice," in *Political Writings*, p. 92; cf. Kant, *Werkausgabe* XI, pp. 171–172.

32. See Kant, "Perpetual Peace," esp. pp. 102–108; *Werkausgabe* XI, pp. 208–217.

33. See ch. 7, "Kant's Idea of Perpetual Peace," pp. 169ff.

34. See ch. 4, "The European Nation State," section V.

35. See D. Grimm, "Does Europe Need a Constitution?" *European Law Journal* 1 (3), 1995: 282–302. In the same issue, see also U. Preuß, "Problems of a Concept of European Identity," pp. 267–281 and J. Weiler, "Does Europe Need a Constitution? Reflections on Demos, Telos, and Ethos in the German Maastricht Decision," pp. 219–258. These papers are reprinted in P. Gowan and P. Anderson, eds., *The Question of Europe* (London, 1997).

36. As Grimm puts it, "The Treaties are not . . . a constitution in the full sense of the term. The difference lies in the reference back to the will of the Member States rather than to the people of the Union . . . The European public power is not one that derives from the people, but one mediated through States. Since the Treaties thus have not an internal but an external reference point, they are also not the expression of a society's self-determination as to the form and objectives of its political unity. Insofar as constitutions are concerned with the legitimation of rule by those subject to it, the Treaties thus fall short" (Grimm, "Does Europe Need a Constitution?" p. 291).

37. The European Union is built around four institutions: the Council of Ministers, the European Commission, the Parliament, and the European Court of Justice. The Commission is in charge of formulating policy, drafting legislation, preparing the budget of the Union, as well as implementing policies accepted by the Council and not vetoed by the Parliament. Part of its power derives from the fact that its drafts are the only basis for decisions in the Council. Commissioners are expected to be loyal to the Union, to which they swear an oath. (In this and the next three footnotes we will be following the papers collected in R. Keohane and S. Hoffman, eds., *The New European Community*, [Boulder, CO, 1991] and the very useful monograph by E. Eriksen, A. Føllesdall, and R. Malnes, *Europeanisation and Normative Political Theory.* ARENA working paper 1/95 [Oslo, 1995].)

38. The *Council of Ministers* is the real decision-making body of the Union. It is made up of representatives of the governments of all member states. Representatives in the Council stand in for the interests of their countries. Thus some commentators argue that the council is the main reason the European Union falls short of a federation.

39. The *European Parliament* is, arguably, the least developed of the Union's major institutions. Originally the Parliament's rights were limited to consultation and limited veto powers. It has slowly gained additional competences, including the right to ask the Commission for legislative initiatives over certain issues, and, most importantly, the right to do second and third readings of some legislative drafts before they are approved by the Council. Even with these enlarged powers, it should be clear that the Parliament is significantly weaker than a normal national Parliament.

40. That is, precisely what Grimm attacks; see chapter 6, below, "Does Europe Need a Constitution? Response to Dieter Grimm," p. 156.

41. Ibid.

42. Ibid., p. 161.

43. See chapter 8, below, "Struggles for Recognition in the Democratic Constitutional State," p. 210.

44. See "Struggles for Recognition," pp. 208, and "Individuation through Socialization," pp. 221ff.

45. See C. Taylor, "The Struggle for Recognition," in A. Gutmann, ed. *Multiculturalism: Examining the Politics of Recognition,* expanded edition (Princeton, NJ, 1994).

46. There is an important difference between equalizing the risks entailed by the different cultural choices made by different groups on the one hand, and, on the other, minimizing those risks. The latter is an attempt to guarantee through state action the survival of existing cultures. See Michael Walzer, "Comment," in Gutmann, ed., *Multiculturalism,* pp. 99–103. Habermas also argues against treating cultural groups as if they were species under the threat of extinction; see "Struggles for Recognition," section IV, pp. 220ff.

47. K. A. Appiah, "Identity, Authenticity, Survival: Multicultural Societies and Social Reproduction," in Gutmann, ed., *Multiculturalism,* pp. 149–163. Identities are "tightly scripted" when they impose a narrow definition of what it means to be African-American, Quebecois, gay, etc., on those who accept these identifications or who are socially identified (e.g., by skin color or behavior) as belonging to the groups in question regardless of whether they choose to identify with them or not.

48. See Habermas, "On the Pragmatic, the Ethical, and the Moral Employments of Practical Reason."

49. Habermas's vigorous support of procedural democracy puts him at odds not only with those theorists who are skeptical about the effectiveness of democracy in advancing the goals of pluralism, but also with the increasing tendency in our political culture to juridify social issues, that is, to appeal to judges rather than to democratic legislative forums for the resolution of important social problems.

Preface

1. English translation: *Between Facts and Norms: Contributions to a Discourse Theory of Law and Democracy*, trans. W. Rehg (Cambridge, MA, 1996).

2. *Between Facts and Norms*, pp. 491–515.

Chapter 1

1. P. F. Strawson, *Freedom and Resentment* (London, 1974).

2. H. L. A. Hart took this view when he traced the unity of legal systems back to basic rules that legitimate the whole corpus but do not admit of justification themselves. Like the rules of a language game, these "rules of recognition" are rooted in a practice that an observer can only register as a fact, whereas for the participants it has the status of a self-evident cultural commonplace which is accepted and assumed to be valid; see *The Concept of Law*, 2nd. ed. (Oxford, 1994).

3. See the impressive phenomenology of moral consciousness in L. Wingert, *Gemeinsinn und Moral* (Frankfurt am Main, 1993), ch. 3.

4. J. Habermas, "Transcendence from Within, Transcendence in This World," in D. S. Browning and F. Schüssler-Fiorenza, eds., *Habermas, Modernity, and Public Theology* (New York, 1992), pp. 226–250; also Th. M. Schmidt, "Immanente Transzendenz," in L. Hauser and E. Nordhofen, eds., *Im Netz der Begriffe: Religionsphilosophische Analyzen* (Freiburg, 1994), pp. 78–96.

5. On "justice" and "solidarity" see J. Habermas, *Moral Consciousness and Communicative Action*, trans. C. Lenhardt and S. Weber Nicholsen (Cambridge, MA, 1990), pp. 200ff. and "Justice and Solidarity: On the Discussion Concerning 'Stage 6,'" in T. Wren, ed., *The Moral Domain* (Cambridge, MA, 1990), pp. 244ff.; for a different account see L. Wingert, *Gemeinsinn und Moral*, pp. 179ff.

6. J. Habermas, *Postmetaphysical Thinking: Philosophical Essays*, trans. W. M. Hohengarten (Cambridge, MA, 1992).

7. For a critique of this view see J. L. Mackie, *Ethics* (New York, 1977), pp. 38ff. Today the balance of the argument has shifted in favor of realism. J. McDowell has developed the most subtle version of a value-ethic which starts from epistemological premises but is grounded in a philosophy of nature drawing on Plato and Aristotle, in *Mind and World* (Cambridge, MA, 1994), p. 82: "The ethical is a domain of rational requirements, which are there in any case, whether or not we are responsive to them. We are alerted to these demands by acquiring appropriate conceptual capacities. When a decent upbringing initiates us into the relevant way of thinking, our eyes are opened to the very existence of this tract of the space of reasons." McDowell makes the transition to objective idealism by assuming an organically based formation process (*Bildungsprozeß*), in light of which practical reason appears as a natural faculty that can claim objective validity: "Our *Bildung* actualizes some of the potentialities we are born with; we do not have to suppose it introduces a nonanimal ingredient into our constitution. And although the structure of the space of reasons cannot be reconstructed out of facts about our involvement in the realm of law, it can be the

Notes

framework within which meaning comes into view only because our eyes can be opened to it by *Bildung*, which is an element in the normal coming to maturity of the kind of animals we are. Meaning is not a mysterious gift from outside nature" (p. 88). McDowell frankly acknowledges the metaphysical claim of this conception, which I cannot go into in detail here: "The position is a naturalism of second nature, and I suggested that we can equally see it as a naturalized platonism. The idea is that the dictates of reason are there anyway, whether or not one's eyes are opened to them; that is what happens in a proper upbringing" (p. 91).

8. H. Lenk, "Kann die sprachanalytische Moralphilosophie neutral sein?" in M. Riedel, ed., *Rehabilitierung der praktischen Philosophie*, vol. II (Freiburg, 1974), pp. 405–422.

9. See E. Tugendhat, *Vorlesungen über Ethik* (Frankfurt am Main, 1993), pp. 199ff.

10. On the opposition between objective and subjective reason, see M. Horkheimer, *Critique of Instrumental Reason*, trans. M. J. O'Connell et al. (New York, 1974); H. Schnädelbach, "Vernunft," in E. Martens, H. Schnädelbach, eds., *Philosophie* (Heidelberg, 1985), pp. 77–115.

11. Kant, *Foundations of the Metaphysics of Morals*, trans. L. W. Beck (New York, 1990), p. 34 (Akad. ed., p. 417).

12. A. C. Baier, *Moral Prejudices* (Cambridge, MA, 1994), ch. 9, pp. 184ff. Instead of sympathy Baier goes back to the phenomenon of childhood trust: "Trust . . . is letting other persons . . . take care of something the truster cares about, where such 'caring for' involves some exercise of discretionary powers" (p. 105). This has the advantage of allowing moral concern to be described, true to experience, as a multifaceted compensating mechanism for dependency and vulnerability; but at the same time by transferring a model developed for asymmetrical parent-child relations to the symmetrical relations between adults, it has the disadvantage that it gives rise to the problem of trustworthiness and the abuse of trust (cf. chs. 6, 7, and 8).

13. Nor can the problem of affective ties to strangers be solved through a shift in focus from sympathy or trust to compassion. Although our capacity for empathetic identification with creatures capable of suffering undoubtedly extends farther than positive feelings toward people who are useful, agreeable, and trustworthy, compassion cannot ground equal respect for others *even, and especially, in their empathetically unbridgeable otherness.*

14. Cf. Mackie, *Ethics;* also "Can There be a Right-based Moral Theory?" in J. Waldron, ed., *Theories of Rights* (Oxford, 1984), pp. 168–181.

15. E. Tugendhat, "Zum Begriff und zur Begründung von Moral," in *Philosophische Aufsätze* (Frankfurt am Main, 1992), pp. 315–333.

16. E. Tugendhat, *Vorlesungen über Ethik*, p. 75.

17. J. Elster, *The Cement of Society* (Cambridge, 1989), Ch. 3.

18. E. Tugendhat, *Vorlesungen über Ethik*, pp. 29 and 91.

19. A. Gibbard, *Wise Choices, Apt Feelings* (Cambridge, MA, 1992), p. 296.

20. Ibid., p. 84.

21. Ibid., pp. 72f.

22. Ibid., p. 193: "[A] speaker treats what he is saying as an objective matter of rationality if he can demand its acceptance by everybody. More precisely, the test is this: could he coherently make his demands, revealing their grounds, and still not browbeat his audience? What makes for browbeating in this test is a question of conversational inhibitions and embarrassments. . . ."

23. Ibid., p. 195 n. 2 refers to the theory of discourse.

24. Ibid., p. 223 (my emphasis).

25. Nor can this be achieved by the participants in discourse making the biological description their own; for such an objectifying self-description would either destroy the practical self-understanding of subjects capable of action or undergo a fundamental change in meaning with the switch from the observer's to the participant's perspective.

26. Tugendhat, *Vorlesungen über Ethik*, p. 29.

27. M. Seel, *Versuch über die Form des Glücks* (Frankfurt am Main, 1995), p. 206.

28. Ibid., pp. 203f.

29. Ibid., p. 203: "It is true that the question 'Why be moral?' can still—indeed, can only—be answered by appealing to preferences, because moral conduct alone makes possible a form of social existence based on friendship and solidarity; but while this step may be motivated by preferences it commits us to modes of conduct that cannot be traced back to orientations grounded in preferences."

30. Tugendhat, *Vorlesungen über Ethik*, pp. 87f.

31. This is even clearer in E. Tugendhat, "Gibt es eine moderne Moral?" in *Zeitschrift für philosophische Forschung* 50 (1996): 323–338.

32. B. Williams, *Ethics and the Limits of Philosophy* (Cambridge, MA, 1985), ch. 8.

33. Rawls speaks in this connection of "reflective equilibrium."

34. McDowell rejects an objectivistic interpretation of these "salient features" of situations: "The relevant notion of salience cannot be understood except in terms of seeing something as a reason for acting which silences all others." "Virtue and Reason," *The Monist* 62 (1979): p. 345. He explains ethical insights in terms of the interaction between the way of life and self-understanding of individuals, on the one hand, and their evaluatively charged understanding of the particular situation, on the other. These analyses can still be understood—without embracing realism—in terms of a neo-Aristotelian ethics informed by Wittgenstein.

35. J. McDowell, "Are Moral Requirements Hypothetical Imperatives?" *Proceedings of the Aristotelian Society*, Supplementary Volume 5 (1978): 13–29.

36. Ch. Taylor, *The Sources of the Self* (Cambridge, MA, 1989).

37. Theories also raise a "higher-level" or more complex validity claim; they are not "true" or "false" in the same sense as the singular propositions that are derivable from them.

38. The existentialist sharpening of this decision into a radical choice fails to grasp the character of this freedom as an epistemically guided *process*.

39. Williams, *Ethics and the Limits of Philosophy*, pp. 184f.

40. Ibid., p. 187.

41. M. Seel (*Versuch über die Form des Glücks*) tries to develop such a formal concept of the good. But the idea of a formal determination of the good—distinct from morality in the Kantian sense—is a self-contradiction. Seel's attempt to explain the nature and conditions of the successful life cannot avoid privileging certain basic goods (security, health, freedom of movement), contents (work, interaction, play, and contemplation), and ends (self-determination that is responsive to external impulses). These ideas reflect fallible anthropological assumptions and valuations which are not only matters of dispute between different cultures but remain controversial, and for good reasons, in intercultural dialogue. A noncriterial understanding of such a projection of human potentialities has paternalistic implications, even when it is only offered as well-meaning advice: "What if someone does not want this good? We will tell her that she is rejecting what is best for her" (p. 189). The descriptive content of an anthropology of the good that goes beyond the analysis of the form of hermeneutic discourses of self-understanding in terms of a logic of argumentation remains bound to its context of discovery in a specific way—as is shown by the example of Heidegger whose existential ontology betrays not only the jargon but also the political prejudices of its time to any attentive reader one or two generations later (cf. R. Wolin, *The Politics of Being* [New York, 1990]).

42. Seel, *Versuch über die Form des Glücks*, p. 223.

43. R. Dworkin develops a similar approach in "Foundations of Liberal Equality," G. B. Peterson, ed., *The Tanner Lectures on Human Values* XI (Salt Lake City, 1990).

44. See n. 41 above.

45. Kant, *Foundations of the Metaphysics of Morals*, p. 55 (438).

46. Ibid., p. 29 (412) (translation modified).

47. C. Korsgaard misunderstands this point; see "The Sources of Normativity," *The Tanner Lectures on Human Values* XV (Salt Lake City, 1994), pp. 88ff.

48. Kant, *Foundations of the Metaphysics of Morals*, p. 52 (435).

49. The same holds true for Tugendhat (see above IV, 2).

50. J. Habermas, "Discourse Ethics: Notes on a Program of Philosophical Justification," in *Moral Consciousness and Communicative Action*, p. 66.

51. This is why, in important sectors of social life, the weak motivating force of morality must be supplemented by coercive positive law; cf. Habermas, *Between Facts and Norms*, trans. W. Rehg (Cambridge, MA, 1996), pp. 104ff.

52. On the following, cf. J. Heath, "Morality and Social Action" (Dissertation, Northwestern University, 1995), pp. 86–102.

53. D. Davidson, *Inquiries into Truth and Interpretation* (Oxford, 1983).

54. Habermas, "An Excursus on the Theory of Argumentation," in *The Theory of Communicative Action*, Vol. 1, trans. T. McCarthy (Cambridge, MA, 1984), pp. 22–42.

55. R. Rorty, "Pragmatism, Davidson, and Truth," in E. LePore, ed., *Truth and Interpretation* (Oxford, 1981), pp. 333–353.

56. This reactive concept of "discursive redeemability," which is not oriented to ideal conditions [of complete justification] but to potential objections, is similar to the notion of "superassertibility;" cf. C. Wright, *Truth and Objectivity* (Cambridge, MA, 1992), pp. 33ff. For a critique of my earlier conception of truth which was still influenced by Peirce, see A. Wellmer, *The Persistence of Modernity*, trans. D. Midgley (Cambridge, MA, 1991), pp. 160ff.; also Wingert, *Gemeinsinn und Moral*, pp. 264ff.

57. For a pragmatist interpretation of the discourse-concept of truth, cf. J. Habermas, "Rorty's Pragmatic Turn" (forthcoming).

58. This also explains why moral discourses of justification must be supplemented by discourses of application; cf. K. Günther, *The Sense of Appropriateness*, trans. J. Farrell (Albany, NY, 1993); also J. Habermas, *Between Facts and Norms*, p. 109.

59. Cf. J. Rawls, "Kantian Constructivism in Moral Theory," *The Journal of Philosophy* 77 (9) (1980): 515–572, p. 519.

60. A. Honneth, *The Struggle for Recognition*, trans. J. Anderson (Cambridge, 1992); R. Forst, *Kontexte der Gerechtigkeit* (Frankfurt am Main, 1994).

61. Wingert, *Gemeinsinn und Moral*, pp. 295ff. On the perspective structure of action oriented to reaching understanding see the title essay in Habermas, *Moral Consciousness and Communicative Action*, pp. 116ff., especially pp. 133–141.

62. Wingert has rigorously explored the implications of this duality in *Gemeinsinn und Moral*.

63. For this reason, the condition of impartiality is not satisfied simply by the fact that an impartial judge weighs the goods and harms that are at stake for "any" individual; for a different view see Tugendhat, *Vorlesungen über Ethik*, p. 353.

64. Cf. Seel, *Versuch über die Form des Glücks*, p. 204.

65. Cf. K. Ott, "Wie begründet man ein Diskussionsprinzip der Moral?" in *Vom Begründen zum Handeln* (Tübingen, 1996), pp. 12–50.

66. Cf. M. Niquet, *Transzendentale Argumente* (Frankfurt am Main, 1991); "Nichthintergehbarkeit und Diskurs" (Habilitationsschrift, Frankfurt am Main, 1995).

67. E. Tugendhat, *Vorlesungen über Ethik* (Frankfurt am Main, 1993), pp. 161ff. Tugendhat's criticism refers to a version of my argument which I revised already in the second [German] edition of *Moral Consciousness and Communicative Action*, that is, in 1984 (!); cf. Habermas, *Justification and Application*, p. 179, n. 17.

68. This point is emphasized by W. Rehg in *Insight and Solidarity* (Berkeley, CA, 1994), pp. 65ff.; cf. S. Benhabib, "Autonomy, Modernity and Community," in *Situating the Self* (New York, 1992), pp. 68–88.

69. K. O. Apel, "Die transzendentalpragmatische Begründung der Kommunikation-sethik," in *Diskurs und Verantwortung* (Frankfurt am Main, 1988), pp. 306–369.

70. See n. 57 above.

71. Habermas, *Between Facts and Norms*, pp. 106ff. and "Postscript," (pp. 459ff).

72. See R. Alexy, *Theorie der juristischen Argumentation* (Frankfurt am Main, 1991); K. Baynes, *The Normative Grounds of Social Criticism* (Albany, NY, 1992); S. Benhabib, "Deliberative Rationality and Models of Democratic Legitimacy," *Constellations* 1 (1994): 26–52; and especially R. Forst, *Kontexte der Gerechtigkeit*.

Chapter 2

1. *A Theory of Justice* (Cambridge, MA, 1971) (hereafter TJ).

2. John Rawls, *Political Liberalism* (New York, 1993) IV, section 1, p. 137 (hereafter PL).

3. In preparing this essay the following works were especially helpful: K. Baynes, *The Normative Grounds of Social Criticism* (Albany, NY, 1992); R. Forst, *Kontexte der Gerechtigkeit* (Frankfurt am Main, 1994).

4. Rawls, "The Basic Liberties and Their Priority," in S. McMurrin, ed., *The Tanner Lectures on Human Values* III (Salt Lake City, 1982), p. 16.

5. Rawls, "Justice as Fairness: Political not Metaphysical," *Philosophy and Public Affairs* 14 (1985): 223–251, p. 237 n. 20.

6. Thomas Scanlon also criticizes the traces of a decision-theoretical orientation, though from a different standpoint, in "Contractualism and Utilitarianism," in A. Sen and B. Williams, eds., *Utilitarianism and Beyond* (Cambridge, 1982), pp. 123ff.

7. I. M. Young, *Justice and the Politics of Difference* (Princeton, 1990), p. 25.

8. This objection is not based on the thesis of the primacy of duties over rights, as in O. O'Neill, *Constructions of Reason* (Cambridge, 1989), Ch. 12, pp. 206ff.

9. H. L. A. Hart, "Rawls On Liberty and its Priority," in N. Daniels, ed., *Reading Rawls* (New York, 1975), pp. 230ff.

10. See W. Hinsch, "Einleitung" to Rawls, *Die Idee des politischen Liberalismus* (Frankfurt am Main, 1992), pp. 38ff.

11. Rawls, "The Basic Liberties and Their Priority," pp. 21ff. and 39ff.

12. See, e.g., *Taking Rights Seriously* (Cambridge, MA, 1977).

13. Cf. J. Habermas, *Moral Consciousness and Communicative Action*, trans. C. Lenhardt and S. Weber Nicholsen (Cambridge, MA, 1990), and *Justification and Application: Remarks on Discourse Ethics*, trans. C. Cronin (Cambridge, MA, 1993); on the location of discourse ethics in contemporary American discussions, see S. Benhabib, "In the Shadow of Aristotle and Hegel: Communicative Ethics and Current Controversies in Practical Philosophy," in *Situating the Self* (New York, 1992), pp. 23–67. See also D. Rasmussen, ed., *Universalism vs. Communitarianism: Contemporary Debates in Ethics* (Cambridge, MA, 1990).

14. Cf. W. Rehg, *Insight and Solidarity: The Idea of a Discourse Ethics* (Berkeley, forthcoming).

15. *The Journal of Philosophy* 78 (9) (1980): 515–572.

16. Rawls, "The Domain of the Political and Overlapping Consensus," *New York University Law Review* 64 (1988): 223–255, p. 246

17. "Justice as Fairness: Political not Metaphysical," p. 230.

18. Rawls, "The Idea of an Overlapping Consensus," *Oxford Journal of Legal Studies* 7 (1987): 1–25, p. 6.

19. "What rational agents lack is the particular form of moral sensibility that underlies the desire to engage in fair cooperation as such, and to do so on terms that others as equals might reasonably be expected to endorse" (PL 51).

20. Cf. my reflections in *Justification and Application*, pp. 25ff.

21. Rawls, "The Idea of an Overlapping Consensus," p. 25.

22. Habermas, "Themes in Postmetaphysical Thinking," in *Postmetaphysical Thinking*, trans. W. M. Hohengarten (Cambridge, MA, 1992), pp. 28–53.

23. Cf. the Tanner Lectures, where he writes at the end of section VII: "The idea is to incorporate into the basic structure of society an effective political procedure which mirrors in that structure the fair representation of persons achieved by the original position" (p. 45).

24. "The Basic Liberties and Their Priority," p. 13.

25. S. Benhabib, "Models of Public Space," in *Situating the Self* (New York, 1992), pp. 89–120.

26. This principle of Kantian legal theory is taken up in Rawls's first principle.

27. Cf. "On the Internal Relation between the Rule of Law and Democracy," below pp. 256ff.

Chapter 3

1. I am grateful to Rainer Forst, Thomas McCarthy, and Lutz Wingert for instructive criticism.

2. J. Rawls, *Political Liberalism* (New York, 1993), p. 12 (hereafter PL).

3. J. Rawls, "Reply to Habermas," *The Journal of Philosophy* 92 (3) (1995): 132–180, p. 141, n. 16 (hereafter R). [This essay, which contains Rawls's response to the criticisms raised in the previous essay in this volume, has been reprinted as an appendix to the paperback edition of *Political Liberalism,* pp. 372–434. Trans.]

4. See Rawls, "Reply to Habermas."

5. This is a further development of the objections outlined in the second part of the previous essay.

6. J. Habermas, *The Theory of Communicative Action,* trans. T. McCarthy, 2 vols. (Boston, 1984, 1987). See also my essay "Sprechakttheoretischen Erläuterungen zum Begriff der kommunikativen Rationalität," *Zeitschrift für philosophische Vorschung* 50 (1996): 65–91.

7. T. M. Scanlon, "Contractualism and Utilitarianism," in A. K. Sen and B. Williams, eds., *Utilitarianism and Beyond* (Cambridge, 1982), p. 119.

8. J. Rawls, "Kantian Constructivism in Moral Theory," *The Journal of Philosophy* 77 (1980): 515–573; this approach is taken up by R. Milo, "Contractarian Constructivism," *The Journal of Philosophy* 92 (1995): 181–204.

9. L. Wingert, *Gemeinsinn und Moral* (Frankfurt am Main, 1993), Pt. II, pp. 166ff.

10. I follow the sequence of "three kinds" of justification outlined by Rawls. This logical sequence should not be understood as a temporal sequence of stages but sketches the path along which any member of contemporary society can radicalize her stance on current questions of political justice. Once her criticism places in question the relevant underlying political consensus from the perspective of a competing conception of justice, her defense of this alternative must follow the path of this logical genesis.

11. Cf. Habermas, "On the Pragmatic, the Ethical, and the Moral Employments of Practical Reason," in *Justification and Application,* trans. C. Cronin (Cambridge, MA, 1993), pp. 6f.

12. Forst, *Kontexte der Gerechtigkeit* (Frankfurt am Main, 1994), p. 159.

13. Ibid., pp. 152–161 and 72ff.

14. [That is, the German counterpart of the Supreme Court of the United States. Trans.]

15. "The particular meaning of the priority of right is that comprehensive conceptions of the good are admissible . . . only if their pursuit conforms to the political conception of justice" (PL 176, n. 2).

16. "In this case [i.e., when an overlapping consensus is achieved], citizens embed their shared political conception in their reasonable comprehensive doctrines. Then we hope that citizens will judge (by their comprehensive view) that political values are normally (though not always) ordered prior to, or outweigh, whatever nonpolitical values may conflict with them" (R 147).

17. I owe this argument to R. Forst, *Kontexte der Gerechtigkeit*.

18. I agree with Rawls's observations on procedural vs. substantive justice (R 170–180); but his remarks do not capture the sense in which I use the expressions "procedure" and "procedural rationality" when I assert that a practice of argumentation instituted in a certain way tends to support the assumption that its results are rationally acceptable.

19. As does R. Rorty's contextualist reading of Rawls's theory; see "The Priority of Democracy to Politics," in R. Vaughn, ed., *The Virginia Statute of Religious Freedom: Two Hundred Years After* (Madison, Wis., 1988); also R. J. Bernstein, "One Step Forward, Two Steps Backwards: Rorty On Liberal Democracy and Philosophy," *Political Theory* 15 (1987).

20. Of course I agree with Charles Larmore's suggestion in *The Morals of Modernity*, p. 216: "that our vision of the good life is the object of reasonable disagreement does not entail that we should withdraw our allegiance to it or regard it as henceforth a mere article of faith. . . . We should remember only that such reasons are not likely to be acceptable to other people, who are equally reasonable but have a different history of experience and reflection." Larmore evidently misunderstands my conception of the ethical use of practical reason; cf. Habermas, *Justification and Application*, pp. 1–17.

21. Forst, *Kontexte der Gerechtigkeit*, p. 283.

22. On the internal relation between the rule of law and democracy, see below, ch. 10.

Chapter 4

1. M. R. Lepsius, "Der europäische Nationalstaat," in *Interessen, Ideen und Institutionen* (Opladen, 1990), pp. 256–269.

2. In his essay "On the Common Saying: 'This May be True in Theory, But it Does Not Apply in Practice,'" Kant famously distinguished "the equality (of the individual) with everyone else as a subject" from the "freedom of the human being" and the "independence of the citizen;" Kant, *Political Writings*, ed. H. Reiss (Cambridge, 1991), p. 74.

3. "The model of nations made its entry into European history under the guise of asymmetrical contrasting concepts;" H. Münkler, "Die Nation als Modell politischer Ordnung," *Staatswissenschaft und Staatspraxis* 5, 3 (1994), p. 381.

4. H. Schulze, *Staat und Nation in der Europäischen Geschichte* (Munich, 1994), p. 189.

5. This mistake was already made by the liberal constitutional theorist Johann Caspar Bluntschli: "Every nation is called and therefore authorized to form a state. . . . Just as humanity is divided into a number of nations, so should [!] the world be divided into just as many states. Each nation a state. Each state a national entity" (quoted in H. Schulze, *Staat und Nation,* p. 225).

6. Cf. H. Schulze, *Staat und Nation,* p. 243ff.

7. Cf. J. Habermas, *Between Facts and Norms* (Cambridge, MA, 1996), pp. 409ff.

8. A. Giddens, *The Consequences of Modernity* (Cambridge, 1990), p. 64; *Beyond Left and Right* (Cambridge, 1994), pp. 78ff.

9. I. Wallerstein, *The Modern World System* (New York, 1974).

10. Knieper, *Nationale Souveränität* (Frankfurt am Main, 1991), p. 85.

11. J. M. Guéhenno, *The End of the Nation-State,* trans. V. Elliott (Minneapolis, 1995), p. 58.

12. Guéhenno, *The End of the Nation-State,* p. 99.

13. Today probably ten countries possess nuclear weapons, more than twenty chemical weapons, and it is suspected that some Middle Eastern countries already possess bacteriological weapons; cf. E. O. Czempiel, *Weltpolitik im Umbruch* (Munich, 1993), p. 93.

Chapter 5

1. H. Lübbe, *Abschied vom Superstaat* (Berlin, 1994), pp. 33f.

2. Cf. M. R. Lepsius, "'Ethnos' und 'Demos,'" in *Interessen, Ideen und Institutionen* (Opladen, 1990), pp. 247–256; *Demokratie in Deutschland* (Göttingen, 1993).

3. Cf. C. Leggewie, "Ethnizität, Nationalismus und multikulturelle Gesellschaft," in H. Berding, ed., *Nationales Bewußtsein und kollektive Identität* (Frankfurt am Main, 1995), p. 54.

4. W. Connor, *Ethnonationalism* (Princeton, NJ, 1994), p. 202: "Our answer to that often asked question, 'What is a nation?', is that it is a group of people who feel they are ancestrally related."

5. Cf. H. Schulze, *Staat und Nation in der Europäischen Geschichte* (Munich, 1994).

6. See, e.g., P. Sahlins, *Boundaries* (Berkeley, CA, 1989).

7. W. Böckenförde, "Die Nation," *Frankfurter Allegmeine Zeitung,* September 30, 1995.

8. Bökenförde, "Die Nation."

Notes

9. J. Habermas, *Die Normalität einer Berliner Republik* (Frankfurt am Main, 1995), p. 181.

10. H. Wehler, "Nationalismus und Nation in der deutschen Geschichte," in Berding, ed., *Nationales Bewußtsein*, pp. 174f.

11. Lübbe, *Abschied vom Superstaat*, pp. 38f.

12. C. Schmitt, *Verfassungslehre* (1928) (Berlin, 1983), p. 231.

13. Cf. I. Maus, "Rechtsgleichheit und gesellschaftliche Differenzierung bei Carl Schmitt," in *Rechtstheorie und Poilitische Theorie im Industriekapitalismus* (Munich, 1986), pp. 111–140.

14. Schmitt, *Verfassungslehre*, p. 228.

15. Ibid., p. 229.

16. Ibid., p. 243.

17. Ibid., p. 227.

18. Ibid., p. 234.

19. B. O. Bryde, "Die bundesrepublikanische Volksdemokratie als Irrweg der Demokratietheorie," *Staatswissenschaften und Staatspraxis* 5 (1994): 305–329.

20. Cf. Habermas, *Between Facts and Norms*, trans. W. Rehg (Cambridge, MA, 1996), Ch. 3.

21. I. Mauss, "'Volk' und 'Nation' in Denken der Aufklärung," *Blätter für deutsche und internationale Politik* 5 (1994), p. 604.

22. R. Forst, *Kontexte der Gerechtigkeit* (Frankfurt am Main, 1994), chs. 1 and 3.

23. Cf. Maus, *Zur Aufklärung der Demokratietheorie* (Frankfurt am Main, 1992).

24. R. A. Dahl, *Democracy and Its Critics* (New Haven & London, 1989), p. 193.

25. Schmitt, *Verfassungslehre*, p. 231.

26. Ibid., p. 233.

27. The relevant issues of status were first definitively clarified for the European powers when the unilateral declaration of independence of the United Netherlands was recognized by Spain in the Peace of Westphalia of 1581.

28. J. A. Frowein, "Die Entwicklung der Anerkennung von Staaten und Regierungen im Völkerrecht," *Der Staat* 11 (1972): 145–159.

29. Article 1 of the human rights agreement of December 16, 1966, which is tailored to the era of peaceful decolonization after the Second World War, reads: "All peoples

have the right of self-determination. By virtue of that right they freely determine their political status and freely pursue their economic, social and cultural development."

30. A. Verdross and B. Simma, *Universelles Völkerrecht,* 3rd ed. (Berlin, 1984), p. 318 (section 511).

31. Ch. Taylor, *Multiculturalism and the Politics of Recognition* (Princeton, 1992).

32. J. Habermas, "Struggles for Recognition in Constitutional States," this volume, pp. 219ff.

33. Dahl, *Democracy and Its Critics,* p. 204.

34. Cf. H. J. Puhle, "Vom Bürgerrecht zum Gruppenrecht? Multikulturelle Politik in den USA," in: K. J. Baade, ed., *Menschen über Grenzen* (Herne, 1995), pp. 134–149.

35. J. Raz, "Multiculturalism: A Liberal Perspective," *Dissent* (Winter 1994): 67–79, p. 77.

36. R. Wolfrum, "Die Entwicklung des internationalen Menschenrechtsschutzes," *Europa-Archiv* 23 (1993): 681–690.

37. Schmitt, *The Concept of the Political* (1932) (Chicago, 1996).

38. Schmitt, *Die Wendung zum diskriminierenden Kriegsbegriff* (1938) (Berlin, 1988).

39. For a discussion of this aspect of Walzer's work see B. Jahn, "Humanitäre Intervention und der Selbstbestimmungsrecht der Völker," *Politische Vierteljahresschrift* 34 (1993): 567–587.

40. M. Walzer, *Just and Unjust Wars: A Moral Argument with Historical Illustrations* (1977) (New York, 1992).

41. Walzer, "The Moral Standing of States," *Philosophy and Public Affairs* 9 (1980): 209–229, p. 211.

42. Ibid., p. 214.

43. G. Doppelt, "Walzer's Theory of Morality in International Relations," *Philosophy and Public Affairs* 8 (1978): 3–26, p. 19.

44. Cf. D. Senghaas, *Wohin driftet die Welt?* (Frankfurt am Main, 1994), p. 185.

45. Cf. K. O. Nass, "Grenzen und Gefahren humanitärer Interventionen," *Europa-Archiv* 10 (1993): 279–288.

46. Cf. Ch. Greenwood, "Gibt es ein Recht auf humanitäre Intervention?" *Europa-Archiv* 23 (1993): 93–106.

47. Judgment of the second senate of the Federal Constitutional Court of October 12th, 1993: 2 BvR 2134/92, 2BvR 2159/92, *Europäische Grundrechte Zeitschrift* 1993: 429–447, p. 438.

48. Cf. D. Murswiek, "Maastricht und der Pouvoir Constituant," *Der Staat* (1993): 161–190.

49. On this deflationary concept see H. P. Ipsen, "Zehn Glossen zum Maastricht-Urteil," *Europarecht* 29 (1994): 20: "By introducing the concept 'alliance of states' [*Staatenverbund*] (the judgment) employs a terminology that is inappropriate because of its economic-technical connotations. It ignores unnecessarily the language of the European community and the other member states." [The German word "*Verbund*" means a cooperative alliance among commercial enterprises. Trans.]

50. *Europäische Grundrechte Zeitschrift* (1993), p. 439.

51. J. A. Frowein, "Das Maastricht-Urteil und die Grenzen der Verfassungs-gerichtsbarkeit," *Zeitschrift für ausländisches öffentliches Recht und Völkerrecht* (1994): 1–16.

52. Lübbe, *Abschied vom Superstaat*, p. 100.

53. C. Joppke, *Nation-Building after World War Two* (European University Institute, Florence, 1996), p. 10.

54. The Federal Constitutional Court actually suggested this interpretation at one point in its justification of the Maastricht verdict: "Democracy . . . depends on the presence of certain prelegal preconditions, such as a permanent free debate between conflicting social forces, interests, and ideas, in which political goals are also clarified and transformed, and in which a public opinion preforms the political will. . . . Parties, associations, the press, and the electronic media are both the medium and a factor in this mediation process from which a European public opinion can take shape" (*Europäische Grundrechte Zeitschrift* (1993), pp. 437f.). The reference to the requirement of a common language which follows this statement is supposed to bridge the gap between this communication-theoretical understanding of democracy and the homogeneity of the citizenry which is elsewhere assumed to be necessary.

Chapter 6

1. See D. Grimm, "Does Europe Need a Constitution" in *European Law Journal* 1 (November 1995): 282–302.

Chapter 7

1. I. Kant, "The Contest of Faculties," in *Kant's Political Writings* (Cambridge, 1970), p. 187; *Werke* XI (Frankfurt am Main, 1977), p. 364.

2. D. Held, *Democracy and the Global Order* (Cambridge, 1995).

3. In the "Conclusion" to Rechtslehre of *The Metaphysics of Morals*, trans. & ed. M. Gregor (Cambridge, 1996), p. 123; *Werke* VIII, p. 478.

4. Kant does indeed mention in his "Doctrine of Right" the "unjust enemy" whose "publicly expressed will (whether by word or deed) reveals a maxim by which, if it

were made a universal rule, any condition of peace among nations would be impossible" (*Metaphysics of Morals,* section 60, p. 119; *Werke* VIII, p. 473); but the examples he gives, such as the violation of international treaties or the division of a conquered country (such as Poland in his own time), reveal the accidental character of this conception. A "punitive war" against unjust enemies remains an idea with no real practical consequences so long as we assume that states have unlimited sovereignty. For such states could not recognize a judicial authority that impartially adjudicates transgressions of rules in international relations without jeopardizing their own sovereignty. Only victory and defeat can decide "who is in the right" (*Political Writings,* p. 96; *Werke* XI, p. 200).

5. Kant, *Political Writings,* p. 113; *Werke* XI, p. 212.

6. Kant, "Theory and Practice," in *Political Writings,* p. 92 [translation modified]; *Werke* XI, p. 172.

7. Kant, "Perpetual Peace," in *Political Writings,* p. 105; *Werke* XI, p. 213.

8. In the "Doctrine of Right," *Metaphysics of Morals,* section 61, p. 119.

9. Kant, *Metaphysics of Morals,* p. 120 [translation modified]; *Werke* VIII, p. 475.

10. "Perpetual Peace," p. 104–105; *Werke* XI, p. 212.

11. "Perpetual Peace," p. 113; *Werke* XI, p. 225.

12. "Theory and Practice," p. 90; *Werke* XI, p. 169.

13. "Perpetual Peace," p. 100; *Werke* XI, pp. 205–206.

14. Cf. H. Schulze, *Staat und Nation in der Europäischen Geschichte* (München, 1994).

15. See D. Archibugi and D. Held's "Introduction" to their collection *Cosmopolitan Democracy* (Cambridge, 1995), pp. 10ff.

16. See "The Doctrine of Right," *Metaphysics of Morals,* section 62, p. 121.

17. "Perpetual Peace," 114; Werke XI, p. 226.

18. See G. Lukács, *The Young Hegel,* trans. R. Livingstone (Cambridge, MA, 1976).

19. D. Senghaas, "Internationale Politik im Lichte ihrer strukturellen Dilemmata," in *Wohin driftet die Welt?* (Frankfurt am Main, 1994), pp. 121ff., p. 132.

20. This is Anthony Giddens's definition of globalization in *The Consequences of Modernity* (Cambridge, 1990), p. 64.

21. Cf. R. Knieper, *Nationale Souveränität* (Frankfurt am Main, 1991).

22. J. S. Nye, "Soft Power," *Foreign Policy* 80 (1990): 153–171.

23. "Perpetual Peace," p. 121 [translation modified]; *Werke* XI, p. 238.

24. "Perpetual Peace," p. 115 [translation modified]; *Werke* XI, p. 228.

25. "Perpetual Peace," pp. 107–108; *Werke,* XI, pp. 216f.

26. On the theme "Farewell to the world of nation-states!" see E. O. Czempiel, *Weltpolitik im Umbruch* (München, 1993), pp. 105ff.

27. See the essays by A. Wellmer and A. Honneth in *Gemeinschaft und Gerechtigkeit,* ed. M. Brumlik and H. Brunkhorst (Frankfurt am Main, 1993), pp. 173ff and pp. 260ff.

28. See the title essay of my *Die Normalität einer Berliner Republik* (München, 1995), pp. 165ff.

29. "Perpetual Peace," p. 114; *Werke* XI, p. 226.

30. "Idea for a Universal History," in *Political Writings,* p. 51; "Idee zu einer Allgemeinen Geschichte," in *Werke* XI, pp. 46ff.

31. On the idea of the people as a learning sovereign, see H. Brunkhorst, *Demokratie und Differenz* (Frankfurt am Main, 1994), pp. 199ff.

32. "Idea for a Universal History," p. 45 [translation modified]; *Werke* XI, p. 38.

33. J. Isensee defends a qualified prohibition on intervention "against the increasing tendency to deviate from the norm" in terms of the surprising notion of "basic rights for states" in "Weltpolizei für Menschenrechten," *Juristische Zeitung* 9 (1995): 421–430: "What is valid for the basic rights of individuals also holds *mutatis mutandis* for the 'basic rights' of states, especially for their sovereign equality, their self-determination as the supreme authority over persons and territory" (p. 424; see also p. 429). Drawing an analogy between the sovereignty of states recognized by international law and the constitutionally guaranteed freedom of persons as legal subjects misses not only the fundamental importance of individual rights and the individualist orientation of modern legal orders; it also misses the specifically juridical meaning of human rights as the individual rights of citizens of a cosmopolitan order.

34. See the examples cited by Ch. Greenwood in, "Gibt es ein Recht auf humanitäre Intervention?" *Europa-Archiv* 4 (1993): 93–106, p. 94.

35. See Habermas, *The Past as Future* (Lincoln, Nebraska, 1994), pp. 5–31.

36. "Theory and Practice," p. 77 [translation modified]; *Werke* XI, p. 144.

37. See J. Habermas, "Struggles for Recognition in the Democratic Constitutional State," below pp. 214ff.

38. "Perpetual Peace," p. 112 [translation modified]; *Werke* XI, p. 223.

39. In a discussion of a work by Georges Scelle, *Precis de droit de gens* Vols. I and II (Paris, 1932 & 1934) in C. Schmitt, *Die Wendung zum diskriminierenden Kriegsbegriff* (1938) (Berlin, 1988), p. 16.

40. Schmitt, *Kriegsbegriff,* p. 19.

41. On the Vienna conference on human rights, see R. Wolfrum, "Die Entwicklung des internationalen Menschenrechtsschutzes," *Europa-Archiv* 23 (1993): 681–690; on the status of disputed rights to solidarity, see W. Huber's article "Menschenrechte/Menschenwürde," in *Theologische Realenzyklopädie,* Vol. XXII (Berlin/New York, 1992), pp. 577–602; also E. Riedel, "Menschenrechte der dritten Dimension," *Europäische Grundrechte Zeitschrift* (1989): 9–21.

42. In 1993 the Security Council established such a tribunal to prosecute war crimes and crimes against humanity in the former Yugoslavia.

43. As argued by H. Quaritsch in his postscript to C. Schmitt, *Das internationalrechtliche Verbrechen des Angriffskrieges* (1945) (Berlin, 1994), pp. 125–247; here pp. 236ff.

44. See the analyses and conclusions of Greenwood, "Gibt es ein Recht auf humanitäre Intervention?"

45. Greenwood comes to the following conclusion: "The idea that the UN could use the powers granted in its Charter to intervene in a state on humanitarian grounds now appears to be much more strongly established;" "Gibt es ein Recht auf humanitäre Intervention?" p. 104.

46. Quoted in Greenwood, "Gibt es ein Recht auf humanitäre Intervention?" p. 96.

47. "Perpetual Peace," p. 104; *Werke* XI, pp. 211ff.

48. See R. Cooper, "Gibt es eine neue Weltordnung?" *Europa-Archiv* 18 (1993): 509–516.

49. A reasonable framework for discussing human rights is proposed by T. Lindholm, "The Cross-Cultural Legitimacy of Human Rights," *Norwegian Institute of Human Rights,* No. 3 (Oslo, 1990).

50. D. and E. Senghaas, "Si vis pacem, para pacem," *Leviathan* (1992): 230–247.

51. E. O. Czempiel has investigated these strategies in light of many different examples in "Internationale Politik und der Wandel von Regimen," in G. Schwarz, ed., *Sonderheft der Zeitschrift für Politik* (Zürich, 1989), 55–75.

52. I am here following D. Archibugi, "From the United Nations to Cosmopolitan Democracy," in Archibugi and Held, *Cosmopolitan Democracy,* pp. 121–162.

53. [Here the author has in mind the bicameral parliamentary system typical of European states in which an upper house (in Germany, the *Bundesrat*) exercises legislative competence in a division of labor with the house of representatives (the *Bundestag*). Trans.]

54. See H. Kelsen, *Peace Through Law* (Chapel Hill, 1944).

55. Habermas, *The Philosophical Discourse of Modernity,* trans. F. Lawrence (Cambridge, MA, 1987), pp. 336ff.

56. C. Schmitt, *The Concept of the Political,* trans. G. Schwab (Chicago, 1996), p. 54 [translation modified]. One finds the same argument in Isensee, "Weltpolizei für

Menschenrechten," p. 429: "For as long as there have been interventions, they have served ideologies: religious ideologies in the sixteenth and seventeenth centuries, monarchical, Jacobin, and humanitarian principles, the socialist world revolution. Now human rights and democracy are the order of the day. In the long history of intervention, ideology has served to dissemble the power interests of the interveners and to invest their effectiveness with the aura of legitimacy."

57. Cf. Schmitt, *Glossarium 1947–1951* (Berlin, 1991), p. 76.

58. Schmitt, *Der Begriff des Politischen,* (Berlin, 1963), p. 94. [This passage does not appear in the English translation. Trans.]

59. See S. Schute and S. Hurley, eds., *On Human Rights* (New York, 1993).

60. O. Höffe, "Die Menschenrechte als Legitimation und kritischer Maßstab der Demokratie," in J. Schwardtländer (ed.), *Menschenrechte und Demokratie* (Strasbourg, 1981), p. 250; see also Höffe, *Political Justice,* trans. J.C. Cohen (Cambridge, 1995).

61. S. König, *Zur Begründung der Menschenrechte: Hobbes-Locke-Kant* (Freiburg, 1994), pp. 26ff.

62. The implications of the rights to political participation for human rights are such that everyone has at any rate the right to belong to *one* political community as a citizen.

63. See Hugo Bedau's analysis of the structure of human rights, which draws on Henry Shue's position, in "International Human Rights," T. Regan and D. van de Weer, eds., *And Justice for All* (Totowa, NJ, 1983), p. 279: "The emphasis on duties is meant to avoid leaving the defense of human rights in a vacuum, bereft of any moral significance for the specific conduct of others. But the duties are not intended to explain or generate rights; if anything, the rights are supposed to explain and generate the duties."

64. Cf. S. König, *Zur Begründung der Menschenrechte,* pp. 84ff.

65. Kant, *Metaphysics of Morals,* p. 24; *Werke* VIII, p. 337.

66. *Metaphysics of Morals,* p. 30; *Werke* VIII, 345.

67. On the differentiation of the spheres of ethics, law, and morality, see R. Forst, *Kontexte der Gerechtigkeit* (Frankfurt am Main, 1994), pp. 131–142.

68. Cf. Schmitt, *Das internationalrechtliche Verbrechen des Angriffskrieges.*

69. In both *The Concept of the Political* and *Die Wendung zur diskriminerenden Kriegsbegriff.*

70. Schmitt, *Das internationalrechtliche Verbrechen,* p. 19.

71. Schmitt, *Glossarium,* pp. 113, 265, 146, 282.

72. Schmitt, *Die Wendung zur diskriminerenden Kriegsbegriff,* p. 1.

73. Schmitt, *Der Begriff des Politischen*, p. 110. [This section is not included in the English translations. Trans.]

74. Schmitt, *The Concept of the Political*, p. 33.

75. H. M. Enzensberger, *Aussichten auf den Bürgerkrieg* (Frankfurt am Main, 1993), pp. 73ff. See A. Honneth, "Universalismus as moralische Falle?" *Merkur* 546/7 (1994): 867–883. Enzensberger not only bases his case on a highly selective description of the current international situation which completely ignores the surprising expansion of constitutional regimes in Latin American, Africa, and Eastern Europe in the last twenty years (cf. Czempiel, *Weltpolitik im Umbruch*, pp. 107ff.). He also casually transmutes the complex relationships between fundamentalist politics, on the one hand, and social deprivations and the absence of liberal traditions, on the other, into anthropological features. But precisely the expanded conception of peace points to preventive, nonviolent strategies and highlights the pragmatic limitations to which humanitarian interventions are subject, as is shown both by the example of Somalia and the different situation in the former Yugoslavia. For a case-based analysis of different types of interventions, see D. Senghaas, *Wohin driftet die Welt?*, pp. 185ff.

76. A. Gehlen, *Moral und Hypermoral* (Frankfurt am Main, 1969).

77. Schmitt, *Glossarium*, p. 259.

78. Ibid., p. 229; also *The Concept of the Political*, p. 63.

79. Schmitt, *The Concept of the Political*, p. 54.

80. Ibid., p. 36 [translation modified].

81. See Habermas, *Kleine Politische Schriften* I–IV (Frankfurt am Main, 1981), pp. 328–339.

82. K. Günther, "Kampf gegen das Böse? Wider die ethische Aufrüstung der Kriminalpolitik," *Kritische Justiz* 17 (1994): 135–157.

83. Ibid., p. 144.

84. Ibid., p. 144.

Chapter 8

1. Cf. J. Habermas, *Between Facts and Norms*, trans. W. Rehg (Cambridge, MA, 1996), chap. 3.

2. A. Honneth, *Struggles for Recognition*, trans. J. Andersen (Cambridge, 1994).

3. Cf. Ch. Taylor, "The Politics of Recognition," in *Multiculturalism: Examining the Politics of Recognition*, rev. ed., A. Gutmann, ed., (Princeton, 1994), pp. 25–73.

4. A. Gutmann, "Introduction," *Multiculturalism*, p. 8.

5. Cf. Taylor, in *Multiculturalism*, pp. 58–59.

Notes

6. Ibid.

7. J. Habermas, "Individuation through Socialization," in *Postmetaphysical Thinking*, trans. W. M. Hohengarten (Cambridge, MA, 1992), pp. 149–204.

8. D. L. Rhode, *Justice and Gender* (Cambridge, MA, 1989), Part 1.

9. Nancy Fraser, "Struggle over Needs," in *Unruly Practices* (Minneapolis, 1989), pp. 144–160.

10. S. Benhabib, *Situating the Self* (New York, 1992), Part 2.

11. P. Berman, ed., *Debating P.C.* (New York, 1992); see also J. Searle, "Storm Over the University," in the same volume, pp. 85–123.

12. J. Habermas, *The Philosophical Discourse of Modernity*, trans. F. Lawrence (Cambridge, MA, 1987).

13. As Gutmann remarks of the deconstructionist method, "This reductionist argument about intellectual standards is often made on behalf of groups that are underrepresented in the university and disadvantaged in society, but it is hard to see how it can come to the aid of anyone. The argument is self-undermining, both logically and practically. By its internal logic, deconstructionism has nothing more to say for the view that intellectual standards are masks for the will to political power than that it too reflects the will to power of deconstructionists. But why then bother with intellectual life at all, which is not the fastest, surest, or even most satisfying path to political power, if it is political power that one is really after?" "Introduction," *Multiculturalism*, pp. 18–19.

14. R. Dworkin, *Taking Rights Seriously* (Cambridge, MA, 1977).

15. R. Beiner, *Political Judgment* (Chicago, 1994), p. 138.

16. P. Alter, *Nationalism* (New York, 1989).

17. This essay was written in early 1993.

18. W. Kymlicka, *Liberalism, Community and Culture* (Oxford, 1991).

19. S. Wolf, "Comment," in *Multiculturalism*, p. 79.

20. Cf. the Supreme Court decision in *Wisconsin v. Yoder*, 406 U.S. 205 (1972).

21. D. Cohn-Bendit and T. Schmid, *Heimat Babylon* (Hamburg, 1992), pp. 316ff.

22. J. Habermas, *Justification and Application: Remarks on Discourse Ethics*, trans. C. Cronin (Cambridge, MA, 1993).

23. J. Rawls, "The Idea of an Overlapping Consensus," *Oxford Journal of Legal Studies* 7 (1987): 1–25.

24. J. Habermas, *The New Conservatism: Cultural Criticism and the Historians' Debate*, trans. S. W. Nicholsen (Cambridge, MA, 1989).

25. D. J. van de Kaa, "European Migration at the End of History," *European Review* 1 (January 1993): 94.

26. E. Wiegand, "Ausländerfeindlichkeit in der Festung Europa. Einstellungen zu Fremden im europäischen Vergleich," *Informationsdienst Soziale Indikatoren* (ZUMA), no. 9 (1993): 1–4.

27. M. Walzer, "What Does It Mean to Be an American?" *Social Research* 57 (1990): 591–614. Walzer notes that the communitarian conception does not take account of the complex composition of a multicultural society (p. 613).

28. R. Brubaker, *Citizenship and Nationhood in France and Germany* (Cambridge, MA, 1992), pp. 128ff.

29. Cohn-Bendit and Schmid, *Heimat Babylon*, chap. 8.

30. J. H. Carens, "Aliens and Citizens," *Review of Politics* 49 (1987): 271; cf. also J. Habermas, "Citizenship and National Identity," in *Between Facts and Norms*, pp. 491–515.

31. P. C. Emmer, "Intercontinental Migration," *European Review* 1 (January 1993): 67–74: "After 1800 the dramatic increase in the economic growth of Western Europe could only be maintained as an 'escape hatch.' The escape of sixty-one million Europeans after 1800 allowed the European economies to create such a mix of the factors of production as to allow for record economic growth and to avoid a situation in which economic growth was absorbed by an increase in population. After the Second World War, Europeans also benefitted from intercontinental migration since the colonial empires forced many colonial subjects to migrate to the metropolis. In this particular period there was no danger of overpopulation . . . . Many of the colonial migrants coming to Europe had been well trained and they arrived at exactly the time when skilled labor was at a premium in rebuilding Europe's economy" (pp. 72f.).

32. With a justification that is outrageous from a constitutional point of view, on May 14, 1996 the second senate of the Federal Constitutional Court upheld the constitutionality of the clause concerning "third countries" and the clause defining "safe countries of origin" laid down in the revised version of the Basic Law. This ruling subordinates the constitution to functional imperatives that call for prompt expulsion of asylum seekers. As Heribert Prantl wrote (in the *Süddeutschen Zeitung* of May 14/15, 1996): "Quick expulsion is more important to the constitutional court . . . than the right to asylum, more important than human dignity, more important than the principle of due process."

33. K. J. Bade, "Immigration and Integration in Germany since 1945," *European Review* 1 (January 1993): 75–79.

34. Bade, "Immigration and Integration," p. 77.

35. See the title essay in J. Habermas, *Die Normalität einer Berliner Republik* (Frankfurt am Main, 1995).

Notes

Chapter 9

1. Cf. H. Arendt, *On Revolution* (New York, 1965); *On Violence* (New York, 1970).

2. Cf. F. I. Michelman, "Political Truth and the Rule of Law," *Tel Aviv University Studies in Law* 8 (1988): 283: "The political society envisioned by bumper-sticker republicans is the society of private rights bearers, an association whose first principle is the protection of the lives, liberties, and estates of its individual members. In that society, the state is justified by the protection it gives to those prepolitical interests; the purpose of the constitution is to ensure that the state apparatus, the government, provides such protection for the people at large rather than serves the special interests of the governors or their patrons; the function of citizenship is to operate the constitution and thereby to motivate the governors to act according to that protective purpose; and the value to you of your political franchise—your right to vote and speak, to have your views heard and counted—is the handle it gives you on influencing the system so that it will adequately heed and protect *your* particular, prepolitical rights and other interests."

3. On the distinction between positive and negative freedom see Ch. Taylor, "What is Human Agency?" in *Human Agency and Language: Philosophical Papers 1* (Cambridge, 1985), pp. 15–44.

4. Michelman, "Political Truth and the Rule of Law," p. 284: "In [the] civic constitutional vision, political society is primarily the society not of rights bearers, but of citizens, an association whose first principle is the creation and provision of a public realm within which a people, together, argue and reason about the right terms of social coexistence, terms that they will set together and which they understand as comprising their common good. . . . Hence, the state is justified by its purpose of establishing and ordering the public sphere within which persons can achieve freedom in the sense of self-government by the exercise of reason in public dialogue."

5. Michelman, "Conceptions of Democracy in American Constitutional Argument: Voting Rights," *Florida Law Review* 41 (1989): 446f. (hereafter "Voting Rights").

6. Michelman, "Voting Rights," p. 484.

7. Michelman, "Conceptions of Democracy in American Constitutional Argument: The Case of Pornography Regulation," *Tennessee Law Review* 291 (1989): 293.

8. Cf. J. Habermas, "Popular Sovereignty as Procedure," in *Between Facts and Norms,* trans. W. Rehg (1996), pp. 463–490.

9. Cf. *The Basic Law of the Federal Republic of Germany,* article 20, sec. 2.

Index

Index